CHANGE
OLOGY

**How to enable groups,
communities and societies
to do things they've
never done before**

CHANGE OLOGY

How to enable groups, communities and societies to do things they've never done before

Les Robinson

green books

First published in the UK in 2012
by Green Books Ltd,
Dartington Space, Dartington Hall,
Totnes, Devon TQ9 6EN

ISBN 978 0 85784 061 5

Text printed on Corona Natural 100% recycled paper
by T J International, Padstow, Cornwall, UK

Contents

Introduction
How to change the world

Mickey Weiss was a bare-knuckled, hardheaded vegetable merchant who ran a mushroom company at the Los Angeles Wholesale Produce Market for four decades until he retired at the age of 72.

One day in 1987, after passing a homeless encampment on his way to work, he arrived to see a pallet of perfectly edible but unsold strawberries being tipped into a dumpster. Mickey cried out "Why are we throwing away berries when eight blocks away people are frying stale bread over open fires for their first meal of the day?"

When he retired, Weiss did something extraordinary. At his own expense, he set up shop on 2,500 square feet of dock space at the Los Angeles markets. Then he went to his old competitors and asked them to donate their 'edible-but-not-sellable' produce. Next, he contacted a host of charities and gave them landing rights to back up at his dock at, say, 10.30 to 11.00 a.m., take away whatever they wanted, and distribute it to the poor and homeless.

Weiss's scheme became well known. It won awards and plaudits across the nation. Yet despite the wide publicity, it remained a lonely bright spot. In four years only one other city had managed to copy the idea.

At that time, Peter Clarke and Susan Evans were Dean and Assistant Dean at the Annenberg School for Communication in Los Angeles. They were moved by Weiss's story and, as health communication professionals, decided to take on the task of disseminating his 'orphan innovation' to other cities.

I met Peter Clarke, a lean, vigorous, 60-something in a dimly-lit faux Mexican restaurant off Wilshire Boulevard. In between seemingly endless bowls of guacamole, he described what must be one of the largest, most successful and most uncelebrated change projects ever undertaken by private individuals.

Peter explained that the United States had around 250 food banks that delivered food to 36,000 community pantries, shelters and homeless missions who used it to feed hungry adults and children. In 1991 virtually zero per cent of this food was fresh fruit and vegetables. It was mostly canned and packaged food and beverages, much of it high in salt, fats and added sugar and low in nutrition – two of the largest inventory items were fizzy drinks and salted crackers. Although intended to nourish, this food was itself a public health problem, contributing to epidemic levels of diabetes (affecting 18-24 per cent of low-income people), high blood pressure, and other chronic and potentially deadly conditions.

Meanwhile, wholesale produce markets, growers, retail outlets and other sectors of the US food industry were dumping thousands of tonnes of unwanted but perfectly edible fruit and vegetables every day at their own expense simply because it was unsold and had to be moved off their docks to make way for more.

The angle that impressed Peter and Susan most was putting vast amounts of disease-preventing food like carrots, courgettes, cabbage and sweetcorn into the hands of those who needed it most. "It was the largest public health intervention we could imagine," he said. So they decided to dedicate six months, part-time, to spreading the idea. That was in 1991 and they're still at it.

Peter and Susan began by imagining they faced a problem that could be solved by education. So they wrote a manual based on Weiss's programme and presented it to five food banks. And they held a conference in Los Angeles where participants could see Mickey's programme in action. According to Peter, the food banks were fired up with enthusiasm but six months later nothing had happened.

So they went directly to the food bank industry association, America's Second Harvest, and presented their proposal to its annual convention. They had large, enthusiastic audiences for their talks. But again, nothing happened. Their efforts had amounted to, in Peter's words, "a well-intentioned, well-executed, colossal failure".

Peter and Susan's first big realisation was that they were trying to sell the wrong programme. "It took us a while to learn that Mickey's programme wasn't being replicated because it couldn't be. We'd been trying to get a wholesaler to front a dock like Mickey's but it never worked in the cities where we tried it. It took us three years until we had an ah-ha moment and realised we were trying to sell the wrong thing!" The model couldn't involve a dedicated dock. Instead, the food banks would have to pick up from individual wholesalers.

Their next ah-ha moment came when they started to listen more attentively to the people they'd been trying to persuade. "We heard an off-hand observation from a food bank director who said 'there's no one on my board who thinks we should invest resources on perishable collections.' This was a big realisation for us, that the prospect of adoption would be increased by speaking to all the stakeholders. Just talking to the executive directors wasn't enough. Furthermore, we had to approach each food bank individually, acknowledging its particular food ecology and unique community!"

So they decided to make an offer to food banks: "if you are even mildly interested in fresh food we'll come to you, whether you're in Mobile or Washington or Salt Lake City and spend two days explaining how fresh produce recovery can work in your situation. There's no obligation. The only commitment we ask is a series of meetings, with your executive director, with your key employees, with your board, with a sample of your client agencies, with philanthropic funders, and with produce wholesalers."

Being a change maker began to demand an extraordinary level of commitment from Peter and Susan. "We would finish our classes at 10 p.m. at night, catch a plane first thing the next morning, and spend two days of intensive meetings, collapse on Friday night and fly home on Saturday morning."

Gradually, through trial and error, Peter and Susan pieced together the elements of a successful project. For a start, they knew that credibility was vital. So they brought Mickey Weiss along with them on their visits to prospective food banks. "He radiated credibility when he walked into the room," said Peter. When Mickey died in 1996 they invited managers from adopting food banks to fill his role.

Then Peter and Susan recognised that the executive directors were helpless unless their boards bought into a new vision for their food banks, one that focused more on public health. "We'd tell them: 'We need you to understand you're no longer in the hunger business, you're in the disease-prevention business.' We'd present a mini-lecture on the relationship between diet and illnesses like diabetes. Few of them had understood this before. We were pivoting their mission identity," said Peter.

Next, they were surprised to discover that hardly any food bank staff knew how to pitch for a food donation – the cans and packaged foods had simply arrived year after year. So Peter and Susan had to train them. Their method was to do the pitch to produce wholesalers themselves so food bank staff could see how it was done. "We'd ask the wholesaler to tell us about his business and have a tour of his cool rooms, trucks and dock. And we'd say 'you probably have a lot of food sometimes that you need to get rid of'. They'd agree they had heaps of food going to landfill. Then we'd say 'How about the folks here come and pick it up? You name the time.' And then we'd say to the food bank director 'Can you have a truck on that day?' and he or she would say 'Yes.'" Peter and Susan had become a kind of dating agency, introducing the food bank people to the produce wholesalers, two groups who previously had no idea each other existed.

Another critical discovery was the need for an enthusiast at each food bank who fell in love with the idea. And then there was a final piece in the jigsaw – money. "We'd been cultivating the Baltimore Food Bank," said Peter. "The executive director was positive but kept saying 'I don't know how I'm going to budget to get this started.' We realised he needed some money. We were ignorant about how much so we wrote him personal cheques for US$500 (£300) each, pretending that funds had come from an anonymous donor, called him a week later, and he said 'got your message, we're going to start.'"

Fortunately, they soon found a charitable funder, Helene Soref, who was passionate about nutrition. When a food bank's plans for a pilot programme were finalised, Soref's foundation would cut a cheque, on Peter and Susan's recommendation, for, say, US$18,000 (£10,800) on two weeks notice. This would help a food bank lease a refrigerated truck or pay a driver. Later, Peter and Susan created and ran a grants programme funded by Kraft Foods, and channelled nearly 700 grants to food banks over 12 years, totalling more than US$30 million (£18 million).

By 2007, 16 years after first hearing Mickey Weiss's story, Peter and Susan had kick-started 162 fresh food programmes across the country, 87 per cent of all programmes operating at that time. And they're still doing it.

American food banks now handle more than 500 million pounds of fresh produce every year.

Peter summed up their journey, "Every place was different, so diffusion didn't happen easily. We had to be accommodating about each site's peculiarities and not try one-size-fits-all. We had to become an authority, not just on fresh food, but on fresh food in Dallas, Spokane and Cleveland! Our biggest lesson was, at the end, to step back and let local food banks take the credit. Their ownership had to be affirmed just as if they'd invented it themselves so they'd take full responsibility for their success and not become dependent on us. To be really successful, we had to disappear." [1]

Peter and Susan's story illustrates many things about a successful change effort. First, it shows how, with perseverance and imagination, it really is possible for individuals – even unfunded ones – to change the world in amazing ways.

Second, it demonstrates some of the essential features of a successful change effort: Mickey Weiss provided an inspiring story worth buzzing about. Without that buzz Peter and Susan would never have heard about the idea, and even if they had wanted to make it happen, food bank executive directors and boards would never have listened to them. Building on Mickey's story, Peter and Susan generated a hopeful new vision for food banks: no longer would they be simply feeding the needy, now they would contribute to their health as well. Yet buzz and vision alone did not create the change. New relationships needed to be shepherded into existence. And individuals including local champions, board members and food bank staff needed specific kinds of assistance to learn how acting for change might really be within their power. Meanwhile the programme itself changed dramatically as Peter and Susan learnt hard lessons along the way. These are the vital themes we'll be coming back to in this book.

Third, it shows how solutions to large-scale social, health and environmental problems always involve people doing things they have never done before. Food bank directors agreed to establish refrigerated stores on their premises and fund new pickups, food bank boards voted to change time-honoured methods of operation, food bank staff found themselves courageously pitching their case to fresh food wholesalers, and the wholesalers found themselves making room on their docks for charitable pickups.

Peter and Susan's effort is a microcosm of how the world changes. The solutions to complex social problems always involve diverse individuals doing things they have never done before and sustaining those changes in their lives and organisations, whether it be politicians voting new programmes, CEOs leading their corporations in new directions, or ordinary folk changing the habits of a lifetime.

When individuals make these kinds of changes their lives usually get better and they might become the stimulus for others to change. When many people make these changes, we may see revolutionary waves that overturn the established order. The action might be eating healthier, joining an action group, letting our children bicycle to school, signing a petition, or investing in green technology. Or it might be speaking up against a bully or a dictator. Whatever it is, broad social changes are the accumulation of millions of such individual changes. And each one of these changes is a person doing something they have never done before.

It's true that technological change and institutional reform, accident and cataclysm all profoundly affect the world. But the result always depends on how humans interpret those events and willingly change and adapt. Boffins may invent new products, and politicians may pass new laws, but whether those products or laws amount to anything depends on whether people invest their time, energy and commitment to adopt them and sustain that change permanently.

Nowadays myriad efforts are under way to influence human behaviour for the better. In every country, at every level of society, small teams in government, business, community organisations, and even private individuals, are working to tackle complex and longstanding social challenges in every field imaginable – energy and water conservation, road safety, obesity, drug and alcohol addiction, hunger and nutrition, emergency preparedness, habitat protection, crime prevention, to name a few.

This book is for all those who wish to be makers of this kind of change.

It aims to answer the question: How can we work successfully to influence the decisions other humans make, and by doing so help solve some of the outstanding social, environmental and health problems of our time?

Humans, as we'll see, are geniuses at resisting change when they think others are trying to impose it on them (and just as well too, or we'd all be living in extraordinarily primitive and oppressive societies). Yet progress happens too: people stop denying and resisting and willingly embrace change when the conditions are right.

There are rarely silver bullets in this kind of work. Instead, change is more like a pattern. A mix of ingredients comes together and we find, often to our great surprise, that people start adopting new practices in their lives, businesses and communities. And what starts as a trickle sometimes turns into a wave.

This book proposes that successful and sustained change efforts happen when six different ingredients come together:

1. Positive buzz
2. An offer of hope
3. An enabling environment
4. A sticky solution
5. Expanded comfort zones
6. The right inviter.

Am I saying that if you utilise these ingredients your project will succeed in its goals? Well, pretty much, yes. Failure to include them will almost certainly tip your effort into a 'so what?' zone where you may struggle to find any observable impact at all. Yet by applying them with zest and imagination, there's a good chance you'll be surprised at the results.

In six sections of this book I examine each ingredient in detail, aiming to capture the collective learning of many practitioners and theorists, giving inspiring examples, and examining the experimental research to explain why some approaches work and others don't.

Following most sections, I've also added a practical tool or method that I've found useful in designing change efforts. I hope you find them useful too.

Popular folk theories
Why it's necessary to slay our assumptions

Five teenagers were sprawled on grubby armchairs in a grimy inner-city youth refuge. They were pallid, fidgety boys, aged between 13 and 16. I was there to collect stories for a comic book about youth health. In the course of the interview one of my colleagues asked these kids what they did for thrills.

What they did was: they broke into homes, rifled through medicine cabinets and swallowed anything that looked remotely like a painkiller or narcotic. They told us stories about intoxicated binges that culminated in unconsciousness or self-harm.

Just as the interview was closing, I thought of one more question. I gave the microphone to the youngest, most drug-damaged one of all and asked "If you could give a message about taking drugs to other kids, what would you say?"

He sobered up, as if assuming a great responsibility, and said "I'd say don't take drugs. They'll fuck you up." He looked perfectly serious. I glanced at the other boys to see what they thought. They stared steadily back as if the answer was self-evident. It seemed they shared his views.

I was shocked by this whole interview. The boys' chemical self-mutilation was astounding and awful but what also confronted me was the attack on one of my own cherished assumptions about the world. Surely people's behaviour follows from their beliefs. But there was no relationship between what these boys believed and what they actually did.

It was my first insight into the awesome chasm that can exist between what I assume about people's motivations and the evidence of real life. I thought these kids were taking drugs because they were ignorant about, or in denial of, the damage they were doing to themselves. I was wrong. It turns out that the beliefs people hold have only the most tenuous connection to the actions they take in their daily lives. The assumption that 'If someone believes A is good and right; they will do A' doesn't apply in the real world. There is overwhelming evidence on this point, and most experienced change makers, if pressed, will admit it's true. Why then is the equation:

$$BELIEF = BEHAVIOUR$$

one of the most commonly held assumptions behind projects that try to change the world?

If we want to change the world then starting with defective thinking about the motivations of other people is likely to be a recipe for failure.

Before we start discussing how people really change, it's good to pause a moment and ask: When it comes to understanding what makes others tick, why are we so often wrong?

Homo romanticus

Michael Gazzaniga was a graduate student assisting neurophysiologist Roger Sperry in his pioneering split-brain experiments in the 1960s when he witnessed something surprising.

The experimenters were working with people who had injuries that had destroyed the tissues connecting the two halves of their brain. This caused their left and right hemispheres to act like independent brains. Because the left hemisphere – which processes language – is connected to only the right eye, it had no idea what the left eye was seeing. In one experiment the instruction 'walk' was shown to the left eye of a split-brain patient. Gazzaniga watched the patient push his chair back and start to leave the room. When asked why he did this, he replied "Going to my house to go get a Coke."[1]

Gazzaniga was awe-struck. This patient's *left* brain – the side that processes language – could have had no idea why its owner had started walking across the room. Yet it instantly created a reasonable explanation: to get a Coke. Gazzaniga later wrote:

> Our species can develop beliefs at lightning speed. We create them almost as a reflex. We now know that the left hemisphere of the brain

– the one that attaches a story to input from the world – creates these beliefs . . . The left-hemisphere interpreter is not only a master of belief creation, but it will stick to its belief system no matter what.

Any time our left brain is confronted with information that does not jibe with our self-image, knowledge, or conceptual framework, our left-hemisphere interpreter creates a belief to enable all incoming information to make sense and mesh with our ongoing idea of our self. The interpreter seeks patterns, order, and causal relationships.[2]

Gazzaniga realised that humans are hardwired to generate stories that justify their actions and explain their worlds.

It's therefore in our nature to be story-makers and story-tellers. It's also in our nature to be enthralled by stories and use stories to rationalise and justify our actions. Stories are (as we'll see) the medium that carries change through societies. Our drive to explain also makes us compulsive inventors of stories that make sense of the actions of other people.

Because stories are usually about people doing things, they have behavioural explanations woven into them. That makes stories predictive. They act just like behavioural theories. For instance, we would rarely say "Ruth smokes a lot" and leave it at that. Instead, we would say "Ruth smokes a lot because her husband Ted is such a creep." This leads to the automatic behavioural prediction that "If Ruth wants to stop smoking, she should dump Ted." Now we have a theory about the cause of Ruth's problem, and also a theory about how to fix it.

Stories like this are theories of change. We make them up all the time. We just can't help it, we're designed that way. And our stories are mostly self-serving – they justify our own interests, fears and prejudices.

Unfortunately, practically no one has enough evidence to invent truly well-informed explanations for the behaviour of others. As a result, self-serving theories tend to be the norm.

That would be enough of a problem, but we don't limit our theorising to the lives of our friends and acquaintances. We love theorising about the behaviour of whole groups, communities and societies. And when some of us become politicians, presidents, CEOs, managers and Pentagon strategists the consequences of our self-serving theories of change can become very serious indeed.

Why theories are often wrong

Try this quick quiz.

Most litterers:
1. Don't care about the environment.
2. Don't care what anyone thinks about them.
3. Do care about the environment and what others think about them.

Surrogate mothers:
1. Are poor and easily exploited.
2. Are mercenary.
3. Enjoy bearing children and have empathy for women who can't.

Middle-class college students become lawyers:
1. To make money.
2. To please their parents.
3. Because they've always dreamt about being lawyers.

The answer, according to credible social research, is 3. in each case.[3] Yet I expect some readers would find these answers surprising and counter-intuitive. Why? Because common theories about the motivations of litterers, surrogate mothers and law students have in-built, unconscious biases.

When it comes to predicting what might change human behaviour, biases apply. Here are some common generic theories of change:

People will change if they learn the correct facts.
People will change if we sell the case harder.
People will change if they feel enough pain.
People will change if they are shocked into action.
People will change if the rewards are big enough.

The problem with all these theories is that they are wrong most of the time. There's overwhelming evidence – from psychological experiments and from the systematic failure of real-life programmes based on these theories – that humans rarely change for these reasons. We'll touch on the evidence in this book, but first it's valuable to consider what makes us want to believe such theories in the first place.

Part of the reason is that these theories emerge from widely held worldviews. For example, when 1,000 Americans were asked to rate reasons why Americans were poor, their reasons fitted into three kinds of theory:

> *Individualistic theories:* people are poor because of their own lack of thrift and effort, loose morals and drunkenness;
> *Structural theories:* people are poor because of low wages, lack of jobs, poor schools and prejudice;
> *Fatalistic theories:* people are poor because of bad luck.[4]

These kinds of generic theory are examples of *worldviews*. They are the lenses through which we humans have learnt to view our worlds. Worldviews tend to be culturally inherited and are very slow to change. Because we often apply worldviews in a blanket way, no matter what the situation, they systematically bias our judgements about other people.

And, of course, those worldviews are also the platforms of political parties. When parties come to power, their worldviews are transformed into large-scale social-change programmes. Conservatives, famously, like to fund tough-minded programmes based on the theory that people are best controlled by strong laws, harsh punishments and hierarchical authority. Liberals, mostly, like to fund more tender-hearted programmes based on the theory that people can be encouraged to be their best through love, care and being given responsibility.[5]

We are quite well acquainted with these grand worldviews, but there are also a number of deeper 'attributional biases' that are intrinsic to human perception and exceptionally hard to avoid.

According to attributional bias theorists, there are natural, automatic, and almost unavoidable biases in the way we think about the motivations of other people. Wikipedia has an interesting list of the attributional biases recognised by psychologists. One of the most common of these, called 'Fundamental Attribution Error', says we have an inbuilt tendency to assume that a person's actions are caused by the *kind* of person they are, rather than as a result of their abilities, self-confidence, fears or social pressures.

For instance, if we know that Jasmine drives a lot, we might jump to the conclusion that Jasmine doesn't care about the environment, or if she neglects her children we might say she doesn't love them. If Jasmine was us, however, we'd probably say we drive because the public transport is woefully inadequate, and that we spend time away from our children because of work pressures.

I recently saw a survey that asked whether the legalisation of drugs would cause people to use more drugs. Three per cent of people said they would probably use drugs more often, but 62 per cent said they thought other people would![6] That's attributional bias.

It's easy to see why attributional biases exist. We know a lot about our own motivations because we have access to our own mental processes (which, of course, we interpret in a self-serving way). But the only evidence we have of other people's mental processes is what we see them do (and which we also interpret in a self-serving way!). The result is a tendency to be comprehensively wrong about the motivations of others (while not necessarily being right about our own motivations either!).

Worldview bias and attributional bias react together to produce two pervasive biases that have toxic effects on change efforts. I call them 'Man is Bad Bias' and 'Heroic Agent Bias'.

Man is Bad Bias

Man is Bad Bias is a cynical view of human nature that imagines people as lazy, greedy consumers who eat up resources with little concern for the wellbeing of others; who gaily dump waste and costs onto others; who form exclusive groups that compete ruthlessly; and who do the right thing only when someone is checking on them.

Here's an example. When students at the State University of New York were asked whether they would donate blood for free 63 per cent said yes. But when the same students were asked to estimate whether their peers would donate blood, they said that only 33 per cent would do it for free, a difference of 30 per cent. That's an almost 100 per cent misjudgement of the self-interest factor in the motivation in their peers.[7]

If you don't hold that bias, you probably know someone who does. It's so legitimate and respectable that it's practically hardwired into modern culture. Robert Wuthnow in his book *Acts of Compassion* noticed that many people who performed genuine acts of compassion seemed embarrassed about their altruistic motives. Instead, they were more comfortable using the language of self-interest. People's accounts of volunteering for charities, he noted, tended to overemphasise selfish motives: "It gave me something to do." "I liked the other volunteers." "It got me out of the house." If our culture makes us ashamed to admit our own altruism then it's easy to understand why we might overestimate the self-interest of others.

Interestingly, it's also possible that Man is Bad Bias is self-fulfilling. A study by Robert Frank asked Cornell students whether they would report being undercharged for a purchase and whether they would return a lost envelope containing US$100. Three months later they were asked the same questions again. Those who had taken an introductory course in economics in the meantime became less honest, while astronomy students became more honest![8]

The problem with Man is Bad Bias is not just that it's frequently wrong, but that it *always* blinds us to the great, and often unexpected, richness of motives that truly drive human behaviour. From the Declaration of Independence to classical economic theory, the self-interested pursuit of happiness is supposed to be the sovereign human motivation. But of course it's not. Here are some of the other equally fundamental motivations which have emerged in studies of human behaviour: altruism, skill mastery, frugality, bettering one's community, relationships, self-esteem, autonomy, freedom from fear, freedom from coercion, loyalty, doing the right thing, playfulness, and curiosity. Depending on the situation, these motives have been shown to drive human behaviour far more powerfully than narrow self-interest.

Heroic Agent Bias

Heroic Agent Bias is summed up by the phrase 'to a hammer every problem looks like a nail'. In other words, for a given problem, we inevitably tend to overestimate the effectiveness of our own bubble of knowledge and expertise. When it comes to solving human problems, Heroic Agent Bias causes legislators to overestimate the effects of laws; scientists to overestimate the effect of research; planners to overestimate the effect of plans; engineers to overestimate the effect of built structures; educators to overestimate the effect of knowledge; marketers to overestimate the effect of messages; doctors to overestimate the effect of drugs; air force generals to overestimate the effect of bombing; theologians to overestimate the power of faith; artists to overestimate the effect of art; and CEOs to overestimate the effect of corporate restructuring.

Heroic Agent Bias conveniently allows trained professionals to star in their own dramas, feeling relevant and important at the same time.

When it comes to influencing the behaviour of a particular group of people, Heroic Agent Bias causes change makers to simultaneously overestimate their own power and underestimate the power of those people's inner motivations and the situational forces that affect them. At its worst, it leads to a 'we know what you need' arrogance that practically ensures failure.

Heroic Agent Bias is marvellously adaptable. When thwarted, it can swing wildly in the opposite direction. It causes us to take responsibility for success but deny responsibility for failure, deftly shifting blame to others. When the failure is particularly stinging, the blame can be vitriolic. "We gave the Iraqis their freedom," pronounced liberal Californian Senator Barbara Boxer in 2006. "What are they doing with this freedom? They're killing each other."[9]

We want to live in a world where we exercise control over what happens. As a result, we are all biased in favour of theories that see ourselves as controlling the course of events and we are naturally prejudiced against theories that see ourselves as powerless or irrelevant.

For engineers, managers, politicians and generals it's especially galling. They have to believe they can control events. It's a matter of professional pride. If human beings turn out to be more strongly influenced by their inner motivations and forces beyond the control of professionals then those professionals face the awful truth of their own feebleness. It's so much more comforting to believe they are in control and have the answers. I suspect Heroic Agent Bias is the explanation for many failed change projects, both laughable and tragic.

A few years ago, I was trekking in a remote part of the island of Sulawesi in Indonesia. One village lay beside a fast-flowing, crystal-clear river on a rainforest plateau. I asked our guide about swimming in the river. He said it was OK, provided we swam on the upstream side of the village. The down-stream side was for something else. And, sure enough, it was the villagers' bathroom; in fact, we were expected to crap in the water as well. Later, walking around the village at dusk, I noticed a big new TV satellite dish and the guide told the story of how it came to be there. A couple of years earlier, two Dutch tourists had visited the village and were appalled when they saw the river being used as a latrine. So they went back to the Netherlands and raised money for the villagers to build sanitary facilities away from the river. You guessed it . . . the villagers spent the money on satellite TV, something they clearly valued more.

A similar thing happened to the Chinese eco-village designed by the famous American green architect William McDonough. It was "a classic case of good intentions gone horribly wrong" wrote an investigating journalist about the project to turn the village of Huangbaiyu in north-east China into the nation's first ecologically sustainable village. The plan called for a new village of 'eco-dwellings' to be made from hay and pressed earth bricks, fully insulated, solar-powered and facing south, clustered together in the centre of the village so the villagers' higgledy-piggledy plots of farm-land could be consolidated into more efficient lots. But no one bothered to ask the villagers about the project and they refused to pay for the houses once they were built. "Why would I want to pay 50,000 to 60,000 yuan, which I don't have, for this new house? The whole village has no relation-ship to us," said one. The dismayed anthropologist who evaluated the project commented, "Even if the houses were more affordable and even if you raised people's income, they may not want to spend the money on a new house, they might want to send their daughter to high school or get surgery for grandma or open a small store." [10]

In order to be better change makers, the safest starting point is to admit that we don't know best, and that our theories are often wrong.

How to make better theories

Being theory-less, however, is not an option. It would mean leaping into expensive and time-consuming efforts with no idea why they might succeed. Being theory-less is also impossible. Our actions are *always* guided by our mental theories or models, even when we don't think they are. The trick is to be conscious and versatile in our theory-making. After all, the real failure is not making mistakes, it's failing to learn from them. Failures are essential. As sixteenth-century philosopher Francis Bacon put it, "Truth emerges more readily from error than from confusion." The trick is to be able to figure out what caused the failure. Having a conscious theory of change makes that possible.

The 'So what?' test

Barry Hamilton, then community safety director at Western Australia's Fire and Emergency Services Authority, told me about his cruel and unusual habit. His staff were supposed to convince communities across Western Australia, a state the size of western Europe, to prepare for emergencies such as cyclones and bushfires. Whenever one of them presented a campaign idea, Hamilton's standard response was "So what?" It was infuriating but brilliant because it shook his people out of their easy assumptions.

Try it. Ask someone: "What could you do to cause A to change their behaviour?" And when they pop out a confident reply, say "So what?" When they come back with a different theory, say "So what?" again. Repeat until they try to strangle you. This method is excellent at exposing and demolishing the assumptions behind half-baked ideas.

Get a brains trust

Demolishing bad theories is only half the job. We also need to create better ones.

Bad theories are often concocted by lone geniuses sitting in the corners of their rooms or offices and trying to figure out how to save the world in their own private headspaces, with their own private prejudices and their own teeny-weeny stores of knowledge and experience. That's the lone genius theory of change. Lone geniuses might, just occasionally, produce a better light bulb or piston engine, but for every lone genius who succeeds, there are hundreds who fail. The way to maximise your chance of success is never to theorise alone. In other words: get a brains trust. And, to get the best out of your brains trust, make sure it's diverse, informed and inspired, and enjoying itself. Here's why.

Make sure your brains trust is diverse

Many brains beat single brains at solving all sorts of problems. They bring a marvellous collective intelligence as well as a store of knowledge and experiences. And many brains stimulate each other to think with more energy and enthusiasm than lonely brains. Crowds have a natural wisdom which is most famously illustrated by the striking accuracy of election wagering. In the 15 US presidential elections between 1884 and 1940, for instance, the betting firms were wrong just once.[11]

But there is also a dark side to the wisdom of crowds. The wisdom only works when the starting point is more than 50 per cent of people being more than 50 per cent right. If more than 50 per cent of people are more than 50 per cent wrong, a crowd may not produce wise results. Instead, it may produce nutty, counter-productive and unjust results.[12] A fascinating experiment on the dynamics of jury deliberation showed just how far the wisdom of deliberating groups is sensitive to the pre-existing prejudices of the majority.[13]

The 2005 experiment brought together 60 residents of Colorado who were divided into ten groups. The members of both groups were asked to debate three of the most controversial issues of the day: Should states allow same-sex couples to enter into civil union? Should employers engage in affirmative action by giving preference to members of disadvantaged groups? Should the US sign an international treaty to combat global warming?

The groups were selected to ensure that all their members started with either liberal or conservative views on the issues at stake.

Here's the interesting thing: after just 15 minutes of discussion, most members became more extreme in their views. The liberals became more strongly in favour of civil unions, affirmative action and a treaty on global warming, and the conservatives became more strongly opposed to those things. The discussion also produced more homogenous views. Before people began to talk there was a certain amount of disagreement. After talking, that diversity of views was lost.

It's all about the natural dynamics of groups. Some people compete for recognition by advocating stronger views. Others shift their positions to avoid disharmony and rejection. And everyone feels better when their views are corroborated by others, no matter whether they are right or wrong. In almost no time, just 15 minutes in this case, the common prejudices of the group were exaggerated. That's 'group think' at work.

When a group of people come together to tackle a problem, their worst enemy is their own unconscious biases. It's therefore vital to ensure that the group is diverse – drawn from a mix of backgrounds and life experiences – to ensure that no one set of prejudices dominates and that assumptions can get challenged.

Ideally, you'd want a mix of ages, genders, educational backgrounds and life experiences. And maybe a wild card or two – how about a graffiti artist, a theatre director, or a dance party enthusiast – to add a little creativity to the mix.

Make sure your brains trust is informed and inspired

Another shocking demonstration of how groups can go wrong comes from an experiment that showed how knowledge held in common can prejudice a discussion. In this case, groups of four people were asked to select the best political candidate.

In some groups most of the important information was known by every member. Those groups uniformly made the best decision, choosing the candidate who was clearly best fitted for public office. In the other groups vital pieces of information were known only to single members of each group, while the commonly held information favoured the inferior candidates. Here the discussion took a weird turn: after discussion far fewer groups favoured the best candidate. The reason for this change was that the information which had a biggest influence on group members was the information that was held in common.[14]

In other words, the quality of decision-making depends on the quality of the knowledge that's *shared* before the group starts deliberating. Or, put more simply, garbage in, garbage out.

Imagine a dotted line around you that's the sum of your ideas and experiences. It's not very big. You're just one person and there's a hell of a lot you haven't experienced or heard about. Now imagine the dotted lines around each member of your brains trust. Each of them adds a pile of knowledge and stories and strengths to your effort, but, even then, it's tiny compared to what they don't know. And they might easily be infected by a commonly held misconception or prejudice that biases the results of their discussion.

So, making sure relevant knowledge is shared *before* the brains trust starts deliberating is one of your most important jobs. That means doing wide preliminary research and presenting it to the group. What is known to influence change? What is the baseline data on the problem? What are people saying about the problem and their role in it? What are the technical, scientific, regulatory and legislative aspects you'll need to be aware of?

Worse still, their shared prejudice may be a belief that the problem cannot be solved. If no one they know has ever tackled this problem successfully, the group as a whole may be pessimistic about the possibility of success. They won't let themselves dream. They'll censor their imaginations. The thoughts that need to be spoken might seem ludicrous and impossible because they don't have optimistic stories that contradict the accumulated history of failure.

So your role is to inspire your brains trust. Inspiring means blowing away the limitations imposed by their small circles of experience. "Nearly every problem has been solved by someone, somewhere," wrote Bill Clinton. So start by blowing their minds about possibilities and ideas they have never imagined – surprising and stereotype-challenging solutions from Buenos Aires, London, Stockholm and Lagos. Google puts us a few clicks away from all this knowledge. So, before you start, spend time exploring the world and don't stop until you're genuinely excited by the methods others have used, no matter how seemingly wacky and unfamiliar. If you're inspired, your brains trust will be too.

Once you've got a brains trust that's diverse, informed and inspired, there's one more quality that will make the difference between boring, conventional thinking and bold, creative thinking. That's whether they are enjoying themselves.

Make sure your brains trust is happy

In 1998 a psychologist named Barbara Fredrickson asked a question no psychologist had apparently thought to ask before: "What good are positive emotions?"[15] She was intrigued by an experiment by Marcial Losada, an organisational psychologist who had observed business teams developing their annual plans. He used one-way mirrors and had his researchers categorise every utterance the teams made. Strikingly, the biggest factor that predicted successful performance by each team in the following months was the number of emotionally positive remarks they made.

Fredrickson looked around for other research into the effect of positive emotions and discovered that enjoyment makes a tremendous difference to people's performance and creativity. She cited research that found that when students were in a positive mood they performed better in tests; when negotiators felt positive they found win-win solutions more often; and when doctors felt positive they solved complex medical dilemmas without getting stuck on their initial diagnosis.

Fredrickson wrote:

> Joy sparks the urge to play, interest sparks the urge to explore, contentment sparks the urge to savor and integrate, and love sparks a recurring cycle of each of these urges within safe, close relationships. [This contrasts with] the narrowed mindsets sparked by many negative emotions . . . such as attack or flee. By broadening an individual's momentary thought-action repertoire . . . positive emotions promote discovery of novel and creative actions, ideas and social bonds, which in turn build that individual's personal resources.[16]

Which is a complicated way of saying that enjoyment opens people up to their own memories and experiences and encourages playful "exploration, invention and just plain fooling around" so that problems get solved more imaginatively.

This suggests you can shift a group towards creativity simply by increasing their enjoyment while they're doing an activity.

Enjoyment is an easy thing for a leader or facilitator to produce. It simply takes a light-hearted touch, food, games, ground rules against negativity, and processes that focus relentlessly on positive outcomes, assets and strengths, and above all, freedom from the pressure of goals and timetables, which are death for creativity.[17]

Watching a team brainstorming a tricky creative challenge recently, I noticed their knotted brows and unhappy faces. Then they got their first creative spark and started laughing. The happier they got, the more creative they were and this made them even happier until they were a five-person riot. And I noticed it was a two-way flow. Happiness increased creativity. But creativity also increased happiness! It's possible that, once a group experiences success on a creative task, it's a virtuous circle.

What follows

Now you've got a diverse, informed, inspired and creative brains trust, you'll want to give them some work to do. Scattered through this book are Method sections that give step-by-step instructions for activities you can do with your brains trust that use their collective minds to generate your next change project. The most important of these activities will be creating theories of change.

Keep in mind, however, that someone wise once said "All theories are wrong but some are useful." Even with a diverse, informed, inspired and imaginative brains trust, theorising about human beings will always be an uncertain business. No theory can ever be perfect. Every theory is only a provisional step towards a better theory. Yet, inevitably, most of what we do as change makers is based on our theories. Since, despite our best intentions, our unconscious theories are often biased or half-baked, it's valuable to turn theory-making into a conscious activity. At the start of any attempt to influence the behaviour of others we should be able to say: "I believe this effort will succeed because . . ." and then make the effort a test of the theory.

Improving the way we theorise about human change is the purpose of this book. It's designed to provide insight into what makes people tick and change. It's a compilation of what's been shown to work, or not work, when it comes to influencing groups of people to adopt new behaviours. Incidentally, the book also IS a theory of change (although that may not be clear until the end). Despite that, it's not meant to be a substitute for your own imagination. Instead, it's a stockpile of ideas that helps you avoid biases and saves you the trouble of testing and demolishing commonly held theories that don't work, while suggesting some unexpected ones that might.

What, then, does the accumulated knowledge of change makers, psychologists and scholars tell us about changing the behaviour of groups, communities and societies? Let's start with a critical look at the dubious track record of some of the most common theories of change.

Method

Establish a brains trust

When setting out to change the world, a little bit of process goes a long way. A great change effort rarely crystallises out of thin air in a moment of brilliance. Good results depend on teamwork, even if it's just a team of two. Working with a team and keeping them on the same page can benefit immensely from a step-by-step process. So, here is one you might like to follow or feel free to modify to suit your needs and situation.

Who develops a project is vital. You and your immediate circle of colleagues will be too similar in your unconscious assumptions to avoid the hazards of group-think. You'll need a wider circle of brains, one that has enough diversity of life experience and expertise to ensure that unconscious assumptions get challenged. To achieve this, invite a diverse mix of people to be your brains trust – perhaps between 10 and 20 individuals. They'll need to meet a few times during the project. They might include:

- people whose lives are affected by the environmental, social or health problem
- a mixture of professional experts who can help to devise a wide range of interventions; for example engineers, facilitators, urban planners, designers or educators
- academics who have researched the problem and its solutions
- creative types; for example, a poet, a theatre director, an artist, an architect, or a cartoonist (they'll be essential when it comes to inventing funny and engaging tactics)
- government managers (not fence-sitters but people with a passion to solve the problem)
- internal players in your organisation (again, you will need people with passion).

Don't be afraid to invite senior people and decision-makers. They might only come along once but their buy-in might prove decisive later on.

By the way, avoid having opponents in your brains trust. You don't want to spend your precious time squabbling.

Inspire and inform your brains trust

Before you start strategising, it's vital you and your brains trust have all the background information and inspiration you need to think wisely and creatively. That means plenty of Googling and talking to knowledgeable people, then collating what you find and sharing it with your brains trust.

A useful first job for your brains trust is to help you develop your research agenda.

Instructions for your brains trust

Invite your brains trust to brainstorm two questions:

1. "What do we need to know before we start planning?"
2. "How could we get insight into the lives and needs of the people we hope will act?"

Here's a simple exercise to begin the process:

- First, each member of the brains trust silently jots down their thoughts or ideas on the two questions above (2 minutes).
- Then the group brainstorms answers to those questions (15 minutes).
- Finally, there is a group discussion, looking for points of consensus (15 minutes).

Some of the research items they might identify could include:

- Baseline data on the problem
- Known causes of the problem
- What is known to influence change? (Try Google Scholar.)
- What the affected people say and think. (Conduct interviews or focus

groups, observe how people act in real life, look for published social research, talk to experts or informants who know their community well.)

- Lessons from similar projects. (Try Google Scholar, speak directly to experienced project staff in other places, get hold of evaluation reports from other projects.)
- Lessons from dissimilar projects. (Google outside your discipline, e.g. if you're starting a health project, look beyond the health field to community dance, street art, community gardening and so on – you might be surprised at what you find!)
- What are your stakeholders and potential partners thinking? What is the link to their core business? How do they define success? What resources and people could they provide?
- Technical, scientific, regulatory and legislative aspects of the problem.
- Intersecting strategies, plans and projects of other organisations.
- Money: where could you get more from?

Now do the research and share what you've discovered

Now take the list of research ideas your brains trust has generated, and carry out the research. When you've finished, collate what you've found and report it back to your brains trust. Give them a detailed account of what you've discovered about the problem, the people and the possible solutions. To increase their immersion, why not let them hear from experts or people who are living with the problem, or take them on a tour to see, smell and touch the problem, or to see imaginative solutions in action?

And while it's important to look at the problem, it's even more important to look at possible solutions. As their facilitator, your job is to provide a rich, tasty and nutritious mixture of positive images and stories to feed their imaginations. Discover how other communities have tackled similar problems and created better futures. It's a big planet and it's full of inspirations – people in Denmark, Oregon, Guangzhou, Saskatoon and Christchurch are wrestling with exactly the same problems. Find out what they are creating and fill your brains trust's imaginations with positive and exciting ideas. Now they are ready to strategise.

The social immune system
Why tell, sell and threaten rarely work

Fear of salsa

If you've ever run a training course you'll know the post-lunch pit of doom. It's when students zone out following the apparently exhausting effort of digesting those tiny savoury sandwiches. Rows of blank faces peer back with empty 'Do-we-have-to-be-here?' eyes.

It's time for an energiser. The trainer invites his undead students to rise for some playful physical activity designed to jolt them out of their death-like stupor.

Usually it's not so hard. As long as it doesn't involve mental effort, most people will willingly rise to the challenge of jumping around a bit after lunch.

But not always. Once, while teaching a class of adult educators, my invitation to be energised met with total, intransigent resistance.

During the morning introductions it emerged that the tallest, most glamorous woman in the class was a salsa instructor. When the pit of doom arrived, I invited her to lead the class in a few salsa steps. First she demonstrated a couple of steps. Then I joined her, incompetently. Next I invited the class to join in. And here's what happened: they froze in their seats. I repeated the invitation. Blank stares. "It's easy," I coaxed, "just stand up and take two steps forward and two steps back, like this", with a clumsy wiggle of the hips.

Sullen silence. A room full of intelligent, competent adults had switched from easy-going compliance to truculent insurrection. In the end I had to give up and get them to play a game that involved a lot of running around and dodging each other. That was OK. Salsa wasn't.

I think that was an apt illustration of the comfort zone at work. Salsa-ing in public, it seems, is outside most people's comfort zone. It's located, quite firmly, in their scary zone.

Comfort zones aren't places; they're sets of behaviours that aren't going to get us into trouble. We love our comfort zones precisely because they feel safe and certain. And what lies outside the comfort zone? A scary wilderness of potential embarrassment, humiliation, rejection, social annihilation, not to mention bother, lost time, cost, injury, pain, uncertainty and anxiety. The scary zone is scary because it involves unfamiliar behaviours, and even seemingly simple behaviours can be frightening for those who have never done them before.

Of course, what also lies outside the comfort zone is hope: the possibility of bettering oneself. We intuitively know this and so the scary zone has a dread fascination. At its best and worst, it's a dizzying swirl of hope and fear, where exultation and terror intermingle. We may dream of going there, but most of the time we prefer to stick with behaviours that are tried and safe.

Arrogantly, those of us who can already salsa (or don't care what other people think of us), routinely discount the fears sparked by even this simple act.

Humiliation

It could just be me, but I suspect that of all the terrors that lurk in the scary zone, humiliation might be the worst. Here's how Evelin Lindner of the University of Oslo described humiliation in her study of the Rwandan genocide:[1]

> To be humiliated is to be placed, against your will . . . and often in a deeply hurtful way, in a situation that is greatly inferior to what you feel you should expect. Humiliation entails demeaning treatment that transgresses established expectations . . . one of the defining characteristics of humiliation . . . is that the victim is forced into passivity, acted upon, made helpless.

Humiliation is a multi-headed beast. It often involves loss of control, damaged self-image and awful feelings of rejection.

Humiliation is hurtful because it damages our sense of self. Cruel looks, words or actions (or our own bumbling) make us out to be weaker, dumber, plainer, less astute and more inept than we believe ourselves to be.

For some reason, psychologists haven't yet explored humiliation but they have studied its accompanying state: rejection. Brain scans show that rejection lights up the same regions of the brain as physical pain.[2]

Rejection hurts because it eats away at the social connections that affirm our identity. How do we know we are good, attractive, loved, popular, smart, creative or hip? It's the opinions, words and responses of others that give us the social proof that we are who we imagine ourselves to be. Without that affirmation, our sense of self can disintegrate.

As identity fragments, so does behaviour. In experiments over many years, Roy Baumeister of Florida State University and his colleagues showed that rejected individuals have less self-regulation, less problem-solving ability,[3] more aggression,[4] and more self-defeating activity than connected individuals. Rejected people tend to make fewer healthy choices and more unhealthy choices, and they have a greater tendency to give up when faced with frustration.[5]

Studies have shown that men without meaningful close relationships are more likely to be arrested for speeding and be involved in car accidents, especially those involving alcohol. Single women are more likely to abuse alcohol and drugs. Individuals suffering from the social pain of grief or loss are more likely to die from risky behaviour including accidents and alcohol abuse.[6] Prolonged social exclusion can lead to depression, suicide, association with anti-social fringe groups, and, rarely, mass killings such as the Columbine High School massacre in 1999.[7] A 2004 analysis showed that 13 out of 15 recent killings in American schools were carried out by adolescent males who had experienced repeated social rejection. A study of over 12,000 adolescents by Michael Resnick and his colleagues found that connectedness was the single biggest factor protecting adolescents from violence.[8]

On the scale of nations, humiliation and fear of humiliation are associated with atrocities and civil wars. The Arab-Israeli conflict, the Chechen wars, riots by alienated Muslim youths in France, and the breakdown of civil order in Kenya are cases in point. Humiliation is a significant factor in the psychology of genocide. Evelin Lindner, in her cross-cultural study of genocides, noted that "it was the fear of imagined future destitution and humiliating subjugation of one group at the hands of another" that formed the motivation for genocidal killings in Rwanda, Somalia and Nazi Germany.[9]

In short, the fear of humiliation puts humans in a bad place.

The fear of humiliation is not just something that happens during civil wars, schoolyard bullying and racial discrimination. If, like me, you're a keen fan of *Funniest Home Videos* or similar TV programmes, you'll be aware that each of us hovers only an inch away from humiliation as we go about our daily lives. And it's unfamiliar activities, like salsa dancing, that are most likely to reveal our ineptitude and inferiority.

The potential for humiliation, along with a host of other fears, costs and unwelcome bothers, is present whenever someone faces a decision to do something new, even a simple, benign act like volunteering, going to the gym, starting a garden, cutting down on alcohol or fatty foods, or picking up their dog poop.

For example, consider the decision to quit smoking. Quitting not only involves the emotional and physical pain of giving up an addiction but also the threat of social rejection. A study of young smokers in New York City observed that:

> youth had to cope with temptation, frequent and often intense urges or cravings for cigarettes, and lack of social support from their family and friends. The young participants not only had to cope with general life stresses without being able to use cigarettes to reduce tensions but also had to contend with new stressful situations, such as friends who put them down for not smoking. In addition, the teens had to give up things that were important to them, such as friendships, during their quit attempts.[10]

Put simply: change can be scary and hard. Change makers miss something vital when they discount the fears, costs, difficulties and potential humiliations people face when contemplating change in their lives.

Why education fails

In 1984, the United States Congress passed laws encouraging the states to raise the legal drinking age to 21 years. Underage drinking did indeed change as states began to comply with the laws, but not in the way they expected. Before the laws came into force, it was clear that alcohol consumption tended to increase gradually with age. Following the laws, however, numerous studies showed that under-21s began to drink more heavily than over-21s. Alcohol consumption increased, binge-drinking increased, and drink-driving arrests increased for 18- to 21-year-olds, while there were no similar increases for 21 to 23-year-olds.[11]

A large study of students in 56 US colleges in 1987 found that 24 per cent of students under the age of 21 were heavy drinkers, compared with 15 per cent of students aged over 21. This pattern was in complete contrast to patterns extending back to the early 1950s. The researchers concluded that raising the minimum legal purchasing age did not reduce underage drinking. "In fact, the legislation may actually have contributed to increased drinking among underage students."[12]

This example is one of many that illustrate how well-meaning attempts to influence people's behaviour can produce exactly the opposite results, what has been called a 'boomerang effect'.[13]

It turns out that we humans are manufactured with a special feature – standard in all models – that protects us against attempts by others to drag us out of our comfort zones. It's a kind of social immune system which produces two powerful immune responses: denial and resistance – the cognitive equivalents of flight and fight.

Denial is when people turn a blind eye to information that threatens their identity or interests. They decide "it's not my problem" or "I can't stop it" or "my wife won't let me" or "it won't make any difference anyway" and continue doing what they do, often concocting elaborate arguments to convince themselves there's no need to change.

Resistance is a more active state. It involves purposefully rebellious behaviour. It occurs whenever people feel their familiar behaviours are actively threatened. They reassert their right to continue those behaviours by doing them more often, with greater energy, commitment, zest and enjoyment than before. A recent study in the *Journal of Personality and Social Psychology* found that men are more likely to stray if their significant other scolds them for checking out other women. That's resistance.[14]

Denial and resistance are everywhere. If you're a parent, a child, a spouse, an employer or an employee, you experience them every day (or every few minutes). The cycle of threat–resistance–counter-threat–more resistance explains wars, revolutions, strikes and family breakdowns.

Denial and resistance explain why change projects fail to get results as advertised and often produce boomerang effects where undesirable behaviours get worse.

Professionals who design education programmes aren't immune from denial when it comes to judging the effectiveness of their programmes. Just how stunningly they've been in denial has become visible in recent years with the arrival of a new form of evaluation: the systematic review.

Rigorous evaluation is a rarity in most fields of social change – except health promotion. Health promoters have been professionally evaluating their efforts for decades, and there's now a large body of published data about the effectiveness of different approaches to influencing people's health behaviours. In recent years, independent statisticians have begun to pore over this data, collating scores of published evaluations into massive systematic reviews (sometimes called meta-evaluations or reviews-of-reviews). The result is a growing body of knowledge that lets us make judgements about the merits of various approaches.

The results are depressing news for anyone advocating 'tell' or 'sell' approaches to behaviour change. By 'tell', I mean approaches that focus on imparting information, and by 'sell' I mean approaches drawn from marketing that often use emotions such as fear and humour to influence behaviour.

In 2002, for instance, a group of medical researchers at McMasters University in Canada analysed 26 evaluations of sex education programmes targeted at adolescents.[15] They found the programmes "did not delay initiation of sexual intercourse in young women or young men; did not improve use of birth control . . . and did not reduce pregnancy rates in young women. Four abstinence programmes and one school-based sex education programme were associated with an increase in number of pregnancies among partners of young male participants."

In 2004, a group of British researchers examined 144 anti-smoking programmes targeting young people in the USA, UK and Finland.[16] They found little evidence of success, except for a minority of programmes that involved peer support or social learning interventions.*

---

* We'll talk more about social learning, or modelling, later. It's a promising approach.

A 2002 review compared 56 anti-drinking programmes from around the world aimed at under-25-year-olds. They found 36 had detectable effects on drinking behaviours but the effects had evaporated in less than 12 months. Four of the programmes actually seemed to increase drinking behaviour. Only three showed evidence of changes lasting up to three years.[17]

In 2002 the Scottish Executive commissioned a world-wide review of the effectiveness of mass-media alcohol education campaigns. The programmes, the researchers concluded, raised people's knowledge about alcohol but had virtually no impact on their behaviour. "The balance of evidence suggests mass media educational campaigns on their own have . . . no impact on drinking behaviour."[18]

Drug education programmes fared no better. A 1998 review examined 62 drug education programmes targeting people aged 8 to 25 years, mainly in the USA. They found only 18 showed evidence of change in drug use, but "the impact . . . was small with dissipation of programme gains over time". The average effect of the programmes was equivalent to just 3.7 per cent of participants delaying taking up drugs or never using them.[19]

In 2007, a study of 13 HIV education programmes based on sexual abstinence involving 15,940 US youths found not one programme reduced the incidence of unprotected sex, number of partners, condom use, or age of starting sex.[20] The researchers concluded that programmes "that exclusively encourage abstinence from sex do not seem to affect the risk of HIV infection in high income countries".

A 2007 review of evaluations of 57 nutrition education programmes targeting schoolchildren found "mostly failure. Just four showed any real success in changing the way kids eat or any promise as weapons against the growing epidemic of childhood obesity." "Any person looking at the published literature about these programmes would have to conclude that they are generally not working," wrote Dr Tom Baranowski, paediatrics professor at Baylor College of Medicine in Houston, Texas.[21]

Even in the face of serious and imminent threats to their health, people still seem remarkably resistant to being told how to behave.

A 1996 New Zealand study of asthma sufferers found that few would use peak flow meters or use emergency services during an asthma attack. The disappointed researchers concluded "For many of us who place education at the highest priority, it is a difficult concept to accept that the acquisition of knowledge is not necessarily followed by the initiation of appropriate action. The access to knowledge . . . about a disease such as asthma should not be assumed to translate into changes in behavioural practices, even if these actions would be of direct benefit to the involved persons."[22]

In 2004, Australian road safety researchers drew a similar chastening conclusion: "One of the disturbing problems with speeding is that while most people accept that speeding increases crash risk, most people continue to speed. Researchers have found that most campaigns are more successful in conveying information and changing attitudes than in altering behaviour."[23]

I could go on, but you get the message.

Systematic reviews are rare in fields like climate change, water conservation, sustainable farm management and so on, but my hunch is we'd see similar results. The conclusion is that programmes that aim to inform people how they should behave are unlikely to show positive effects on behaviour.

Systematic reviews of thousands of evaluated educational efforts reveal an ordinary truth: we humans don't like being given unwanted advice about how we should behave. We have a powerful immune system that protects us from just such attempts to influence our behaviour. It turns out that threatening ideas are just like physical threats. They cause normal, reasonable human beings like you and me to respond with flight (denial) or fight (resistance).

Denial theory

Back in the 1950s a young Californian psychologist named Leon Festinger was hired by the Behavioral Sciences Division of the Ford Foundation to audit all published knowledge about communication and social influence. Not surprisingly, he soon found a way to avoid such an onerous task. Instead, he developed a fascination with a perplexing problem.

After the Indian earthquake of 1934 rumours spread among the survivors that an even more horrible earthquake was to come. Why, Festinger wondered, would traumatised people willingly believe a rumour that had the effect of increasing their anxiety? Eventually he realised that the answer might not be that the rumour was anxiety-provoking, but that it was anxiety justifying. He was on the verge of developing one of the most influential theories in psychology.

His theory sought to explain what happens when there is an inconsistency between what people know and what they do. This inconsistency, he said, causes psychological discomfort. The term 'psychological discomfort', as Festinger used it, was a catch-all for feelings of frustration, guilt, unease, anguish, disgust or emotional pain, feelings we now know are processed in a deep brain structure called the insular cortex which, tellingly, is also involved with bodily representation or self-image.

According to Festinger, people respond to this psychological pain in one of two ways. They either change their behaviour, or they avoid situations or information that remind them of the inconsistency.[24] Since behaviour is often hard to change, people usually prefer to modify their beliefs, attitudes and sources of information to avoid the discomfort. They do this quite unconsciously and automatically. The economist J. K. Galbraith said it perfectly: "Faced with the choice between changing one's mind and proving there is no need to do so, almost everyone gets busy on the proof." Festinger called his theory 'cognitive dissonance', although a better name would be 'denial theory'.

One of Festinger's most interesting studies involved a UFO cult. The cult consisted of about 25 middle-class followers of a suburban housewife who prophesied that a great flood would sweep away civilisation at midnight on a certain day in 1956. Only her small group of believers would be rescued by a flying saucer.

On the night of the predicted flood the group gathered in the home of the leader to await the alien rescuers. Unfortunately, neither flood nor flying saucer materialised. From midnight to almost five a.m. the group struggled to find an explanation. Then, at 4.45 a.m. their leader received a message from God, saying that He had saved the world because of the light and strength of the group. The group accepted the message, and from that moment they became devoted advocates of the new belief. Moreover, they completely transformed the character of their cult, abandoning their previous secretive existence, and embarking on a very public media campaign to obtain new adherents.

Festinger's explanation is that the group suffered huge dissonance – psychological discomfort – when the prophecy failed. They had two choices, either give up their beliefs and dissolve the group, or invent a new justification to continue their existence. Rather than abandoning the social support of their tightly knit group, they grasped at a new justification for continuing the life of their cult. What's more, the extreme dissonance that they felt motivated them to embark on an equally extreme campaign of public self-justification.

The point of Festinger's theory was that the UFO cult members were not freaks. Although their beliefs were wacky, their behaviour was quite normal. They liked belonging to their group and wanted to avoid change at all costs. When faced with a personal threat they eagerly grasped whatever argument would help avoid unpleasant truths, and then over-justified their behaviour with extravagant assertions of righteousness. It all sounds quite familiar.*

Festinger's theory was very controversial at the time. It challenged conventional wisdoms about human behaviour. There have since been many experiments to either disprove it or to understand it. The current consensus among psychologists seems to be that dissonance, at its core, is about a challenge to people's identity or self-concept. We humans are at our most defensive when we feel our sense of self is under attack. The psychologist Elliot Aronson wrote that most people have favourable views of themselves: they want to see themselves as competent, moral, and able to predict their own behaviour.[25] When they're given evidence that contradicts those self-perceptions, dissonance and denial are the result.

Festinger's theory helps explain why inconvenient truths tend to have so little effect on human behaviour. Information that challenges people's identity causes something close to physical pain. The quickest and easiest way to reduce that pain is to deny the inconsistency and avoid information that reminds them of it.

When our status quo is challenged, our instinct is to defend it. Our marvellous human storytelling ability means we are superbly equipped to rationalise our current behaviours and so protect our comfort zones from the kind of bad news delivered by well-meaning educators.

---

* Economists have their own take on this phenomenon. They call it the 'sunk-costs effect'. People make investments in certain courses of action and may defend those investments to the point of absurdity even when the prospective gains outweigh the benefits. Loss aversion, the tendency to overestimate potential losses compared to potential gains, is the result.

Educational campaigns that offer unsolicited advice about behaviour are therefore likely to force people to voice counter-arguments. And the more people argue for a position, the firmer the position becomes. As psychotherapists William Miller and Steven Rollnick explain, that is exactly the reverse of what a change maker should be doing. "It is the client who should be voicing the arguments for change. When you find yourself in the role of arguing for change while your client (patient, student, child) is voicing arguments against it, you're in precisely the wrong role."[26]

As Festinger found in later experiments, the tendency to ignore inconvenient truths is even stronger when acting on them might be socially humiliating.[27] If our friends get used to our behaving a certain way then there are social costs in being different. The fear of embarrassment or rejection can make it even harder to invest time and effort in making a personal change.

Why threats fail

Supernanny is a popular reality TV show about toddler-taming in which out-of-control children are civilised by the loving use of threats and punishments.

Each episode follows a similar format. It starts with a fly-on-the-wall view of a middle-class family where chaos rules. There is a teary exasperated mum, a disengaged dad and a blur of hideously misbehaving children aged between two and eight.

These kids are not just non-compliant. They are monsters. They throw tantrums, assault siblings, bite parents, smash toys. They are masters of emotional tyranny and use their skills to manipulate their parents into supplying torrents of sweets and junk food that drive them into even more frenzied exhibitions of savagery. These children are so ruthlessly disobedient and self-interested that you just want to reach inside your TV and strangle them. But Supernanny knows better.

Supernanny is Jo Frost, a professional English nanny with a steely resolve. She always arrives at the family's home in a London taxi, introduces herself and promptly humiliates the parents by forcing them to watch a video of the wreckage of their family life. The shaken adults promise to follow her instructions and the fun begins.

Jo follows the family around for a day, uttering gasps of horror and theatrical looks of disgust. Then she gets down to business. A family meeting is called. Everyone gathers around a big chart in the kitchen. Jo has made a strict schedule of daily activities and a list of house rules. She patiently explains how everything is going to change. The parents are sceptical, but the kids are bug-eyed with the sort of 'uh-oh' awareness that suggests they know their days of omnipotence are numbered.

Jo explains that from now on there will be consequences for breaking the rules, and that will be timeout in a 'naughty spot'. The naughty spot is a lonely corner devoid of amusement. The parents, meanwhile, have responsibilities. They must enforce the rules in a special way. When bad behaviour occurs they must issue a single clear warning. They must crouch down to the child's eye level and, without using physical intimidation, calmly explain that repeated bad behaviour will incur time in the naughty spot. To be released from the naughty spot the child must apologise for his or her actions. And the apology must be rewarded with a warm hug.

A magnificent contest of wills ensues. Cynthia whacks Johnny. Off she goes to the naughty spot. Johnny kicks Cynthia's Barbie *American Idol* Doll. Off he goes. There are dizzying tantrums. We see Johnny or Cynthia fidgeting in the naughty spot, their little faces squeezed into a "you'll never break me" mask of determination.

Meanwhile, the parents are not only battling with their offspring but with their own souls. Will their hearts be broken by the anguished tears of little Cynthia and Johnny? Will they have Supernanny's iron will to endure?

The mighty soap opera teeters back and forth, before finally, the contest subsides. The kids seem to have figured something out: resistance is futile, compliance is surprisingly painless and brings rewards.

The show invariably ends with a touching scene. Jo is departing. The parents are tearful. They say "Thank you, Supernanny. You've given us back our family" or words to that effect. Supernanny offers a final admonition to stick to the rules. Meanwhile, the children – and here's what's remarkable – seem calm, content and apparently quite happy. Maybe they're just relieved the power-tripping English lady is going so they can get back to being the Sopranos. But I think the transformation is too complete to be just theatre. Even though it's only a TV show, something dramatic has happened. You can guess that the war against chaos is far from over, but this family has been altered by the thoughtful use of threats and punishments.

I'm addicted to this morality play of torment and redemption. I guess there are some families that are so dysfunctional that even Supernanny's iron determination cannot mend them. I suppose their footage ends up in the bin. But for the families we get to see, the transformation is striking.

Supernanny looks like a demonstration of the civilising power of appropriate threats and punishments. Her system seems to work like this:

- there are specific, agreed rules, permanently visible on the kitchen wall
- the rules are for the common good, not just the convenience of the parents
- physical intimidation is avoided: the adults crouch down to the child's eye level and issue calm, firm warnings before punishment is applied
- punishment is immediate
- punishment is real, not just a threat
- punishment matters to the child (loss of social interaction and activity)
- punishment relates to breaking a specific rule, it's not personal and it's not casual or random
- punishment is repeated consistently until compliance occurs
- there are rewards for compliance.

These seem to be the Supernanny principles. Not surprisingly, they concur with what psychologists have figured out in experiments with animals, children and adults. The same principles are well established to control classroom behaviour (just Google 'child behaviour modification'). And there's plenty of evidence they work.[28]

Now let's change the scale. What happens when threats and punishments are taken out of relatively controllable environments like homes and classrooms and applied to free-range populations in the larger world?

In the late 1990s the Australian government performed an accidental experiment that illuminated the effectiveness of threats and punishments as tools for changing people's behaviour on a society-wide scale.

The Federal government at that time believed unemployment payments were a privilege not a right. Government ministers were incensed at the number of 'cruising dole bludgers', people who were said to be completely uninterested in working. The employment minister coined the term 'embuggerance' to describe the government's new approach to encourage the long-term unemployed to look for work. It's a military term for making someone's life a torment.[29]

It was decreed that the unemployed must prove they were actively looking for work or suffer loss of payments. The arrangement was called 'mutual obligation'.

At the time, there were about 386,600 people who'd been receiving benefits for more than 12 months.[30] They were the prime targets of embuggerance. The main tool was partial or complete suspension of benefits, known as 'breaching'.

The most common cause for breaching was failure to do certain job-search activities. For example, every unemployed person was supposed to approach ten employers per fortnight to ask for work. They were expected to keep a job search diary, transfer the details onto a form, and present the form fortnightly to the government agency. Failure to complete the diary, to attend official appointments, or to obey instructions would result in loss of benefits.

From 1996 to 2001 the government engaged in a veritable frenzy of breaching. The scale of the campaign was extraordinary. The number of breaches more than quadrupled, reaching 387,000 per year. Many of these were multiple breaches. Amazingly, some 200,000 people were punished for behavioural infringements in a single year.[31] By 2001 the figures were causing widespread outrage and sparked a campaign by church and welfare groups. Embarrassed, the government drastically cut back on breaching, admitting that breaching "could be too harsh on vulnerable people".[32] Breaching rates then fell back to their original level.

Putting aside moral qualms, let's ask: did this society-wide experiment in social change work? Did the vast programme of threats and punishment alter people's behaviour in the intended direction?

Remember, the primary reason for embuggerance was to drive the jobless into job-seeking activity. If pursued with genuine diligence the result should logically have been more long-term unemployed shifting into jobs.

The graph below compares the breaching rate with the long-term unemployment rate (i.e. people unemployed for 12 months or more) during the relevant period.

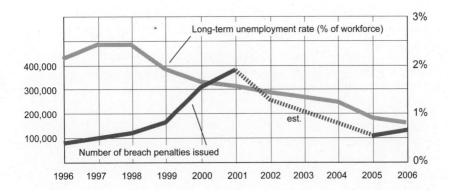

Non-interacting trends. The number of breaches compared with the unemployment rate. The dashed line is an estimate because the government has never released the data.[33]

Compare the two trends. What do you notice? What leaps off the page is that the trends do not interact. The level of breaching seems unrelated to the rate at which the long-term unemployed were getting into jobs. The strongest indicator of this is what happened in 2000-2001. In that year the rate of breaching dramatically spiked but the spike had no detectable effect on the rate of long-term jobless moving into employment. The jobless rate continued gently drifting down in response to a strongly running economy that was creating more jobs. Whatever else was happening here, breaching was not producing the intended behaviour. But, intriguingly, it may have been producing a quite different kind of behaviour.

Look at the next two graphs (see next page). They show robberies in New South Wales over the same period, compared with the breaching rate.

I'm no criminologist, but this seems to be a remarkable coincidence. The rates of robberies without weapons follow eerily similar trajectories to the breaching rates. As breaching increased, so did robbery rates. And as soon as the government backed off, so the robbery rate plummeted rapidly back to below its former level.

It's not hard to make a theory about what may have happened. The loss of income for breaching typically ranged from 18 per cent reduction for 6 months for a first breach, to 2 months with no payment.[34] Breaching was therefore a serious financial punishment for people already on the economic margin. It could be expected to, and did, drive some into homelessness.[35]

Robbery rates per 1,000 population

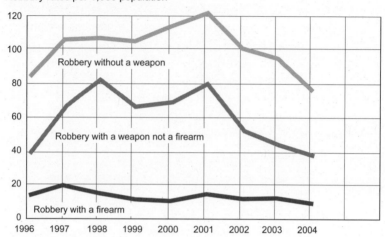

Number of breach penalties issued

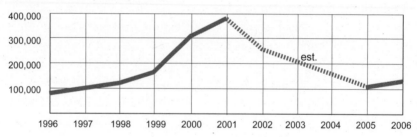

An interesting coincidence. Rates of breaching and robbery without weapons follow strikingly similar trends.[36]

Most people probably borrowed money or slept on friends' floors. But some may have found illegal ways to maintain the normalcy of their lives. Yet their tilt into criminality seems to have been temporary. Once the rate of breaching returned to below its former level, so did the rates of robbery without weapons. If people were criminalised: it was a temporary reaction to a short-term external pressure, not the result of a permanent internal motivation.

Supernanny shows how humanely administered threats and punishments can work in the controllable world of classrooms and family homes.

The Australian embuggerance experiment, however, shows how this approach may fail in the larger, free-range world. High levels of control simply aren't possible. Authorities lack Jo Frost's finely honed social skills. The respectful one-on-one relationships that make behavioural control possible in the home or classroom don't exist in the real world. People feel bullied and that feeling causes determined, sustained resistance.

Resistance theory

Psychologists, bless them, have been delivering electric shocks to animals for decades to understand how punishments modify behaviour. Others have looked at the effect of punishment in classrooms. Meanwhile, economists have been experimenting with economic rewards and punishments.

Whatever their differences, social psychologists and economists agree on one point. Punishment causes anger, hostility, resistance, retaliation and retreat from the punisher.[37]

Resistance is a danger in all kinds of change efforts. The reason is that change is always about substitution. Each time we ask people to adopt a new behaviour, we are also asking them to stop an established behaviour. Before people can adopt healthier, more social, eco-friendly behaviours they have to give up established freedoms like smoking, littering, unprotected sex, speeding, spitting in public, or letting their dogs crap on your lawn. You may think these freedoms suck. It doesn't matter. They are still freedoms and people hate losing them. They hate losing them so much that, even if the freedoms are merely threatened, people will reassert them by doing them with more energy and enjoyment than before.

The original work on the psychology of resistance was done by husband and wife team, Jack and Sharon Brehm, at the University of Kansas. Their theory is a simple one that goes like this: People are motivated to restore free behaviours which are threatened or eliminated.[38]

The result is the 'boomerang effect' or 'forbidden fruit effect' where an educational effort produces the opposite effect.

It's a common and well-documented phenomenon.[39] As early as 1979, experimenters found that health warnings could produce the opposite results. When smokers were given cigarette packets with the statement "Warning by HM Government. Smoking can damage your health", their desire to smoke increased.[40] Similar effects were found with anti-drug warnings. Repeated exposure to the messages: "Using amphetamines and barbiturates can lead to serious trouble. If you're using them – stop now – before it's too late" made people more positive towards drugs.[41]

And warnings about violent films caused audiences to express a greater desire to watch violent films. When these warnings came from an authoritative source, in this case the US Surgeon General, the desire to watch violent films was even greater.[42]

The same for fatty foods. "Warning people about the harmful effects of fatty products only made them want to eat the fatty product more". The researcher concluded, "Although people don't mind being informed about the potentially harmful risks associated with products, they don't like to receive unwanted advice about how they should behave."[43]

Don't muck with comfort zones

"The common people's minds are like clean paper, fit to receive whatsoever by public authorities shall be imprinted in them," wrote that crusty old control freak, Thomas Hobbes, in *Leviathan*, his famous justification for authoritarian government, published in 1651.

After 360 years, tell, sell and threaten continue to be the instinctual responses when authorities try to solve tricky behavioural issues like teen sex, nutrition, drugs and alcohol, climate change, saving water, reducing waste, emergency management, road safety and so on.

The problem with these approaches is that they fail to respect people's comfort zones. Human beings are heroic at resisting changes they don't want. They deny and resist because of the perfectly natural fear of losing control in a dangerous, unpredictable world.

How then do we go about changing the world? Is it even possible?

An aim of this book is to show that change need not be an attack on people's badness. It will always be better to treat people with kindness and respect, recognising their need to remain safe, in control of their lives, and feel good about themselves. Instead of imposing new motivations on people, it will always be better to work with people's existing motivations. Instead of trying to drag people out of their comfort zones, it will always be better to expand those comfort zones by lowering people's fears. Rather than trying to change people, it will always be better to help people change themselves.

I think, from the evidence I can find, that successful change efforts exhibit six ingredients which are very different from tell, sell or threaten. Those ingredients are:

1. *Positive buzz* – when people share optimistic stories about change
2. *An offer of hope* – when people make the connection between a novel action and their own hopes and frustrations
3. *An enabling environment* – when people's environments make new behaviours easy to do and sustain
4. *A sticky solution* – when behaviours are reinvented to better fit people's lives
5. *Expanded comfort zones* – when people are helped to reduce their fears
6. *The right inviter* – when inspiring, trusted peers invite action.

Each of the next six chapters explains one of these ingredients.

Ingredient 1

First, start a buzz

How nothing happens without conversation

Conversation as revolution

Britain's boom commodity of the 1780s was human beings. Tens of thousands of African men, women and children were kidnapped and transported across the Atlantic each year in crowded, filthy slave ships. Those who survived were put to work on Caribbean plantations that produced the second boom commodity of the era, slave-grown sugar.

The elites of the British society – aristocrats, parliamentarians, merchants – made their fortunes from this trade as shareholders in shipping companies or as owners of plantations. Meanwhile, it was an article of faith in British society that the slave trade and slave-grown sugar were cornerstones of national prosperity. In 1773 the value of British imports from the island of Jamaica alone was five times that of the thirteen American colonies put together.

"If, in 1787, you had stood on a London street corner and insisted that slavery was morally wrong and should be stopped, nine out of ten listeners would have laughed you off as a crackpot," wrote historian Adam Hochschild in *Bury the Chains*, his gripping account of the British anti-slavery campaign.[1]

Yet Britain was soon to be engulfed in one of the great social change campaigns in history. Within a year, abolition committees had sprung up in every major city and town. Parliament received more petitions against slavery than on every other issue combined. Anti-slavery tracts packed bookshop shelves. Anti-slavery debates filled newspaper columns and the agendas of debating societies. More than 300,000 Britons were refusing to eat slave-grown sugar. Young barrister Samuel Romilly wrote to a friend about a dinner party he attended in 1789 "The abolition of the slave trade was the subject of conversation, as it is indeed of almost all conversations".[2]

The anti-slavery campaign, however, faced a powerful, well-financed, exceptionally well-connected industry fighting for its survival. The House of Lords was dominated by pro-slavers and sugar lobbyists who formed a seemingly immovable obstacle to change. The abolitionists came achingly close to achieving their goals in the next few years, but then suffered a tremendous setback. The Napoleonic Wars commenced and conservatives used the war hysteria to taint abolitionists as pro-French. Soon, leading anti-slavery activists were in jail and the rest went underground or withdrew from public life.

It appeared the slavers had won. But then history turned again. Nelson's victory over the French at Trafalgar transformed public hysteria into elation and an extraordinary thing happened. The anti-slavery crusade reignited with such ferocity that it was as if the decade of suppression had never occurred. Finally, in 1807 a bill banning the slave trade passed both houses of Parliament. Within a few years, the same Royal Navy that had been protecting the slave ships was hunting them down in the waters of the Atlantic.

What caused this extraordinary social revolution? Quakers, a tiny, often persecuted, religious minority on the margins of British society had campaigned passionately against slavery for decades. But as outsiders their voices counted for little. In the great campaign that arose after 1788 the Quakers would be the hard-working footsoldiers, but abolition did not gain traction until a fortuitous chain of human interactions occurred.

The change seemed to begin in 1783 when news of an atrocity began to circulate in anti-slavery circles. The captain of the slave ship, *The Zong*, had cast into the sea 133 slaves who were too ill to be sold. He fraudulently attempted to recoup the loss through an insurance claim. The insurance company disputed the claim and the matter ended up in court. The story received little attention in the press, but Quakers rapidly spread the news through a letter-writing campaign.

The story eventually reached a prominent Anglican clergyman, Dr Peter Peckard, and it so disturbed him that he preached a sermon condemning the slave trade as a "most barbarous and cruel traffick".[3] Not long afterwards, he was appointed Vice-Chancellor of Cambridge University and in 1785 he set as the topic of Cambridge's prestigious Latin essay contest the question *Anne liceat invitos in servitutem dare?* Is it lawful to makes slaves of others against their will? A 25-year-old divinity student named Thomas Clarkson entered the contest. He knew little about slavery and entered with the sole ambition of winning. Yet as he researched the topic, he became overwhelmed with horror at the barbaric stories he discovered – which included, for instance, the routine burning alive of rebellious slaves on plantations.

He won the Latin essay competition, and, still seething with outrage, marched into the London office of the Quakers who had long campaigned in the wilderness. At last they had an Anglican clergyman – that respectable cornerstone of English society – on their team. It was Clarkson who sought out and recruited William Wilberforce, friend of Prime Minister William Pitt, the powerful and popular orator who would lead the anti-slavery campaign in Parliament. And it was Clarkson who tirelessly crisscrossed Britain, addressing tens of thousands of people in abolitionist groups and public meetings.

Clarkson took to those meetings not just his moral indignation but real-life stories he had meticulously collected from sailors and slave traders. He took objects people could see and touch: slavers' implements of torture and mementoes of African life. And he took a dramatic visual prop: the plan of 482 slaves tightly packed in the slave ship *Brookes*. The plan had fallen into the hands of activists in the port city of Plymouth and was quickly transported to Clarkson and the Quakers who realised its value, reworked it into a poster and distributed thousands of copies. The image soon appeared in newspapers, magazines, books and pamphlets. It "seemed to make an instantaneous impression of horror upon all who saw it," and became one of the most influential campaign posters of all time.[4]

The abolitionists invented the whole armoury of tools modern activists take for granted: the campaign logo, direct mail fundraising, the campaign newsletter, the trade boycott, investigative journalism. However, at the core of their campaign were human interactions. In public meetings, debating societies, coffee houses and at dinner parties people met other like-minded individuals who shared credible stories that sparked outrage and hope.

Hochschild's account demonstrates how a social and political transformation is really built out of interconnected chains of person-to-person interactions. Stories, outrage and hope pass, like a contagion, from person to person. Highly connected, credible individuals play a vital role in this process. It was not, as the Quakers discovered to their discomfort, enough to be right. Social change is a human phenomenon with its own rules and

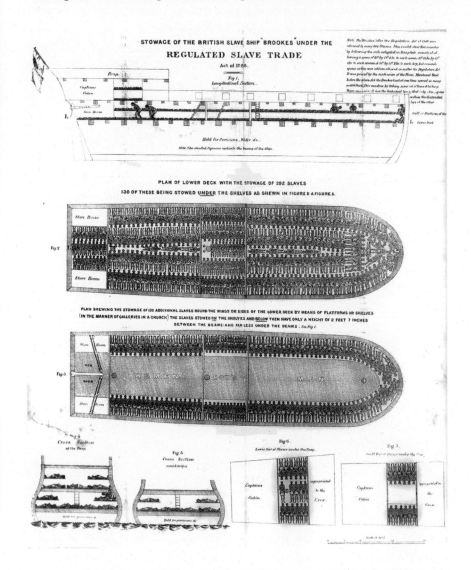

The power of a confronting image. The abolitionists' poster of 482 slaves tightly packed in the slave ship *Brookes* became one of the most influential campaign posters of all time. It "seemed to make an instantaneous impression of horror upon all who saw it."

momentum. The most important of these rules was, clearly, that change must be something people want to talk to each other about.

But not all talk is the same. In the anti-slavery debate a pivotal change took place around 1788. Before 1788 slavery was widely known and disapproved of in polite circles. Yet few people believed anything could be done about it. Before 1788 the talk was all about inaction and blame. It was disempowered talk. But then something changed. People began to hear stories about others just like themselves signing petitions – enormous petitions that were a buzz item in their own right. And there were the stories about Englishmen refusing to buy slave-grown sugar. Refusing to buy sugar! Amazing. No one had ever heard of such a thing.

Around 1788, the talk turned from stories about passivity and failure to stories about action. It was like a dam had burst. Suddenly enormous numbers of people in every social class found it possible to imagine themselves actually doing something about slavery. And, when opportunities arrived, they did. They signed petitions, attended meetings, wrote letters and marched until the pressure on Parliament was immense.

The anti-slavery campaign shows how conversations start revolutions. As historian Theodore Zeldin wrote in his book *Conversation*,

> Humans have already changed the world several times by the way they had conversations. There have been conversational revolutions which have been as important as wars or riots or famines. When problems have appeared insoluble, when life has seemed to be meaningless, when governments have been powerless, people have sometimes found a way out by changing the subject of their conversation, or the way they talked, or the persons they talked to.[5]

Zeldin's comment arose from his study of intimate conversations in history. The ideas of Voltaire and Rousseau, for instance, circulated for decades in polite intellectual circles, but it was only when ordinary people began to talk about inalienable human rights and the corruption of monarchy that the old Absolutist regimes of Europe tottered and collapsed. A handful of courageous women campaigned for female suffrage for years, but it was only when the subject became a ubiquitous subject for dinner conversation that laws began to be passed. Eastern European intellectuals circulated *samizdat* literature in secret for decades, but it was only when ordinary people openly criticised the communist gerontocracies that the Iron Curtain states collapsed. Talk, it seems, can make history.

Conversation as problem-solving

Conversation is how communities face up to their challenges. Groups of people are always being challenged by new circumstances. Politicians make new policies. Natural disasters occur. The climate changes. There are new ideas, technologies and threats. Change looms and societies have to figure out what it means and how to respond. A period of fluid, buzzing conversation follows and then opinions set like custard, and people act on the basis of what they have heard others (and themselves) say.

The story of one community facing a natural disaster illustrates the process. In March 2001 a powerful low-pressure system swept over the north coast of New South Wales, bringing torrential rains that flooded rivers, burst levees and caused tremendous stock and crop losses.

In the town of Grafton, all 12,000 residents knew a flood surge was rushing down the Clarence River towards the city. All that stood between that community and disaster was an 8.2-metre flood levee. On Saturday evening, the Bureau of Meteorology issued a warning that the Clarence would rise to 8.1 metres. At that point, the State Emergency Service gave the order to evacuate the town.

The order was issued by radio. It was reinforced by police cars with loudhailers cruising the streets. Alert to the danger and glued to their radios, virtually the whole community heard the evacuation order. Yet to the bewilderment of the authorities the order was systematically disobeyed. Fewer than 13 per cent of flood-prone residents left their homes during the nine hours the order was in effect. As it happened, the flood topped at 7.75 metres, which was just as well because the real height of the levee turned out to be only 7.95 metres. The city came within a handspan of calamity.

What caused this episode of mass disobedience? A few weeks later the authorities asked a social researcher to find out.[6] He discovered that 97 per cent of residents heard and understood the evacuation order. What's more, they understood the danger they were in. Virtually everyone knew the levee could be overtopped and were keenly following radio announcements.

So why didn't they obey the direction? The researcher uncovered two significant facts. First, after residents heard the evacuation message, they talked it over with people they knew. They especially sought the views of longer-term residents, many of whom, it transpired, replied that the water "never gets up to here".

Second, they looked around for evidence to confirm whether an evacuation was really taking place. They saw that despite queues at service stations, and supermarkets selling out of batteries, bread and milk, most aspects of life were continuing as normal. The pubs, for instance, were full, and the Royal Hotel disco was going full tilt, giving the impression that it was just another Saturday night in Grafton. The effect of those conversations, reinforced by the evidence of their eyes, caused people to discount the instruction they received from the emergency authorities. And it certainly hadn't helped that the authorities had called it a "voluntary evacuation", sowing the seeds of uncertainty in many people's minds.

So here's what probably happened. The authorities issued an order that, despite their best intentions, was ambiguous. Was there a real threat or not? Trying to make sense of the situation, the city buzzed and people looked around for evidence of what others were doing. Conversation by conversation, phone call by phone call, the city made up its own mind and decided that the official order could be safely flouted.

The Grafton flood story illustrates how, in uncertain times, the buzz of conversation is how communities decide how to act and think. It also shows the importance of trust and personal relationships in this process. Family, friends, neighbours are the credible sources people turn to when deciding how to behave when challenged by new ideas, events or threats.

The science of buzz

Are there rules about how conversation makes change? It turns out there's an entire discipline, called Diffusion of Innovations, that's dedicated to the subject.

It's rare that a new branch of science is born almost whole from a single research project. Yet in 1943 two perceptive researchers at Iowa State University did just that. They not only invented modern diffusion theory, they also nailed most of its principles in a nine-page, plain English, research paper.[7]

During the 1930s a superior hybrid corn seed had spread rapidly throughout the Corn Belt of the American Midwest. These were the hard years of the Great Depression. It was no time to expect broadacre farmers – a notoriously risk-averse lot – to invest in a new innovation, especially one that fundamentally altered traditional farming practices. The new seed was, in theory, drought-hardy and offered a 20 per cent increase on current yields. However, it was a hybrid and that meant it had to be purchased anew every year from an agribusiness company. This replaced the time-honoured practice of farmers saving their own seed from their best corn plants after each harvest.

Bryce Ryan and Neal Gross, researchers at Iowa State University, were struck by the relatively rapid and complete triumph of this revolutionary innovation. They decided to trace the process of its adoption in two Iowa communities, Grand Junction and Scranton.

Below is the hand-drawn graph they produced. The white bars show the number of farmers who first heard about the seed in a given year. The black bars show the number who started planting the seed in a given year. Ryan and Gross's first striking discovery was that hearing about an innovation and doing it are separate processes.

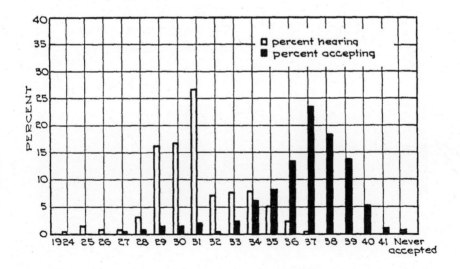

The Iowa hybrid corn study: hearing of a new idea and doing it are separate processes.[8]

Ryan and Gross realised they were looking at two normal distribution curves or 'bell curves'. What's more, they noticed that each curve tended to be caused by a different kind of communication. Although most farmers first heard about the hybrid seed from seed salesmen, they first adopted the new seed as a result of conversations with their peers. Ryan and Gross also noticed that print materials such as farm journals and advertisements had very little role in either process: there was an "almost complete lack of influence of impersonal agencies", they wrote.[9]

The relative influence of the different communication channels on the decision to adopt is shown in the graph below. Ryan and Gross found that two-thirds of *early adopters* credited salesmen for their decision to adopt. But two-thirds of *later adopters* attributed their decision to conversations with their neighbours.

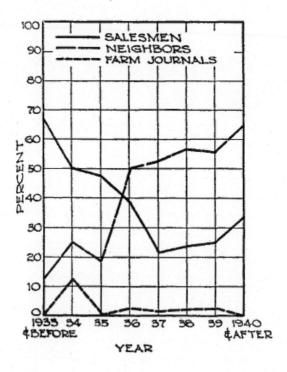

What were the biggest influences on farmers' decisions? Early adopters listened to salesmen; the majority listened to each other; virtually no one attributed their decision to print materials.

This discovery became a key principle in social diffusion: marketing can help spread knowledge, but conversation is the key to changing behaviour.[10] Frank Bass, a marketing professor at Purdue University in Indiana, later formalised this idea in the Bass Forecasting Model.

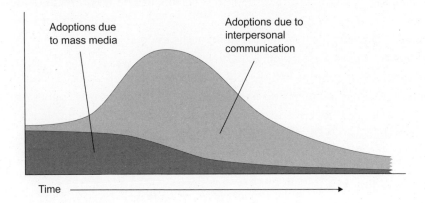

Adoptions due to mass media

Adoptions due to interpersonal communication

Time

Yes, it is who you know. The Bass Forecasting Model.[11]

What were those Iowa farmers saying to each other about the new corn seed? We can't tell from Ryan and Gross's study but it's not hard to imagine. In the beginning, buzz was probably about the first farmers who planted the seed. Were they idiots or prophets?

"Joe Blow is nuts. He'll go broke with that newfangled seed!"
And then, as Joe Blow is seen driving around in his shiny new red pickup.
"Joe Blow is a lucky guy. But it'll never work on my land, the soil's all wrong."
And then, a couple of years later:
"I've gone hybrid. I was just waiting for the right time." *

---

* In reality, few people plunge headlong into a new technology. Every farmer in Ryan and Gross's study experimented on a few acres of their own before large-scale adoption. "Acceptance of the hybrid was far from a conversion: individual and time-consuming self-demonstration was required even after visible evidence and objective comparisons were readily available to all." Ryan and Gross (1943) pp.18-19.

In a single study, Ryan and Gross discovered many of the key principles of how behaviours and products spread, including interpersonal networks, the bell curve, and early adopters versus late adopters.

Recent confirmation of the power of personal networks comes from fascinating work undertaken by social scientists Nicolas Christakis and James Fowler.

For the past 32 years the population of the town of Framingham in Massachusetts, some 12,000 people, participated in regular medical check-ups as part of a long-running health study. At the same time, their social contacts were recorded. Christakis and Fowler realised that this was an opportunity to examine the effect of social networks on people's health. They had the data digitised and constructed three-dimensional maps of the town's social networks. So far, they've drawn three compelling papers out of the data.

First, they watched people's body weight increase as the American obesity epidemic occurred. They noticed that people became obese in clusters in the network. Doing the maths, they found that when one Framingham resident became obese, there was a 45 per cent chance their contacts would become obese, a 20 per cent chance their contacts' contacts would become obese, and a 10 per cent chance their contacts' contacts' contacts would become obese, with the effect only reducing to zero at the third remove. If the first contact was classed as a friend, the chance increased to 57 per cent. Terrifyingly, if a man became obese, the chance of his male friends becoming obese was 100 per cent, although the contagion rate between female friends was lower at 38 per cent.[12]

Then they studied happiness and found the same effect. If a Framingham resident was happy, their contacts had an extra 15% chance of being happy, the contact's contacts an extra 10% chance, and so on, reducing to zero at the third remove. If a Framingham resident got happier, there was a 25% chance their friends living within one mile would be happier too. Between mutual friends the increase in happiness was 63 per cent.[13]

And the same for smoking. If one Framingham resident smoked, there was a 61% chance their contacts smoked, and so on. And friendship had a strong influence on quitting smoking. Between mutual friends, if one quit, there was a 43% per cent chance the other would quit too. Between spouses, the rate was 67 per cent.[14]

	Contacts	Contacts' contacts	Contacts' contacts' contacts
Obesity	45%	20%	10%
Happiness	15%	10%	5.6%
Smoking	61%	29%	11%

How beahviours travel along social networks. From the work of Christakis and Fowler.

Social change, they discovered, follows the same rules as an epidemic, except the mode of transmission is not bodily fluids but social interaction.

The implication for anyone trying to influence behaviour is obvious: no buzz, no change. And that buzz, of course, will be between people who know each other: family, friends, colleagues and advisors (though not neighbours). We'll focus more on the qualities of these trusted peers later.

Buzz agents

If word of mouth is the key to behaviour change, is it possible to spread a new behaviour or product solely by word of mouth, dispensing with expensive mass-media advertising or public relations efforts? Absolutely.

SMS texting is a ubiquitous badge of youth. It's indispensable for gossip and flirting. It's also how my bank sends me security codes. And it's fantastic for the deaf. SMS messages are now supposed to be worth more than $US80 billion (£44 billion) a year.[15]

Yet texting spread with virtually no marketing. Why? Its speed, cheapness, buzz value and social value (and the critical fact that it allowed teenagers to avoid parental supervision) gave it a crushing advantage over its competition, the slower, less hip, more laborious and expensive voice call. As a result, it spread like a virus through interconnected networks of adolescents.

'Going viral' depends on identifying 'buzz agents', 'opinion leaders' or 'mavens' in a social network. These are well-connected people who enjoy buzzing to their friends and acquaintances about their latest ideas and gizmos. With a little training, and some free samples, opinion leaders can be a potent marketing tactic that's been used successfully for HIV prevention, breast cancer screening, the prevention of heart disease, as well as selling alcohol and gadgets.

Diffusion scholar Everett Rogers gives an example of a pioneering marketing campaign built entirely on buzz.[16] In the early 1990s, the governments of California and Arizona mandated that at least 10 per cent of automobiles sold should have zero emissions. In response, General Motors invested $2 billion to develop an electric car. GM's engineers designed a sleek, powerful car that operated entirely on battery power. Named (bizarrely) the IMPACT, it was limited to a range of 100 miles and had to be plugged into a 220-volt electrical outlet for three or four hours to recharge the batteries. It was silent and lightweight. It was different from a conventional auto in almost every respect.

When 150 prototype IMPACTS were built, GM's marketers, with the help of diffusion experts, rolled out a radically new kind of marketing campaign in 18 cities in California and Arizona. The local energy utility, in conjunction with GM, placed ads in newspapers, inviting interested people to apply for an opportunity to test-drive the new vehicle. The response was overwhelming. In Sacramento, for instance, a city of almost half a million people, 7,000 applied. Each applicant was sent a long questionnaire to measure their level of opinion leadership and innovativeness. From the responses, several hundred people were selected in each city and invited for a 30-minute test-drive of the IMPACT.

These individuals, wrote Rogers, "were what most people would call 'car nuts' but marketing experts call them mavens, individuals who possess a high degree of interest and expertise about some type of product." Because mavens know so much about specific products they're often sought out as opinion leaders by other consumers.

After the test-drive, the mavens were given 30 minutes to question GM engineers about the IMPACT. Their curiosity was inexhaustible. They wanted to know every detail of the IMPACT's performance: its wheelbase; its weight; the power of its electric motor.

Each maven was sent home with an eight-by-ten-inch colour photo of a bright-red IMPACT which they were urged to pin on a bulletin board at their place of work. They also received a set of 50 two-by-three inch cards with a colour photo of a red IMPACT on one side and detailed performance data on the other. They were asked to hand these out to their friends. Each card had a unique identification number and a toll-free number the receiver could call to register for their own test-drive.

The idea was to kick off a word-of-mouth diffusion process in those 18 cities. Many of the mavens were longing to buy their own IMPACT. The environmental friendliness, streamlined look, and the status of having the slickest car on the road were all consumer draws. In late autumn 1997, the IMPACT (now sensibly renamed EV1), went on sale in the 18 cities. Sales however, were modest. The EV1, it seems, was just too unfamiliar for Californian motorists (something the diffusion scholars probably told the GM executives, since it's a diffusion principle that 'compatibility' is a quality of successful innovations).

Sadly, within a year, the two state governments had watered down their zero-emission laws, and the EV1 was quietly killed – a sensational story of corporate skulduggery recounted in the 2006 documentary *Who Killed the Electric Car?*.

The EV1 wasn't one of the great sales success stories of history, but the marketing methods it pioneered, based on diffusion principles, entered the mainstream as word-of-mouth or viral marketing.

Popular opinion leader technique

The spread of blogs, Facebook, Myspace, Ning, Flickr, and YouTube, and the audience decline of radio and TV, has made viral marketing a matter of life and death for marketers. The subject of viral marketing has its own blogosphere where you can check out some of the latest tactics. Take a look at some of the examples below:

- Coca-Cola used 30 bloggers from 15 countries, all operating from the same small flat in Berlin, to blog for Coke and football during the 2006 World Cup.[17]
- Dave Balter runs BzzAgent, a company that recruits and trains 'volunteer brand evangelists' to go out and talk to their social networks about a product. They are encouraged to honestly share opinions with their friends. They then get debriefed to provide feedback to the company about its product.
- Tobacco companies place 'stealth videos' of attractive young women

smoking cigarettes on YouTube. Meanwhile, Jeff, a first-year medical student in Boston strikes back with a YouTube video exposing the deception.[18]

One viral technique is Popular Opinion Leader method or POL. In hospitals, POL has been widely used to raise the standards of practice by medical doctors.[19] One experiment aimed to compare a medical opinion leader's approach with a more traditional intervention. The aim was to encourage 76 doctors in 16 community hospitals to adopt best practice guidelines for vaginal birth to minimise the rate of caesarean deliveries. Half the doctors were approached by opinion leaders among the group. The others were subjected to a method called 'audit and feedback' where their patient medical charts were examined and they received feedback on best methods. After two years, the audit intervention had no measurable results, while the POL intervention led to an 85 per cent increase in the rate of vaginal delivery.[20]

The POL method has often been used with high-risk groups that can't be influenced by traditional marketing methods, such as drug addicts, sex workers, high-risk gay men, teenage binge-drinkers and smokers, rave dance drug-takers, homeless youth and children with poor reading skills.[21]

POL approaches have also been used, to good effect, in prisons, with prisoners trained to discuss drug use, HIV prevention, suicide prevention, suicide and mental health with other prisoners.[22]

POL projects can be modest. One simple project aimed to get pre-schoolers to eat vegetables they disliked. The kids were sorted in categories according to the foods they liked. Then the kids were mixed up in the lunchroom, so that, for instance, a 'target' child who disliked carrots was seated with three or four who liked carrots. Four days later, most of the target children were eating vegetables they'd previously rejected.[23]

Or they can be ambitious. Here's an example that demonstrates the power of the POL approach to set social norms on a large scale.

A programme that started in 1991 selected eight US cities for a large-scale experiment into the effectiveness of POL to alter the behaviours of high-risk gay men. Four cities were chosen as a control group, and the other four cities were the intervention group.[24]

The gay bars in all eight cities were fitted with glossy posters and brochures displaying safe sex and HIV messages. In the four intervention cities, well-liked men who regularly visited gay bars were recruited to slip safe-sex talk into their social conversations.

How did the researchers know who was well liked? Well, they asked the bartenders to spot visitors who were greeted the most, or greeted other visitors the most, and find out their names.

The well-liked guys, who formed about 8 per cent of visitors to gay bars, were recruited and given training in communication skills and how to deliver safe-sex messages such as carrying condoms, not having sex while drunk, and how to resist unwanted sexual advances. Each POL was also given a safe-sex badge to act as a conversation starter. Over the next three weeks each POL had about ten conversations with members of their social circle.

To make sure they were measuring significant changes, the researchers waited 12 months to return and survey the effects. The impact was dramatic. Condom use by gay men jumped from 45 per cent to 67 per cent in the intervention cities, but stayed the same in the control cities. And condom-taking from dispensers increased by 65 per cent in the intervention cities but halved in the control cities. Overall, the odds of a visitor to a gay bar in an intervention city having unprotected anal sex was half that in the control cities. Considering these results were measured 12 months after an intervention lasting just three weeks, this was an impressive result. It demonstrates how a POL approach can shift behaviour on a large scale.

POL methods have also been tested in the environment field. For example, the Hood River Weatherizing Project by energy utility Pacific Northwest had an initial sign-up rate of less than 10 per cent of customers. But when the project switched to recruiting local residents and members of Citizen Advisory Councils to be speakers at schools and churches, 85 per cent of households enrolled within two years.[25]

In other cases, anglers have been trained to talk to other anglers about legal fish sizes, dog-owners trained to talk to other dog-owners about picking up their dog's faeces, and gardeners trained to talk to other gardeners about home composting.

Everett Rogers noted that by 2003 there had been eight randomised controlled trials – the gold standard in evaluation – which demonstrated the success of POL tactics in changing behaviour.[26]

Despite the evident success of some POL programmes, the approach nevertheless has a checkered history.[27] I suspect the reason some POL programmes fail is that insufficient attention is given to the personal qualities of the individuals chosen to be POLs. If they lack charisma and credibility, their efforts may prove fruitless.

A recipe for buzz

Are there rules for what makes something buzzworthy?

Did you read the story about the British man who set off to walk to India without any money, relying instead on the goodwill of people along the way or working for his bed and board? Mark Boyle is a former dot.com businessman who aimed to prove the philosophy of 'Freeconomics' that people can live by trading skills instead of cash. He expected the 14,500-km journey would take two-and-a-half years, ending up in Mahatma Gandhi's birthplace.

"I've got some sunscreen, a good knife, a spoon, a bandage . . . no Visa card, no travellers' cheques, no bank account. I won't actually touch money along the way," a news story quoted him saying.

I looked up his blog. He wrote with touching simplicity, and the most inspiring part is the effect he had on other people. Friends and strangers were driving all over the country to find him, give him provisions, look after him, offer him a bed for the night. On his first few days he was so burdened by gifts of food he hardly knew what to do with them. One day he mentioned in his blog that he'd broken his sandals, so friends took time off work and scoured the countryside to find him a new pair. "It was deeply moving. Sometimes when you are walking on your own you can feel quite isolated and you have no idea what is going on in the rest of the world. And to see so many people go out of their way for me without me knowing about it was so touching. You get a huge sense of being cared about and that is the greatest feeling in the world," he wrote.

I felt genuinely moved by Mark's journey and bookmarked his blog so I could keep an eye on his progress. It was an inspiring story. And one that was easy to share. *The Daily Times*, Pakistan, *ABC News*, Australia, *The Gulf Daily News*, Bahrain, *The Sun*, London (which of course called him a 'barmy Brit'), and *The Examiner*, Tasmania were among scores of media outlets that snapped it up. If you read it, I bet you shared it with someone. It's the kind of story that spreads. It's contagious. It doesn't need a marketing budget. I bet people in the Ural Mountains heard about it.

If we accept that it's a change maker's job to create buzz, then it would be good to know if there are rules for making this kind of contagious information.

It turns out there's a simple good-enough rule: surprise+emotion.

Surprise+emotion

Our brains are on the alert for things that violate our expectations of what's normal.

I recently had a chat with a young woman who had just completed a placement with Africa Now, a development agency based in Oxford, England. She told me about The Chilli Project: it raised funds for villages in Zimbabwe and Zambia to plant chillies. Chillies are an excellent cash crop, she said, but the real advantage is they make elephants sneeze. It turns out that chilli powder, mixed with elephant dung and burnt, makes elephants sneeze and helps keep them away from vegetable gardens. Getting donations for this project was a 'snap' she said. "People loved it." Together with funds from trusts and the European Union, they'd raised £260,000 in a few months. By comparison, her Goat Project had really struggled. It was an important project, she said, but donors just weren't interested.

What makes sneezing elephants more interesting than goats? The brain has an organ called the amygdala (two actually, one on each side) that, in the words of Daniel Goleman, author of *Social Intelligence*, "acts as a radar for the brain, calling attention to whatever might be new, puzzling, or important to learn about. The amygdala operates as the brain's early warning system, scanning everything that happens, ever vigilant for emotionally salient events – especially for potential threats."[28]

Our amygdalas ensure that, though we may be drowning in stimulation and myriad demands on our attention, one kind of information will always get through – the one that confronts our expectations. 'Sneezing', 'elephants' and 'chilli' don't normally exist in the same sentence. That combination of words is a little bit startling, so it cuts through the predictable noise that surrounds us.

Surprising, shocking, unexpected stories startle our ever-alert amygdalas which trigger a squirt of adrenalin into the brain, focusing attention, and making us buzz with our family and friends as we try to make sense of the new reality. Hence surprising, shocking, stereotype-busting news travels quickly, spreading from person to person in a wave of conversation. The attack on the World Trade Center was an outstanding example. News services all over the world broke their programming to cover it. It seemed as if no one talked about anything else for weeks. And within days, the buzz was turning into action. People were holding prayer vigils, offering assistance, organising fundraisers.

9/11 was arresting news. It grabbed people's attention and raised puzzling questions we all wanted to buzz about: Who organised the attacks? Why was no wreckage visible at the Pentagon? How many people died? How did President Bush perform? Was it a conspiracy?

Unarresting facts, such as 'Smoking causes lung disease'; 'Fatty foods make you fat'; 'Burning fossil fuels causes climate change', and so on, are stuff we already know about. We are practically drowning in that kind of information. It becomes invisible because we've heard it all before.

Psychologists call this quality of noticeability 'salience'. Salience is the first step in the chain of mental events that leads to behaviour change. Until people focus their attention on something, they can't even begin to respond to it.

Activists intuitively understand the power of salience. Demonstrations, marches, sit-ins, rallies and boycotts, disrupt people's sense of predictable normalcy. The more passionate, even violent, the protest, the more powerful its complacency-busting effect. Political scientist Jon Agnone showed how sharp public protests have successfully increased the passage of legislation in Congress. He analysed the number of pro-environmental laws passed through the United States Congress between 1960 and 1980 and found that the number of new environmental laws corresponded directly to the number of disruptive public protests by activists.[29]

Changing the world, it seems, requires disrupting people's expectations and assumptions, and breaking stereotypes is the key.

It's also the alchemical secret to turning boring facts or claims into fascinating ones. Here are two slogans from my career as a social marketer:

'Create Your Own Eden – Compost.'
and
'Don't buy your best friend their last drink.'

I didn't realise it at the time, but the reason these slogans cut through the clutter was their unexpectedness. 'Eden' doesn't belong in the same sentence as 'compost'. 'Best friend' doesn't belong in the same sentence as 'last drink'.

Although salience matters greatly, the motivational heft of a message comes from another quality – its emotion. We are hardwired to interpret the world through the lens of our emotions. Things that elicit fear, disgust, desire, wonder, dread or delight focus our attention and spark reactions in ways that neutral information can never achieve.

Back in the 1970s, American power utilities were trying to figure out why nuclear power plants were so unpopular. Nuclear energy promised limitless power and wealth, it would usher in a new age of technological progress, and the artists' impressions looked fabulous. Yet, to the mystification of power-utility executives, communities fought long and bitter battles to prevent these facilities being built near their towns.

The executives wanted to find out how to persuade people to accept their scientific assessments about the risks of power plants, rather than going to the barricades in a storm of emotion. So they hired some psychologists who'd been working on risk perception for the insurance industry.[30] Those psychologists spent the next two decades trying to understand how the public understood risk. Along the way, they invented a new science, Risk Communication.

They concluded that, far from being irrational, there is an underlying logic to the way people perceive risk. One team, led by Melissa Finucane, tried to explain how emotion affects judgement. It came up with the idea that people might use a sort of emotional rule of thumb (which, being scientists, they called an 'affect heuristic') to make judgements about benefit and risk.[31] The idea was that images or events in our memories are tagged with positive or negative emotions. When we need to make a judgement about, for instance, the risks and benefits of a nuclear power plant, we pool the emotive tags from our memories concerning nuclear power. If the sum of the emotional tags is positive, we're happy with the proposition. If it's negative, we reject it. This rule of thumb is far more rapid and efficient than wading through the pros and cons of complex arguments that even scientists can't resolve.[32]

So, the theory went, when people were presented with the idea of a nuclear power plant being built near their town, they would instantly consult their mental database of stories and images about nuclear power. What did they see? Skin peeling off Hiroshima victims, cancer, death and destruction. They added up the emotive tags and instantly formed an attitude somewhere to the right of dread.

All this would have remained just theory if it wasn't for brain-scanning machines. There's now plenty of evidence that positive and negative emotional assessments are processed in the same area of the brain that helps create long-term memories, the orbitofrontal cortex.[33] As Melissa Finucane's team proposed, and as our own experience of life suggests, there's no such thing as an objective memory. Everything we know is tagged with positive and negative emotions. That explains why marketers have such a strong interest in emotion.

Contagious communications are almost always surprise+emotion stories. They are never facts, lists, tables, graphs or diagrams (unless, like the diagram of the slave-ship *Brookes*, they tell a surprise+emotion story). Emotionally arousing, out-of-the-ordinary stories grasp people's attention and create drama and anticipation. And, because they are stories, people can imagine themselves as actors in the drama of change.

As Michael Gazzaniga realised with his split-brain patients (see the earlier chapter 'Popular folk theories'), humans are designed to be storytellers. But they are also story-believers, so it's possible to change people by changing the stories they tell each other. Positive, hopeful stories about change enlarge the possibilities available to people, widening their sense of what may be within their power. And it's handy that stories are also educational, demonstrating causes, effects and consequences.

Here are two print advertisements that demonstrate how stories with surprise+emotion can produce powerful communications. Notice how, in both ads, the stories are so potent that the tag lines are superfluous.

The first, from Cease Fire, scored the highest for 'stopping power' in an analysis of 195 non-profit ads.[34] The design is arresting and nothing gets in the way of the message, which is a simple surprising+emotional story.

A gun in the home triples the risk of
a homicide in the home.

CEASE FIRE

Think about your family before you think about getting a handgun.

Cease Fire, Inc. P.O. Box 33824, Washington, D.C. 20033-0424.

The text reads: "Suburban Dallas, TX. 15-yr-old female. Killed by 10-yr-old brother with gun found in parents' room. Boy thought gun was unloaded, tried to scare sister as she talked on phone." The tag line is: "A gun in the home triples the risk of a homicide in the home." [35]

The second ad is from Amnesty International Hungary. It speaks more eloquently about the genocide in Darfur than any number of facts.[36]

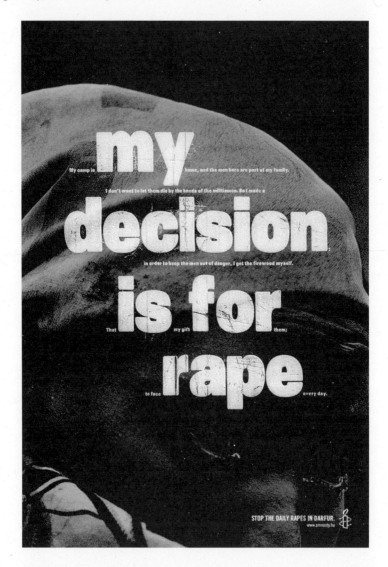

The text reads": "My camp is my home, and the men here are part of my family. I don't want to let them die by the hands of the militiamen. So I made a decision: in order to keep the men out of danger, I get the firewood myself. That is my gift for them; to face rape every day." The tag line is: "Stop the daily rapes in Darfur." Reproduced with permission from Amnesty International Hungary and DDB Budapest.

Down buzz, up buzz

Surprise+emotion might get people buzzing, but buzz alone can't guarantee people will act. Buzz might, for instance, achieve the opposite, reinforcing passivity and helplessness.

Whether buzz sparks or blocks change depends on a special quality of the story that's carried by the buzz: its optimism.

I suspect 2007 was, for global warming activists, something like 1788 was for anti-slavery activists. I can only speak for my own society and circle, but a sea change seemed to sweep over the kinds of discussion I was hearing about climate change.

For years, the talk about climate change in the media and among my friends was all horror stories and complaints about complicit politicians, greedy coal companies, self-serving freeway agencies, corrupt greenhouse sceptics, the useless, lazy, apathetic public, and so on.

Then, suddenly, something changed. I began to hear people talk about *doing things*. A rural town replaced every light bulb with a compact fluoro. Virgin Airlines launched carbon-neutral flights. Rock bands bought emission credits. My friends began to talk about home insulation and fridge ventilation. Frankly, I could hardly believe I was having conversations about fridge ventilation. Why on earth would I find that interesting?

Maybe it was Al Gore's astonishing one-man global crusade, a tale so quixotic that it was moving, irrespective of his message. Maybe it was the wall-to-wall media coverage of Nicholas Stern's 700-page report on the economics of climate change. Maybe it was a thousand small, heroic efforts by activists. Maybe it's because the Arctic is, quite obviously, melting.

Whatever the cause, the conversation flipped decisively in two dimensions. It flipped from blame to action. And it flipped from other to self. And now nearly everyone seems to be doing something, however small, to reduce their energy use, and big businesses are among the most vigorous actors.

Psychologists talk about 'locus of control'. Those with an internal locus of control tend to believe they control their own choices. They are more optimistic,[37] healthier,[38] less depressed,[39] less stressed,[40] more resilient,[41] less prone to taking dangerous risks,[42] suffer less burnout,[43] recover more quickly from injury[44] and are more likely to seek help when they need it.[45] Those with an external locus of control, by comparison, tend to feel others control their choices. They tend to be more depressed, less healthy[46] and have a poorer view of their own capacities.

Psychologist Martin Seligman and others have shown how it's possible to become more optimistic just by changing the kinds of story we tell ourselves, shaking off negative talk that assumes we will always fail and, instead, talking up our own abilities to achieve the things we hope for.[47]

I call this making the shift from 'down buzz', where we talk negatively about our abilities and destinies, to 'up buzz', where we talk ourselves up.

How much 'up buzz' do we need? Amazingly, someone has actually answered this question. Research by psychologists Barbara Fredrickson and Marcial Losada showed that the flip is likely to happen when the ratio of positive to negative day-to-day conversations exceeds 3:1. In other words, three emotionally positive conversations for each emotionally negative conversation. Below three, they concluded, people tended to languish in a self-absorbed, predictable rut. Above three, they tended to flourish, becoming "generative, creative, resilient, ripe with possibility and beautifully complex." [48]

Tellingly, the ratio did not have to fall much below 3:1 before the decline set in. A ratio of 2.3:1 was enough to pitch people into a rut. And interestingly, they also found that too much positivity might be a bad thing. When the ratio exceeded around 11:1 the "dynamic of human flourishing" started to disintegrate. It seems we all need a little negativity and conflict in our lives.

Talk may be cheap, but it has profound psychological consequences. Our buzz tells us what we're good at and what we're not good at, what we can achieve and where we will fail. It tells us who we are: weak or powerful, smart or stupid, loved or neglected. And it tends to be self-fulfilling. "As a person argues on behalf of one position, he or she becomes more committed to it . . . 'As I hear myself talk, I learn what I believe.' In everyday language, we literally talk ourselves into (or out of) things," wrote Miller and Rollnick in *Motivational Interviewing*.[49]

Most people I know are still pessimistic about the global effort to combat climate change, but in their own lives they've become markedly more hopeful since 2007. Suddenly, the microscopic size of individual actions, the enormity of the challenge, and nagging voices of sceptics, stopped being reasons not to act. It was the year climate change talk flipped from 'down buzz' to 'up buzz' in my social networks.

I suspect the flip from down buzz to up buzz might be behind every kind of social change, large and small, whether it's farmers talking about zero tillage or wetland protection, fast-food executives talking about salads, or students talking about overthrowing dictatorships.

But what drives this flip? It's probably a mistake to assume it's entirely due to outside forces. Remember Heroic Agent Bias? That's the bias that assumes we, the change makers, are the effective causes of changes in society. More probably, the cause of the flip will be motivations happening inside people. We can get a clue to this from taking a closer look at down buzz.

Down buzz is the moaning, complaining, griping and bitching that dominates a lot of everyday conversation. It's the muzak of thwarted souls. Although it can be annoying and dispiriting to listen to, whining and bitching tells us something – that people are frustrated and wish for something better. And the more intense and chronic the moaning, probably the greater the thwarted hopes. Down buzz is never apathetic or neutral. It points to intense, muffled passions. So when people complain and gripe (as they do so often) we know there is a pool of hot emotion beneath the surface, ready to erupt into hopeful action.

Down buzz is evidence of people's suppressed passions and hopes for change. Creating conditions where those hopes can break free is the job of the change maker. Fear creates silence, so the role of change maker has a lot to do with creating emotion+surprise stories that stimulate people to buzz about things and feelings they've been reluctant to discuss.

When that happens extraordinary things become possible. As Theodore Zeldin wrote "throughout history, ordinary people have suddenly come out with the most amazing statements when they find the courage. . . . The most rewarding discovery I have made in my study of history has been about the way people who do not think of themselves as brave forget their reticence, their hesitations, and do brave things. Mice, more often than we realise, have been able to move mountains."[50]

The shift from down buzz to up buzz precedes movements for social change, both large and small. But is it possible to intervene and kick-start or speed up this shift?

I think so. The first step is to understand the importance of hope.

Method

How to start a buzz

Talk can be enabling or disabling. People literally talk themselves in and out of change. As a change maker you should first listen to the buzz, being careful to notice what people are saying about both the solution and about their own ability to change. Once you've heard the buzz, look for positive, inspiring stories that change the way people imagine the solution and their own ability to adopt a particular change in their lives.

Listen to the current buzz

Before you start strategising, you'll need to find out what people are thinking, feeling and saying. So ask them. It could be a friendly discussion over a cuppa. Or, to get richer ideas, invite up to seven people to a focus group discussion.

Before you run a focus group, think carefully about the questions you'd like to explore and write them down. They should be open-ended questions. For example:

"What have you heard about . . .?"
"How have you experienced . . .?"
"What could be the advantages of . . .?"

HINT: The easiest way to create an open-ended question is just to start with the word "What".

Instructions for a focus group discussion

Here's a script for a simple focus group discussion that aims to create insight into the current buzz.

> "Thanks for coming along today. With your input, this discussion will help [name of group or organisation] design a new project to help tackle [the problem].
> "I'd like to start by asking you your views on a number of questions:
> "Thinking about the [social, health or environmental] problem:
> "What experience have you had with it?"
> "What do you think could be done to improve or fix it?"
> "[The group or organisation] is proposing that people like yourselves might be willing to adopt a new action or practice." [Describe the proposed practice or technology]:
> "What have you heard about it?"
> "Who from?"
> "How have you experienced it?"
> "What do you believe could be the advantages?"
> "What could prevent you from doing it?"
> "How could it be made easier?"
> "Whose views do you trust on this subject?"
> "[The organisation] is proposing a project to encourage people to trial the practice or technology. [Describe the project]. How do you think this project could work better?"

Start a new buzz

Buzz is sparked by surprising+emotional stories that inspire people with new possibilities. The best stories are those with passion, and some of the most credible passionate stories are your own. To recruit others to your cause it's important to share your own stories about the experiences and moments that have inspired you to become active on the issue. So, for practice:

1. Share a moment in your life that inspired you on the issue. Tell it like a story.

2. Remember when you glimpsed a positive vision that excited you. Sketch a word picture.

3. Remember a story that raised your spirits about the issue. Write it down.

Examining what inspires you in your own life will give you the stories you need to enlist and motivate others to support your effort. Then, whenever you have an opportunity, invite others to share their stories too. Some of those stories will be amazing and buzz-worthy in their own right. So collect them. When you start a meeting or a workshop or a media release, you'll have exactly the material you need to inspire yet more people, create buzz and generate hope that change is possible.

HINT: Remember stories only inspire if they end on a positive, uplifting note. Negative stories tend to depress and disable their listeners.

Buzz-generating tactics

The thing to remember about buzz is that no one is interested in hearing about your project. What they are interested in hearing is stories about people like themselves who've broken the accepted norms and done something out of the ordinary.

Authentic stories

The best way to create 'up buzz' is to let people hear the authentic voices of parents, farmers or executives who've seen a solution work in their own lives, farms or businesses and are happy to share their stories. So hand them the microphone, mobilise their stories in print, get them on TV and YouTube, and spread their spoken words in blogs and tweets.

Coffee table meetings, workshops, field days

Bring people together and invite them to share their positive stories and ideas with each other. We often think a public meeting is a chance for us to educate people and answer their questions but change is far more likely when they are the ones who give each other the answers! Instead of educating, our job can be simply to ask open-ended questions.

For a short guide on asking the right questions, see *How to Change the World One Conversation at a Time*:

   www.enablingchange.com.au/One_conversation_at_a_time.pdf

Popular opinion leaders

Identify well-connected opinion leaders who are at the forefront of change in a particular community or group and enlist them to spread the message in their own day-to-day interactions. They are already chattering about their interests and achievements, so let them chatter about your solution as well.

Ingredient 2

Offer hope
How frustration motivates change

In 1999 NATO spent 78 days bombing Serbia's military and civilian infra-structure to smithereens. Power plants, bridges and factories lay in ruins. NATO's superlative display of air supremacy achieved its desired effect: the Serb army packed up and withdrew from the disputed province of Kosovo. However, that air supremacy also achieved an undesirable effect. The mood of war hysteria in Serbia allowed Slobodan Milošević to crush his oppo-nents, many of whom were now in prison or in hiding. NATO had inadvert-ently cemented Milošević's regime more firmly in power than ever before.

The dust had hardly settled when the activists of Otpor, the student democracy movement driven underground by wartime repression, gath-ered secretly in an apartment in the upmarket shopping district of Belgrade.

At this time Otpor was barely more than a loose club of idealists dedi-cated to a philosophy of non-violence. Yet their aims were extravagant, nothing less than the downfall of Milošević and the transformation of Serbia into an open, modern, liberal, European nation.

The apartment became the headquarters for a renewed campaign of political stunts and pranks. One of these stunts involved placing a barrel in the central shopping street of Belgrade with a picture of Milošević on it and offering anyone who would drop a coin in the barrel the right to whack their leader's face with a baseball bat. "In 15 minutes there were a hundred people in Knez Mihailova Street, beating the barrel," recalls one activist. "They were so happy! The police didn't know what to do. They called the station once, twice . . . at the end, we left the barrel in the street, and they didn't know who to arrest, so they arrested the barrel! And they were photographed doing it and were in the newspapers the next day. The whole country laughed."[1]

The students were pleased at the cleverness of their stunt. But it could very easily have backfired. It might, for instance, have demolished their claim to non-violence and played into the hands of the government. But the stunt was wildly successful and the reason was not the stunt itself but the state of mind of Serbians in 1999.

NATO's bombing had ruined the nation's infrastructure. That, plus years of war, had pushed the poor countryside into even deeper poverty. Traumatised soldiers were coming home to impoverished towns with bombed-out factories and intermittent power supplies. At about the same time as Otpor's activists were launching their undergraduate stunts in Belgrade, 20,000 furious people staged a spontaneous demonstration in the small provincial town of Leskovac. Unexpectedly, defiant demonstrations of rage began to crop up all over the country. As news of this defiance, and Otpor's outrages, spread across Serbia, ordinary people found the courage to do things they had never done before. The cascade of disobedience sparked by these first acts led inexorably to the collapse of the dictatorship 18 months later.

Otpor's stunts were funny and audacious. They were magnets for highly charged community frustrations. They did not create rage, but they opened the floodgates for already existing rage, humiliation and disappointment. Without that suppressed rage Otpor's stunts would have been meaningless.

When the tactics of change makers work, we often say "we captured people's imaginations", or "we turned them on". But that devalues what people themselves contribute, which is the force of their personal motivations. It doesn't matter whether the behaviour we want people to display involves changing a government or making a vegetable garden, success happens when our efforts enable motivations that are already present in people's lives.

The biochemistry of motivation

Which begs a question. What is motivation?[2]

According to economists, motivation results from rewards and punishments in people's external environments. Contemporary psychologists, however, don't buy this. To them, motivation is primarily intrinsic. It arises in the imagination and is converted into physical action by biochemical processes in the brain.

Until recently, biochemists made the same assumption as economists. They assumed people were motivated to act by the fear of pain or discomfort and by the rewards of pleasure. When they looked for the biochemistry of fear and stress they found it in the amygdala, the brain organ that alerts us to danger and stimulates a fight or flight response. And when they looked for the biochemistry of rewards they found it in the hypothalamus, the gland that stimulates release of the pleasure transmitter, beta-endorphin.

Meanwhile, another brain chemical, dopamine, also involved in pleasure and pain, was assumed to be a secondary transmitter in the reward system. It was a simple model: pain and pleasure determined behaviour, and dopamine helped make it work. But then doubts crept in. From the late 1980s experimenters were getting results that suggested the reward circuit was more complex. They discovered, for instance, that rats with destroyed dopamine systems still apparently enjoyed their food.[3] It seemed that dopamine might be independent of the pleasure system after all. If that was the case, what was dopamine for?

Brain biochemists now believe that dopamine is not primarily a transmitter of pleasure, but a transmitter of something far more powerful: desire or wanting. It is true that feelings of pleasure are associated with dopamine because it uses some of the same brain structures, but its real function is not satisfaction, but motivation. It's the drug that gets us busy for a purpose.[4]

Dopamine has a remarkable quality. It can be released entirely in response to things which have never been experienced: to fantasies which reside purely in the imagination. When Michelangelo accepted the challenge to paint the ceiling of the Sistine chapel, he had never painted a mural before. When the Australian swimmer Ian Thorpe decided to train to be a world champion, he had never done that before. When I decided to write this book, I had never done something like that before. The dopamine circuit equips us all with the ability to step into the unknown in search of a dream.

A second special quality of the dopamine circuit is its longevity. The pain circuit is especially short-lived, since shock, pain or threat simultaneously release beta-endorphins that numb the hurt. The pleasure circuit burns itself out from habituation. Dopamine, on the other hand, is capable of perpetual motion. Dopamine is probably the drug behind the pleasurable state of 'flow' that creative artists report as they spend days or months steadily directing their whole beings towards a creative goal. It's the chemical behind Xbox addiction, the ceiling of the Sistine Chapel and the four-minute mile.

What about drug addiction? That's dopamine too. Pleasurable drugs hijack the dopamine system, driving an endless cycle of dopamine surges and retreats that drive addicts in search of their next hit. It seems the dopamine system is just waiting to be harnessed by something inside or outside us. The problem is, it has trouble telling the difference between short-term gratification and long-term satisfaction. Dopamine can be harnessed by our dreams, or it can be hijacked by fast food, drugs and pornography. "Everyone is addicted to SOAP: a substance, an object, an activity or a person," said one of my students.[5]

The sustaining power of the dopamine circuit is demonstrated most powerfully by the great freedom struggles in human history. When people's hopes are stifled they are capable of enduring the most frightful punishments and privations to achieve their dreams. The struggle may be brutal and it may last decades, but the dopamine circuit is patient; it keeps pumping for as long as it takes.

Unfortunately, life sucks

The problem with our dreams, of course, is that they are so often frustrated.

Nobody's life is perfect. Most of us yearn to improve our relationships, our health, or our bank balance. Everyone wants to get off the treadmill and see some progress towards that hoped-for future.

Therapists call this state 'discrepancy'. Psychologists call it 'dissonance'.[6] The rest of us call it 'frustration', although 'guilt' – which is a similar thing – runs a close second. Frustration produces feelings that range from mild heartache to teeth-gnashing anguish. Brain-scan experi-

ments show that frustration lights up the same parts of the brain that process emotional pain.[7]

Frustration, unfortunately, is inherent to the human condition. This is
especially true in developed societies where TV and magazines create innumerable opportunities for social comparisons which damage our sense of
self. [8] It's been shown, for instance, that women's moods fall when they're
shown photos of female models.[9] When men are shown the same photos
they feel less good about their wives.[10] In East Germany, where standards of
living have soared since 1990, the level of happiness has nose-dived
because people now compare themselves with West Germans, instead of
with the inhabitants of the Soviet bloc.[11]

Social comparison also affects health. One study by researchers at the
Harvard School of Public Health found that income inequality was closely
correlated with mortality rates, even after allowing for differences of
income, poverty, smoking and race. After excluding those factors, they
found that every one per cent rise in income inequality was associated with
an increase in mortality of 22 deaths per 100,000 in the US population.[12]

Perversely, this awful picture is great news for change makers. The
reason is that people don't change when they are happy; very much the
opposite.[13]

Here's how some of my students talked about their feelings of frustration before making important changes in their lives:

> "I wasn't using my life well. I needed to do something worthwhile."
> (He volunteered to be a child mentor.)
> "A lot of conflict, unhappy, doing my head in, grief, a sense of loss."
> (She stopped trying to control her teenage son.)
> "After having a child I felt and looked flabby." (She started exercising.)
> "Guilty, lost control." (She greened her lifestyle.)
> "My family were tired of only seeing me on weekends." (He changed
> to a less demanding job.)
> "My partner was unhappy because I was so stressed and tired." (She
> learned to delegate at work.)
> "I lacked energy, felt dizzy, confused." (He changed to a low glycemic
> index diet.)
> "I hated the costs and stresses of running a car." (He sold his car.) [14]

Scratch voluntary change and underneath you'll find frustration, guilt or unhappiness – feelings produced by the discrepancy between what we observe about our lives and what we hope for. A number of psychological theories are quite explicit about the role of dissonance or discrepancy in driving personal change.[15] Frustration alone, however, does not cause people to change. People can writhe in a mire of frustration and misery for years, or for their whole lives. Instead, frustration's role is to energise or predispose people for changes that become possible when they come face to face with the exact opposite of frustration – hope.

Hope

'Hope' is a word you won't see much in scientific journals or academic papers. Yet hope is a tremendous force in the lives of individuals and nations. It's the opposite of hopelessness, helplessness and cynicism. It gets people up in the morning to face another day. It causes governments to rise and fall. I suspect it's the force behind every successful change project.

Al Gore trains his climate change presenters to be careful with the 'hope budget' of their audiences. Barack Obama called his political tract *The Audacity of Hope*. The urban sustainability advocate Peter Newman wrote that "a characteristic of good public spaces is hope".

I'd like to resuscitate the word 'hope' and give it a central place in thinking about change. I'm going to use it to mean the desire all people have to better their lives. As such, it's an optimistic act of imagination. It's about being able to positively visualise oneself living in a better future.

We watched amazed throughout 2011 as populations in the Middle East conquered their fear and overthrew a swathe of murderous dictatorships in one of the tremendous hope outbreaks in history. The geopolitical power of hope may explain that other historic mystery, the hypnotic thrall in which Ronald Reagan held so many Americans during the 1980s. He was the hopeful American Dream writ large.

Successful politicians know a lot about hope. Anthropologist Ghassan Hage wrote that Margaret Thatcher's enduring appeal to the British working class was her understanding of the economy of hope.

Hage wrote:

Her message was simple and clear: if you possess the 'British character', you possessed the capacity to experience upward social mobility even if, at the present, you were at the bottom of the scrap heap.

Hope is not related to an income level. It is about the sense of possibility that life can offer. Its enemy is a sense of entrapment not a sense of poverty.[16]

I, for one, am continually amazed by the varieties of human hope and the determination people display to pursue their dreams.

World-champion swimmer Ian Thorpe got up at dawn and trained for 35 hours per week for most of his teenage and early adult life. His race preparations included swimming 120 kilometres a week, for months. Not just plodding along either, but pushing himself through the pain barrier.

Seventeen-year-old yachtsman Michael Perham designed his own yacht and endured weeks of loneliness and exhaustion to be the first teenager to sail solo across the Atlantic.

Bryan Derken is one of the top ten of Wikipedia editors with over 70,000 edits of Wikipedia articles. He claims to spend about a quarter of his spare time on the site, for no return other than the "gratification of fixing something that's broken or unpolished".[17]

The superlative dedication of revolutionaries, athletes and game addicts is very similar. They are driven by the same potent brain mechanism where imagination drives a tireless motivational system based on dopamine.

Here's a simple diagram that I think evokes the tremendous power of this system. It shows the adoption of life-bettering domestic gadgets during the twentieth century. As you can see, apart from a few wobbly years in the 1930s, people wholeheartedly embraced devices that answered their common hopes for relief from tedious and back-breaking chores, for more time, and for more human connection. It looks like a series of unstoppable waves. Admittedly it shows only material gadgets, but if we showed non-material advances, like literacy, female emancipation, environmentalism, or workplace safety, we'd see identical waves of hope.

People have an enormous energy for betterment in their lives. So we change makers have a choice. They can either work with that energy or

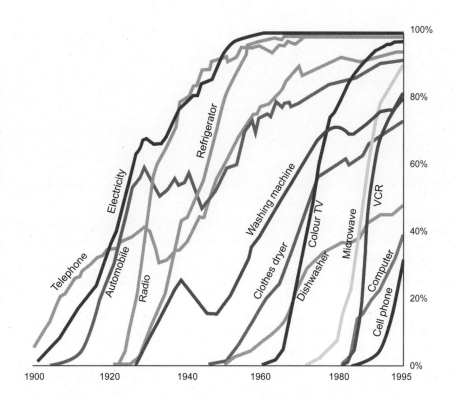

Waves of hope and desire: the adoption of labour-saving gadgets during the twentieth century. Source: Reserve Bank of Dallas, *Annual Report* 1997.

against it. When we offer people a chance to genuinely improve their lives, we'll have access to a surplus of motivation. But when we oppose people's hopes for betterment we're liable to end up like the well-armed but impotent security services of Serbia in 1999 and the Arab Middle East in 2011.

What I take from these stories is that, if we want to change the world, it might be important to start with hopes that are already inside people, instead of trying to impose our own on them. What did *not* happen in the cases I described above is that someone persuaded, manipulated, rewarded or threatened people to change. The desire was already inside them. We humans are like that. We have unique and precious inner hopes that can motivate us in ways that logic and argument, or fear or rewards, can never do.

Yes, it's all about me

Some people sprawl helplessly in front of their TVs while others push the boundaries of human endurance. What seems to make the difference is whether their personal hopes are thwarted or engaged by their environment.

The thing about personal hopes is just that: they are personal. They are unique to each individual. That makes the self the central player in behaviour change. So consider the self.

Each of us has an internal model of who we believe we are and who we want to be. Arguably, the creation, protection and improvement of that model is the most complicated mental activity we humans engage in. It affects every minute of our lives, governs our beliefs, choices and behaviours, and explains why we resist or embrace change. This self is far from the 'rational, utility-maximising individual' imagined by economists.

First, the self is vainglorious

According to psychologist Cordelia Fine:

> For a start, your brain shows you a world massively coloured by vanity. It sets you on a pedestal above your peers. It says you are invincible, invulnerable and omnipotent. It is so very vain that, studies show, it even considers the letters that appear in your name to be more attractive than those that don't. Research shows that these positive illusions are, in fact, essential. They keep your head high and your heart out of your boots. They keep you from contemplating ending it all. If you don't see yourself and your world through the lens of deluded optimism, your immune system begins to wonder whether it's worth the effort of keeping you alive. And, most extraordinary of all, it seems that sometimes your vain brain manages to transform its grandiose beliefs into reality. Buoyed by a brain that loves you like a mother, you struggle and persevere . . . and actually achieve your goals.[18]

In our dreams we are often fantastically conceited and optimistic about our character (honourable, generous etc), our body (beautiful and sexy), our relationships (loved, esteemed and exalted), our abilities (competent and masterful), our dress sense (perfect), our material possessions (the envy of all), our prospects (blinding), our success (majestic), and our perfect partner (Scarlett Johansson, Ewan McGregor etc.).

We imagine ourselves to be better-looking, more interesting, more virtuous, more humane, and more in control of our lives than is ever likely to be the case in real life, and we do this for good reasons.

There is plenty of evidence that people with a strong sense of self do better in life than those who are prone to self-doubt. They are happier. Their optimism gives them stronger social connections to cope with stressful events.[19] They have stronger immune systems.[20] True, they get into more trouble more often, they even start wars more often[21] but when they do, they rarely blame themselves.

A neat illustration of the vainglorious self at work is that our attraction to a sexual partner increases as the partner becomes more similar to our ideal self, but as soon as the partner starts to exceed our ideal self, the attraction turns to repulsion.[22] The vainglorious self may be delusional, but it's also what makes us want to be good, generous and selfless.

Try this experiment. Ask a stranger to help you, say, shift some furniture or push-start your car or carry your shopping. Then, afterwards, offer them, say, a fiver. Observe what happens.

Chances are they'll steadfastly refuse the money. Why? Because you affronted them. Why? Because they did something selfless and good and they liked themselves more for doing it. When you offered them money you threatened that feeling.

What causes altruistic behaviour? One explanation involves empathy. We want to help others because we share their distress and we enjoy their happiness. Recent discoveries about mirror neurons give a lot of weight to this argument.[23] Of course it doesn't explain why we might want to do good in impersonal areas like avoiding pollution, recycling and paying our taxes. I expect the answer may be a notch less than heroic: we want to do good because it agrees with our hopeful, deluded, vainglorious selves. We like to go through life imagining ourselves to be admirable, virtuous, benevolent, upright, unblemished, honourable etc, and it's good to have some supporting evidence. Altruistic acts provide that evidence. Their shining glory is a relief from the soiled compromises that life so often imposes on us.

Second, the self is fragile

A delusional self-image is tricky to maintain in the real world because it's continually threatened with exposure, ignominy and humiliation. So, as we already noted, humans have evolved impressive defence systems: denial and resistance.

These defences are automatic, unconscious, instantaneous and powerful. Their potency points to the vital psychological and physiological functions that the vainglorious self-image performs in managing our health, security and social relationships.

Unfortunately, a threatened self can easily become a behavioural nightmare. If defending a delusional self-image requires our unhealthy and unsociable behaviours to become worse, to assert that black is white, to shoot the messenger, or blame a scapegoat, then we will often find ourselves doing exactly those things to protect the integrity of the self. The lesson for change makers is obvious – don't threaten the self!

Third, the self is emotional

Way back in 1637 mathematician René Descartes wrote "I think therefore I am". Nice try, René. Too bad modern science, arguably his brainchild, now sees the brain as fully lubricated and powered by emotion, including the process of judgement itself. Maths and logic have little to do with the way we humans negotiate our world, and practically nothing to do with our social relationships.

The contemporary understanding of the brain, notably through the work of neurobiologist Antonio Damasio, sees emotion as central to decision-making. When Damasio studied people with damage to only the emotional centres of the brain, he found they were crippled by indecision, unable to make even the simplest choices, like what to wear or eat. He theorised that memories of past events, tagged with emotional markers such as fear, disgust, pleasure and delight, were the guides we use to weigh our choices.[24]

Brain-imaging experiments have been unable to locate a separate logical centre in the brain. Perhaps that's because it's all emotional. In the words of Dr Dean Shibata of the University of Washington, "our imaging research supports the idea that every time you have to make choices in your personal life you need to 'feel' the projected emotional outcome of each choice – subconsciously, or intuitively."[25]

Emotion is, of course, an unreliable lens on the world. We may try to be dispassionate and logical about weighing our choices, but fear, anger, disgust, grief and pleasure colour our thinking. Says neuroscientist Joseph LeDoux, "emotions can flood consciousness because . . . the connections from the emotional systems to the cognitive systems are stronger than from the cognitive systems to the emotional systems".[26]

Emotions have a strong effect on behaviour, partly because they alter our perception of risk. Fear and disgust about, for instance, a dead rat in the compost bin, are liable to make us more risk-averse towards all new ideas while the mood lasts. Liking and delight make us more likely to accept requests and invitations.[27] Anger makes us into more impulsive risk-takers.[28] Fear and anxiety make us cautious.[29] Depression makes us realistic, if gloomy.[30] And disgust makes us morally censorious of everything.[31]

Yes, science has finally discovered that a crappy day at work makes us want to kick the dog. That's because, in the economy of the brain, emotion is the currency.

This vainglorious, fragile, emotional self drives our lives stumblingly in one direction: towards a hopeful vision of the self. Provided it can manage the risks, the self will take almost any opportunity to shift its external reality to be closer to the good, healthy, responsible, sociable, contributive person it imagines itself to be.

Although people are capable of extraordinarily bad behaviours while defending a threatened self, when they do change it's almost always towards that healthy, socially positive self they have always dreamed about. This may explain the many cases where people naturally overcome great difficulties to improve their lives. It may, for instance, explain both the extraordinary courage of dissidents and spontaneous remission of addicts.[32]

It certainly explains why life is infinitely safer, more decent, just and healthier today than it was in, say, the 1600s. People invest tirelessly in improving their lives and their communities – it's an iron law of history. That iron law has implications for change makers. It's an absolute requirement for a change maker to have a believable vision of a dignified life that's consistent with what people dream for themselves (and, which, like it or not, will probably include hip gadgets and comfortable homes).

Yes, I'm afraid it is all about me, though not necessarily in a bad way. When we run a campaign, we are engaging with tens or thousands of vainglorious, fragile, emotional selves who also want to be good and great.

The structure of hopes

A first step in designing a change project is therefore to become acquainted with the hopes of the selves whose behaviour we wish to influence.

Fortunately, hopes are easy to identify. They are usually just the flipside of frustrations. Every frustration implies a hope. If someone is 'tired' they hope to be energised; if they are 'isolated' they hope for company; if they are 'guilty about their energy use' they hope to use less energy!

But there's a problem. All hopes are not equally motivating. Some hopes people are prepared to die for. Others are just daydreams. How do we spot the hopes that have the greatest power to motivate?

In 2001 four psychologists carried out a fascinating experiment that shed light on the character of deep hopes.[33] They asked 907 American and Korean college students to rate 30 qualities that gave them most satisfaction in life, including things like: "Free to do things my own way"; "A strong sense of intimacy with the people I spend time with"; "A strong sense of physical well-being"; and "I had nice things and possessions".

The qualities were divided into ten abstract categories. Five of these categories came out on top, irrespective of nationality:

- *Self-esteem:* having self-respect and many positive qualities
- *Autonomy:* feeling in control of one's life
- *Competence:* success in completing difficult tasks
- *Relatedness:* close connections to people who are important in one's life, especially family and friends
- *Security:* safety from threats

Interestingly, popularity and money/luxury scored near the bottom of the list, suggesting that, although people desire these things, those desires are relatively 'cool'. The only difference between the American and Korean students, by the way, was that 'relatedness' topped the list for the Koreans, whereas it was lower for Americans, pointing to Korea's more collectivist culture.

(In case you're wondering why 'greater purpose' or 'contributing to society' didn't show up, it's because the psychologists forgot to ask! Research on the motivating power of higher purpose is still remarkably thin on the ground.)

Self-esteem, autonomy, competence, relatedness and security: if these hopes are as universal as the study suggests, they may be keys to designing change efforts that motivate large groups of people to change. In other words, if we want to motivate people to volunteer their time, start a new behaviour, or buy a new product, then the effort will be more successful if it delivers on self-respect, autonomy, competence, good relationships and (for those who feel unsafe) safety.[34]

Deep and shallow hopes

Some hopes are deeper than others. It might be useful to think of people's hopes as being in layers, or shells, just like an atom has shells of electrons. The outside layers are where the shallow hopes live; for example, "I'm hoping for a cool new SUV". The inner layers are where the deeper hopes live; for example, "I want to feel healthy and be a good parent".

Shallow hopes are 'means' and deep hopes are 'ends'. A shiny SUV is a means to the end of self-respect. Of course, owning a shiny SUV is only one of many possible paths to achieving that goal. Commerce does a powerful job of providing superficial means, but often a poor job at satisfying the deeper ends that people hope for in their lives. It's the job of progressive change makers to provide healthier, more socially and environmentally desirable means for people to achieve those deep ends.

What's at the centre of the atom? That's a question for philosophers, but I'm putting my money on 'dignity'.

I like to think that dignity is at the centre, and around it is a shell of profound universal values like autonomy, security, health, comfort, family, community, respect, competence and contributing to a better world.

And in the outer layers you have the superficial stuff: jewellery, overseas holidays, white weddings, private schools, whiter teeth and ideology.

Appeals to shallow hopes are everywhere: 'free stuff', 'save money on your energy bills', 'be in the draw for a £50,000 prize'. A possible danger with appeals to shallow hopes is that people who act for shallow reasons might be more liable to offset their new good behaviours with new bad behaviours. So, for instance, they may unconsciously think "I've given to Amnesty International, now I can buy a plasma TV"!

Nevertheless, there's nothing inherently wrong with appeals to shallow hopes. These hopes are perfectly capable of motivating people to do short-term, easy things like sending off an application form or installing a light bulb.

If we only want people to do brief, easy things, then appeals to shallow hopes might be just right. However, if we want people to do things that seem difficult and inconvenient, like consuming less or being politically active, then appeals to deeper hopes are more likely to be successful.[35]

Here's a lovely example of an appeal to deep hopes: UK advertising agency Wieden and Kennedy wanted to cut their office energy use by ten per cent. Instead of exhorting staff to save money, or tonnes of carbon, or black balloons, they teamed up with non-profit SolarAid to donate the money they saved on energy bills to a good cause: installing solar PV panels in Cheryl's Children's Home in Nairobi. Now, turning off the lights in London helps an orphan read at night in Kenya. Every one of Wieden and Kennedy's light switches has a little sign that says: "Wieden+Kennedy Off: Nairobi Children's Home On." Beautiful![36]

(This clever idea shows how switching off a light or any other seemingly mundane act need not be boring, inconsequential and uninspiring. It's not the act itself that matters, it's the story that accompanies it.)

Hot and cool hopes

When deep hopes are frustrated they develop a temperature. They turn into hot desires. Hot hopes are things like curing one's own sick child, saving a wobbly business, or stopping a freeway being built through our own neighbourhood. People passionately desire those things and will work tirelessly to achieve them.

Cool hopes are essentially daydreams. They are things it would be nice to do – volunteering in an orphanage in Bhutan, say – but few people are going to rearrange their lives to do them.

The distinction between hot hopes and cool hopes is valuable for anyone designing a change effort. Which hopes are the ones we should aim to address? The answer is: *the hottest, deepest hopes we can reasonably address*. They are the ones causing the biggest frustration, guilt, humiliation and misery for that group of people.

How do we find out which hopes are hottest? We could pay a social research agency to run focus groups for us. Or we could just ask. Asking people about their day-to-day frustrations, fears and concerns is the easiest way to uncover hot hopes that can form the basis of a change effort.

If I wanted to change the world (or get rich), I'd start by asking people what they are most unhappy about in their lives. If, for instance, I asked housewives about their happiness I might find that commuting, childcare and housework cause their greatest unhappiness, as psychologist Daniel Kahneman did, producing this interesting table:

	HAPPINESS INDEX	AV. HOURS PER DAY
Sex	4.7	0.2
Socialising after work	4.1	1.1
Dinner	4.0	0.8
Relaxing	3.9	2.2
Lunch	3.9	0.6
Exercising	3.8	0.2
Praying	3.8	0.5
Socialising at work	3.8	1.1
Watching TV	3.6	2.2
Phone at home	3.5	0.9
Napping	3.3	0.9
Cooking	3.2	1.1
Shopping	3.2	0.4
Computer at home	3.1	0.5
Housework	3.0	1.1
Childcare	3.0	1.1
Evening communte	2.8	0.6
Working	2.7	6.9
Morning commute	2.0	0.4

Some moments 'suck' more than others. How 909 Texas women rated their moment-to-moment satisfaction during a real day in their lives. Source: Kahneman D. et al. (2004).[37]

Commuting is certainly a human experience that's ripe for improvement. There's research that claims that commuters on Britain's rush-hour roads and railways can be more anxious, as measured by their heart rates, than fighter pilots or riot police facing angry mobs of protesters. David Lewis, who carried out that research for Hewlett-Packard, said commuting made people feel "frustrated, anxious and despondent". Most of his subjects called it an 'ordeal'. Some said it was a 'nightmare'. As a result, "many commuters go into a sort of inner world when they're travelling and don't really notice what's happening around them."[38]

What exactly makes commuting so miserable? One study found that commuters on the most congested and interrupted routes were the most stressed. But, surprisingly, car-poolers had higher blood pressure than single drivers, suggesting that loss of personal control was an important factor.[39]

So, if I wanted to change the world (or make a lot of money), I'd invent a solution to commuters' loss of personal control. I might, for instance, create an itsy-bitsy personal stereo system that gave people back control over their sensory space. Or I might change the transport system itself, maybe make it fast, safe and simple to use. Dr Ela Babalik-Sutcliffe, an urban transport researcher at University College, London, compared new light-rail systems in the USA, Canada and UK and found that the most successful systems were those that were believed to be safe, gave better access to where people wanted to go, were very frequent (with less than five minutes between trains), and had travelcards that allowed unlimited journeys and could be used on other forms of transport such as trains, buses and ferries; all factors which maximise the sense of personal control by commuters.[40]

Loss of control certainly creates unhappiness. But it's not the only cause. Lots of things make people unhappy. The only way we can really know what makes a particular group of people unhappy is to spend time learning about their lives.

Social scientists have become quite sophisticated about doing this. The method du jour is to equip subjects with a beeper and a record book. When the beeper bleeps, say every 20 minutes, subjects are supposed to record what they are doing and how they feel about it. (Just having a beeper go off every 20 minutes would stress me, but I guess they thought about that.)

But the best method of finding out what makes people unhappy is probably just to sit down with them and ask some questions. Here's a question that gets straight to the point:

> "Thinking about how you live your life (or run your business, or care for your family) what are the things you're unhappy about and would like to change?"

Practically everyone will readily answer that question, and, with a little probing, have a moan about the things that bug them. Try it with someone you know. You'll hear a lot of stuff, most of which you won't be able to do anything about. But amongst the complaining and griping, you'll find one or two hot hopes you can begin to construct an answer to, and you'll have the key to a successful change project (or a profitable product).

Here's a real-life example. It's from a project that aimed to reduce smoking amongst Arabic-speaking people in south-west Sydney – a tough challenge because tobacco is deeply entrenched in the social rituals of Arabic culture. The project started with some focus groups (facilitated by local Arabic-speakers) which revealed that this audience didn't need to be told tobacco was a problem: it was already causing plenty of conflict and bitterness in their lives. One pregnant woman felt humiliated because when she asked her guests not to smoke they took it lightly and said "Come on, it's only one cigarette." Another woman hid the ashtrays but was still afraid of family fights. Some smokers felt sad their grandchildren wouldn't kiss them. Others hated the smell in their homes. Heavy smokers felt ostracised when relatives wouldn't visit them.

One of the sharpest points of conflict was the host-guest relationship. Hosts were expected to offer a tray of cigarettes to guests even when the hosts were non-smokers or there were young children in the home. Many were uncomfortable with the practice, but there was so much at stake socially that they tended to swallow their frustration and not complain. Some guests were unhappy too: they wanted to respect the family's health, but were afraid of insulting the host by refusing a cigarette.

It was clear that many in this community felt that tobacco was a threat. The motivation for change was present – in spades. What seemed to be missing was the ability to negotiate solutions to the *social* dilemmas posed by tobacco use. Listening to the focus groups, the agency team began to hear how some Arabic-speakers were inventing their own solutions. One woman put up no smoking signs. Another described how her husband decided to offer sweets instead of cigarettes. These spontaneous social innovations became the seed of the agency's campaign.

The agency hired Arabic-speaking copywriters to create 30-second radio spots in the form of miniature soap operas that demonstrated alternative ways of negotiating tobacco use.

Here's a sample (which was broadcast in colloquial Arabic):

Guest: Cigarette? (offering to host)
Host: No thanks . . . where are you these days?
Guest: I am here and at work . . . Cigarette?
Host: No. No, thank you.
Guest: Have you given it up, or is this not your brand?
Host: My wife does not smoke, and because of the kids I smoke outside. This does not mean you shouldn't. Smoke, man, smoke. Shame on us if you don't.
Guest: Shame on me if I do. Your coffee is more than enough.
Host: More sugar, Hanan (to wife). Thousand welcomes! (to guest)

Reproduced with permission from Sydney South West Area Health Service. The Arabic scripts were created by a multicultural advertising agency, Independent and General.

The key line was "Shame on me if I do. Your coffee is more than enough." It offered a face-saving solution to a common and frustrating social dilemma.

Notice that the ad was not about health risks. And it didn't mention smokers' frustrations. It didn't need to. When people are in a state of anguished frustration there's usually little need to remind them about it. They are already looking for answers and the role of the change maker is simply to provide solutions that are easy to adopt.

The campaign, consisting mostly of short radio spots intensively aired over three years, became one of the most successful anti-smoking campaigns in the agency's history. It was credited with a 5.3 per cent decrease in smoking prevalence and a 7.8 per cent increase in smoke-free homes amongst Arabic-speakers in western Sydney, far ahead of changes in the general population.[41]

So, the first step in designing a change project is to understand what makes a particular group of people unhappy. And the second step is to start looking around for a solution.

Can you shock people into change?

There's a frequently heard theory of change along the lines that people won't change unless they're shocked, "scared straight", hit hard or otherwise had the consequences of their actions pushed firmly into their faces. As one Australian health bureaucrat put it "The research found that smokers wanted to be scared into giving up."[42] That's the theory behind shock advertising.

You've probably seen a TV ad like this: A shiny late-model car is racing along an open country road. It takes the curves beautifully. It's a clear bright day. The eucalyptus trees shoot past. The driver is handsome and happy. The music is hot. The car is hip. It's obviously just another car commercial. Then, before you quite realise it, the car slams into an oncoming vehicle and transforms into a mangled wreck.

Cut to a bleeding figure staggering around in the wreckage. He peers into what's left of the other car and reels back in horror.

It's shocking. It's aversion therapy. I wince whenever I see it and look away from the screen.

Shock ads are the popular weapon of choice for governments whenever morally blameworthy behaviours – like drug-taking, binge-drinking, speeding or drink-driving – need controlling.

The classic shock advertisement was the 1987 'Grim Reaper' TV ad, possibly the most frightening, freakish, ghoulish, horrible, dread-inducing, TV ad of all time (check it out on YouTube).[43]

Unfortunately, there's no evidence that the Grim Reaper made anyone stop having high-risk sex. One study of 77 gay men in Adelaide even showed a dramatic *increase* in the numbers practising unsafe sex from 20 per cent of men to 52 per cent following the ads![44] However, what The Reaper did do was induce an avalanche of anxious calls to the AIDS Hot Line from heterosexuals who weren't actually at risk of getting AIDS[45] and also convince politicians to spend millions on AIDS-prevention programmes (which was its real purpose[46]).

Is it desirable, or even possible, to shock people into change? There's no doubt that shocking news can sometimes force people to face up to the need for change. In 2003, American researchers wondered if showing CT scans to smokers was a 'teachable moment'. They showed 900 smokers scans of their own lungs, almost all of which showed damage. One year later, 14 per cent had kicked the habit, compared with only 5 per cent of smokers who would normally give up in that time.[47]

One advantage of a CT scan is that it's hard to deny. It's a picture of that person's lungs and nobody else's. It's hard work for a smoker to keep thinking "It's not my problem" when it so obviously is.

Ugly CT scans, high electricity bills, poor sales figures and other kinds of 'forensic' bad news can drive personal change because they undermine the self's capacity for denial.

But the self will still work very hard to deny the threat. The self's favourite method is to avoid getting this kind of bad news in the first place. The fear of breast cancer, for instance, causes many women to avoid examining themselves.[48] The high levels of anxiety associated with X-rays, a visit to the dentist, safety inspections, environmental audits, and so on, cause high-risk people to actively avoid being tested.

Most messages, however, aren't as personal as a CT scan of our own lungs. Usually they're generalised information like "25 per cent of smokers die young". That's a breeze to deny because people just tell themselves they're in the other 75 per cent. We all do this (don't bother denying it).

Despite its widespread use, the effectiveness of shock advertising is controversial. Many researchers don't buy its claimed effects. Road safety researchers, for instance, believe that the steady reduction in crashes is primarily due to better police enforcement, safer cars and safer roads.[49]

The use of 'fear appeals' has received a lot of attention from psychologists. The consensus is, in fact, that fear can be quite motivating. Fear arouses the emotions and focuses attention. The bigger the fear, the higher the motivation. But whether that motivation is directed towards hyperdefensiveness or towards positive action depends entirely on another factor: whether the viewer can quickly and easily do something to reduce the threat.

In other words, the threatening message must be immediately followed by an 'escape hatch' – a simple, do-able action that's within a person's abilities and reduces the threat to the self.

The problem with shock ads is that television is a lousy medium for building people's abilities to act. Simplistic exhortations to 'Slow down' or 'Quit now' don't even begin to communicate the complex personal skills and assertiveness people need to implement these changes in their lives.

A large systematic review of HIV education programmes concluded that "Strong fear appeals work only when accompanied by equally strong efficacy messages [that] make target populations believe they are able to perform a recommended response . . ." [50]

A large systematic review of road safety research made almost identical conclusions, [51] quoting ". . . it appears that a key to achieving and sustaining behavioural change lies more in providing the audience with good coping strategies and not simply relying on fear as a source of motivation." [52]

Barry Elliott, an astute social researcher, examined 87 road safety campaigns from the USA, Europe and Australia, most of which would have relied on fear appeals. He found that, despite respectable numbers of drivers becoming aware of mass-media campaigns, far fewer changed their attitudes or intentions. Even fewer changed their behaviours, just 1.3 per cent (and that was for self-reported behaviour: the actual change would have been even lower because people tend to exaggerate their good behaviour). He concluded "you can't sell road safety like soap". [53]

The effect of fear-based anti-smoking ads, by comparison, is a little less clear. The global standard, Australia's *QuitNow* campaign (pus-filled arteries, gangrenous legs etc.) has been thoroughly evaluated. Each burst of ads definitely increased the number of people who called the Quit Line. [54] But they appeared to have had no significant effect on the percentage of people quitting. [55] The weak results contrast oddly with the continued strong advocacy for fear-based campaigns from health authorities. [56] (Though I'm pleased to report that the latest incarnation of the *QuitNow* campaign has the message "Every cigarette you don't smoke is doing you good" which replaces threat with hope. Well done, finally!)

Still, it is possible to have a confronting marketing campaign that works quite well when it provides a simple, immediately do-able escape hatch. Here's an example where the escape hatch was donating money, on-the-spot, to a charity for street kids.

Workers from SUPPORT, an Indian organisation working with street kids, hid pictures of homeless children inside the menu cards in trendy Mumbai coffee shops, together with an appeal to donate. Customers who casually lifted the menu cards were surprised to see a poor street kid crouching inside. The card squarely targeted customers' contradictory values – "Yes, I am a good person who cares about the poor . . .but whoops, I seem to have spent the equivalent of a poor person's weekly income on a piccolo latte".

Sometimes guilt needs a little reminder. Design by Everest Y&R, Mumbai.

SUPPORT collected over 200,000 rupees (£2,400) from 54 cafés in six weeks.[57]

Why does this tactic work? Because a simple, sufficient escape hatch – donating money – is instantly available.

Beyond fundraising, however, shock tactics are high risk. Ham-fisted attempts to highlight people's contradictions fail for a host of reasons. They drive denial, ignite resistance, and erode hope. But their most fatal flaw is that they neglect the escape hatch. Instead, they increase the prominence of bad behaviours while giving no guidance about how to do the good ones.

The one time you can clearly justify shock tactics is to highlight problems that people don't yet know about. The toxic components of indoor air, for example, are horrifying to consider – allergens, residues from cooking, and dust cloaked in a layer of insecticides and poisons! It's scary to think about, but no one is scared because no one is thinking about it. If you face a sleeper issue like this, you're justified in spending time raising the threat level. But don't imagine that the threat alone will change behaviour.

If you want to get people talking, then blatant fear appeals may work. But if you want to change behaviour, you need a more subtle approach. Either follow the bad news with an escape hatch, or forget bad news and, instead, offer hope and build people's abilities to change.

Why there's no need to change people

"The proper question is not, 'Why isn't this person motivated?' but rather, 'For what is this person motivated?'"[58] said Miller and Rollnick in *Motivational Interviewing*, perfectly capturing the point of this chapter.

It's often said that we should aim to 'motivate people' or 'change their values'. I hope I've demonstrated that there's little point in trying to do either of these things, for two reasons.

Firstly, we can't. It's seriously hard work to change people's values and hopes because they are wrapped up in their deepest selves. There's no vaccination for injecting a particular set of healthy or responsible hopes into people's selves. Fortunately, we don't have to change people inside because, although their shallow hopes may differ, most people have pretty much the same deeper hopes, which are about autonomy, safety, health, comfort, family, community, contribution, self-respect, competence, and so on.

Secondly, we don't have to. People already want to change. They are desperate for it. Practically no one has the life they want. Frustration is the human condition and the modern world is a relentless engine of dissonance. No one who watches TV or reads magazines or lives in a city is immune from uncomfortable comparisons with their fellows. It hurts that other people seem to have healthier bodies, happier families, safer neighbourhoods, more prosperous farms, more desirable homes, more customers, more friends, or more respect. The more bitter the pain, the more unpleasant the conflict, the more ignominious the comparison, the more people are motivated to change their lives, families, businesses, farms and communities.

Yet there's little point emphasising this bad news in people's lives. They already know about it. Instead, a vital ingredient in change-making is to offer hope. We are least effective when we try to change people, and most effective when we spot what's not working in people's lives and construct solutions that credibly answer their frustrated hopes.

Recently I talked to some of Al Gore's climate presenters and found they were spontaneously commencing their talks by sharing with their audiences the personal motivations that had driven them to rise to the challenge of global warming. They were talking about their hopes for their children.

Hopeful conversations are essential ingredients in change, but they can't be the whole story. The reason is that we humans take great care, most of the time, to protect ourselves from the threat of failure and humiliation. Inspiration is part of the equation of change, but we are pragmatic creatures who also require practical assurances that our efforts are likely to be crowned with success. That depends to a large extent on whether the surrounding environment enables or disables a particular action, which is the subject of the next chapter.

Method

Sketch a hopeful future

Your project aims to tackle a real-life problem and contribute to a different future, which may be three to five years or more away. Ultimately, your effectiveness will be measured against progress towards that future. The logical starting point for your project is therefore to define the future to which your efforts will contribute. Not just any future, but one that answers people's frustrated hopes.

Defining a future is an excellent creative task for your brains trust. Listed below are some things to keep in mind when instructing them.

1. Think big
A future must inspire hope. Futures are created through the myriad efforts of many players over time; you aren't acting alone. So be hopeful, fill your glass, and imagine a community with zero waste or a valley where every species is protected or a school where every child graduates. Choose futures that are optimistic but not utterly impossible.

2. Make it visual
A future should be easy to visualise. For example: 'More people enjoying cycling, more often'. The more visual you make the description, the better you'll be able to explain yourself, enlist others and measure change. And it helps to keep it short too, ideally 20 words or less.

3. Use plain English
Dump buzzwords like 'efficient', 'sustainable', 'biodiverse', 'accessible', 'resilient', and so on. Let's face it, you're not even sure what they mean.

From the very beginning you should get into the habit of communicating in plain English.

Efficient = smart, savvy, clever
Sustainable = green, earth-friendly
Biodiverse = healthy, complex
Accessible = getting where you want to go
Resilient = strong

4. Use value-ful, emotive language

People aren't motivated by arguments or logic. Instead, they're waiting to be inspired by a future that credibly answers their frustrations. The language that defines that future should be value-ful and emotionally engaging.

Try using words like 'healthy', 'safe', 'productive', 'proud', 'prosperous', 'enjoyable', 'beautiful', or 'wonderful'. Here are some real-life futures defined in value-ful language:

'Housing estates that residents are proud to live in and happy to come home to.' – A public housing improvement programme
'Thriving families. Happy, healthy children.' – A parenting programme
'Giving farmers the edge in their business.' – A farm sustainability programme

Don't worry that your future sounds a little fluffy. The technical rigour will come when you specify the indicators you'll use to measure progress.

5. Choose a feasible scale

This is also a good time to define the geographic scale of your project. There's only one rule for scale: the spread of your efforts should not exceed your resources.

Choose a scale where you have the people and money to make a measurable difference. There's no point spreading your efforts so thinly that you get no observable results. You'll want something to celebrate, an inspiring story to tell, and happy funders. So, when it comes to scale it's helpful to think small.

Decide right now whether you're going to act at the scale of country, state, city, suburb, neighbourhood, street, group, or single household or organisation. And make sure you know exactly which suburb or street. After all, they're all different and one size doesn't fit all.

6. Choose convenient indicators
Remember that the role of indicators is to give an *indication* of progress. Don't get carried away with technical accuracy. Make it easy on yourself by looking for data that someone else is already collecting.

Instructions for your brains trust

Total time = 30 minutes

Step 1. Agree on the concrete environmental, health or social problem you wish to tackle.

> The problem:
> *A dangerous, unfriendly neighbourhood: Upper Sunnyside*

Step 2. What's the evidence for the problem?

> Evidence for the problem:
> *Muggings: 15 in last 12 months (police data)*
> *Vandalism and graffiti: 250 instances in last 12 months (council data)*
> *Most residents believe streets are dangerous after dark: 87% responded 'very dangerous' in recent community survey (council data)*
> *Few people able to name their neighbours: 12% in recent survey (community group data).*

Hint: At this stage don't analyse what might be causing the problem and don't think about solutions. Just define the problem in its *most observable, tactile, easily measurable* form; for example, death and illness data, or pollution data. This step tests whether you have a real, measurable problem, not simply one you dream exists.

By the way, this is the last time you'll refer to a negative problem while you're strategising. From now on you'll be focused solely on how to achieve a positive future.

Step 3. Flip the problem into a desired, positive future.
Don't sweat the process of flipping. It's as simple as converting 'high infant mortality' into 'zero infant mortality'.

The desired future:
A safe, neighbourly Upper Sunnyside.

Step 4. Rewrite the desired future using value-ful language that makes an emotional connection.

The desired future:
Streets we're happy to let our children walk in.

Step 5. Agree on indicator(s), targets and data collection methods.
Indicators are where you build technical rigour into your vision. Targets are where you set out a reasonably staged process for achieving the desired vision.

INDICATORS	TARGETS	DATA SOURCES
Street crime	0 incidents (zero) by 201X	Police records
Vandalism and graffiti	Reduced to 60 cases/year by 201X	Council records
Community safety perception	0% respond 'very dangerous' by 201X	Annual council survey
People able to name their neighbours	60%	Community group survey

Step 6. Agree on the scale of your programme.

Scale:
Upper Sunnyside (1,250 households; 15 businesses)

Now you've defined a future in hopeful terms that's likely to motivate the people you hope will participate in your effort. And you've created objective indicators that rigorously measure progress. You're well on the way to developing a well-designed change project.

Create an enabling environment
It's the system, stupid

On a recent Friday night, I had reason to stop at a notoriously riotous drinking spot, the modern version of what was once called a 'blood house'. Wandering around, anxiety turned to amazement as I saw literally hundreds of well-dressed twenty-somethings quietly chatting in groups without the least hint of danger or aggression. Then I noticed the venue. It was no longer shabby and neglected. It had had a glossy makeover. The stained carpets were gone. There were freshly painted walls and shiny surfaces. And there were disciplined-looking bouncers with wireless headphones and neatly pressed black shirts at all the exits. I thought "It's still early in the evening, maybe the riots don't start until after midnight", so I asked two of the bouncers. They replied that, since the makeover, violence and bad behaviour had almost ceased to exist.

I think I had witnessed one of the many ways that environments influence behaviour. In this case, the well-scrubbed premises and throngs of peaceful patrons were saying "This isn't the kind of place where people behave aggressively." And the disciplined security guards with their high-tech comms gear were saying "This is not the kind of place where aggressive behaviour is tolerated."

There's another way that a pub's environment can influence behaviour, as criminologist Ross Homel and colleagues found out from many hours of observation in Sydney pubs. They concluded that crowding was behind much pub violence. In their article on public drinking and violence, they pointed out:

> Big crowds in most sites usually mean discomfort for many patrons, a problem exacerbated by a lack of seating and by crowded corridors, stairs, and doorways. Patrons in these situations tend to alleviate their discomfort by more rapid drinking, which causes higher levels of drunkenness, and eventually aggressive reactions to discomfort directed at individuals and property. Overcrowding on dance floors appeared to be linked to several arguments and at least one of the severe assaults observed.[1]

Crowding, noise and high temperatures are well-known causes of aggression.[2] Noisy, crowded pubs make patrons uncomfortable. They drink to reduce their discomfort. And then they drink more because the noise and crowding make it impossible to do much else. And then drink more for the same reason – inevitably transforming discomfort into discomfort plus drunkenness, a recipe for aggression.

The design of big Sydney pubs affects not only pub customers, but also the behaviour of people like me – we no longer socialise in them. I doubt a marketing campaign could reverse this. What would need to change is the design of the pub experience, something that might well be under way since 2008 when the NSW State Government, under pressure from the Lord Mayor of Sydney, passed laws lowering the cost of a liquor licence for small bars from $15,000 (£9,800) to $500 (£325), with the aim of encouraging more European-style wine bars. And, of course, that's an environmental change too – a change in the regulatory environment.

Just as crowded pubs are drunk-ogenic, modern cities can be obesogenic, urban designs can be crime-ogenic, and driving environments can be crashogenic.

Whether people exercise, for instance, is related to their proximity to parks, walking trails and safe bicycle routes. One United States study showed that for every quarter-mile increase in distance between a walking trail and people's homes, the likelihood of using the trail decreased by 42 per cent.[3] And more people used the trail when it was well-maintained, with good views, and near shops and cafés, but fewer people used it when there was litter, drainage canals, tunnels and thick vegetation.[4] Another study showed that 43 per cent of park users lived within a quarter-mile of a park, while only 13 per cent lived more than one mile away.[5]

Every behaviour is enabled or disabled by its environment. When we aim to initiate sustained change, therefore, modifying the environment should be a vital part of our efforts.

Message fetish

Did I mention that I think of myself as a 'recovering social marketer'? I mean that, like many in this field, I once worshipped at the altar of The Message. I've noticed that many marketers and public relations professionals, even against their better judgement, tend to operate on a universal Theory of the Message, which works a little like this: "If only we could find the perfectly persuasive message, people would change their behaviours and the social-environmental-health-sales problem would get solved."

Message fetish tends to cause caffeine-fuelled brainstorms by groups of like-minded PR bods (not that I've got anything against coffee). And it tends to produce a predictable result: slogans and tag lines.

Back in 1984, a young marketing academic named Robert Cialdini had suggested a quite different approach. Unsatisfied with the academic literature on marketing, he stepped into the real world and spent three years 'underground' learning from door-to-door salesmen, car dealers, fundraisers and telemarketers, observing the age-old techniques of the sales trade. He then buried himself in back issues of the *Journal of Personality and Social Psychology*, and matched the real-world selling techniques with the experimental literature on social psychology. It was a bold and brilliant approach that generated one of the pivotal books of modern marketing, *Influence: the Psychology of Persuasion*. According to Wikipedia, it's sold over two million copies and been translated into 26 languages.

Reading *Influence* for the first time is quite a revelation. It's like stumbling upon the secret to the human soul. In the six techniques he identified – reciprocity, commitment, social proof, authority, liking and scarcity – seems to lie the answer to every marketer's, and social marketer's, dreams and hopes. Each of these techniques draws its power from social psychology, from the ways human beings interact with each other. In Cialdini's view, behaviour change was less about messages and more about relationships.

A decade later, in 1995, a professor of marketing named Alan Andreasen wrote a book called *Marketing Social Change: Changing Behavior to Promote Health, Social Development, and the Environment* in which he proposed that the methods used to market products could be used to market socially beneficial behaviours. For marketers and marketing academics this was an immensely attractive idea, and Social Marketing has since become a burgeoning field, particularly in health promotion and road safety.

The core of the social marketing concept is to identify the barriers to a behaviour and then develop a message based on the four Ps – product, price, promotion and place – to overcome those barriers. The message should embody a 'value proposition' – it must promise results the customer actually wants. In short, the theory seems to be "Communicate a valued result, at the right price, using the right promotions, in the right place, and people will adopt the behaviour."

A good place to observe contemporary social marketing is on the Osocio website, a rich and constantly growing repository of the efforts of social marketers. There's much to be impressed with here, but one thing I began to notice about these ad campaigns (and my own, for I was now working as a social marketer) was their uniformity. First, they were entirely message-based and, second, they were using those messages to do just two things: they were either arguing facts or they were trying to provoke emotions like fear, anger, disgust or delight, or they were doing both.

Now, there's nothing wrong with presenting facts or provoking emotions. They're the essence of good communication. But, as we've already noted, there's little evidence that communication alone changes people's behaviour.

Something that was not obvious when I first read Cialdini's *Influence* and Andreasen's *Social Marketing* now speaks out loud and clear to me: sales techniques and messages, however well executed, can only ever have short-term effects. At best, they can only get someone to buy a widget, come to a meeting, donate to a cause, or try a behaviour *once*. Of course, one-off actions are important – every change project requires them. But *sustained* change is a longer journey and depends on much more than good marketing.

What sustains a behaviour, I eventually concluded, was the design of the behaviour itself (see the next Ingredient) and also whether that behaviour was enabled or disabled by the environment in which people live and make their day-to-day choices.

Every behaviour is enabled or disabled by its environment

We humans can be addictively motivated to pursue goals beyond the bounds of reason or logic – how else do you explain World of Warcraft, body building or the Tour de France. But most of us have room for only a few such unreasonable obsessions in our lives. Our other behaviours must fit more-or-less conveniently into the rational time-and-motion economy of life. If they fit well, they might be sustained. If they fit badly, they'll probably be dropped.

Good marketing may get us to trial a new behaviour, but if we end up feeling exhausted, unrewarded, anxious or confused, then we'll eventually stop trying and find something less exhausting, scary and humiliating to invest our time in. Those negative experiences train us to be helpless. Effectively, the behaviour becomes literally undo-able. This process of learned helplessness is a profound way that our environments control our actions. It's what stops us exercising, eating healthy foods, driving safely, quitting smoking and going out for a quiet drink with friends on a Friday night, even when we want to.

The other way our environments control us is by rewards. To explain this, consider how our eating habits have been influenced by the stupendous explosion of delicious foods in our environments. People are not obese just because they have suddenly become greedy and lazy but because their environment now presents them with a fabulous cornucopia of delicious, sugary, fatty little dollops of pleasure available at every turn, 24/7. The modern supermarket is to a potential food addict what a casino is to a gambler. And the reverse is true: healthy, sustainable behaviours are also more likely to be taken up if our environment rewards us for them.[6]

Sustained change therefore depends on modifying the environment so that desired behaviours become easy, safe, comfortable, pleasant and rewarding.

- Tackling obesity, for example, has as much to do with making food accessible as it has with people wanting to eat healthy food. As a result, Michelle Obama's *Let's Move* campaign is working with major food retailers to establish 1,500 shops selling healthy food in what are now inner city 'food deserts'.[7]
- Reducing car dependence requires accessible, safe, comfortable public transport, footpaths and bicycle routes that take people where they want to go quickly and pleasurably. That's why light rail is replacing heavy rail all around the world, and why cities like New York and Sydney are constructing multi-million dollar networks of dedicated cycleways. It's one thing to *want* to avoid the car but it's the infrastructure that *enables* us to avoid it.
- Tackling road accidents depends on better road design and layout, better pedestrian facilities, aggressive police enforcement, and safer vehicle design, as well as interventions to reduce drink-driving and denormalise speeding.[8]
- Tackling tobacco smoking depends on tax increases, clinic-based quit programmes, advertising bans and indoor smoking bans, as well as education and promotion campaigns.[9]
- Even rude behaviour by bicyclists has environmental causes. A recent review found that conflict between bicyclists and pedestrians on shared paths "occurs most commonly where lack of clear rules meets poor path design meets people in groups" – all environmental factors.[10]

Environments enable or disable behaviours in at least three ways. First, they shift the balance of convenience, making some behaviours difficult, complex, time-consuming, uncertain, unsafe or irksome and other behaviours easy, simple, quick, certain, safer and more pleasing. Then, through herd behaviour, they create social norms. And, through familiarity, they make unconscious compliance easy.

The enabling or disabling effect of environments has been called 'choice architecture' and it's been a popular topic since Richard Thaler and Cass Sunstein published their book *Nudge* in 2008.[11] In their view, nudging involves altering the environment with an eye to unconscious psychological biases so that good choices get preferred over bad ones. Their most quoted example is the use of opt-out defaults on application forms to increase superannuation contributions and organ donations. Because opting-out requires mental effort most people prefer to leave the default in place. This produces a tremendous difference in levels of organ donation between Germany which has an opt-in system where 12 per cent of citizens give their consent and Austria with an opt-out system where 99 per cent do.[12]

Thaler and Sunstein described a dozen or so environmental nudges. But in fact, the range of possible environmental modifications is numberless.[13] Car-sharing schemes, traffic-calming devices, smart meters, energy-star rating schemes, public-place smoking bans, cigarette taxes, ceiling insulation finance schemes are all examples of environmental modifications that influence behaviour. Fortunately, to make programme design a little easier, it's possible to categorise most environmental modifications into six types.

To enable a desired behaviour, we can:

1. Build a community
2. Create ease
3. Lower the cost

And, to disable an undesired behaviour, we can:

4. Raise the cost
5. Thwart
6. Regulate*

1. Build a community

It's a scientifically proven fact that a lone surfer has a high risk of being attacked by a shark whereas a group of surfers is perfectly safe. Well, of course that's wrong, but if you're a surfer it FEELS that way! Being part of a group lowers people's perceived sense of risk, making them more able to sustain difficult activities and persevere against adversity, while remaining

---

* Thoughtful readers will notice that 'modify norms' doesn't appear on this list. Although influencing norms is always an important goal, I doubt they can be changed directly. Instead, norms get altered indirectly by the gradual accumulation of social proofs resulting from other interventions. Norms and social proof are discussed in Ingredient 5.

happy at the same time.

I had the pleasure of walking down Swanston Street, Melbourne, this morning from Bourke Street Mall to Federation Square – surely one of the hippest, most delightfully 'happening' urban strips in the world.

First I passed four nondescript-looking folks setting up a literature stall, three middle-aged men and a young woman. Although they looked ordinary, their publications bore lurid titles like *Awake!* and *Armageddon*. Jehovah's Witnesses. I thought, it can't be easy to stand up in public in a busy street in the big city, risking ridicule and challenging Satan in the lives of the entire population. They seemed so small and humble compared with the mighty task they had set for themselves.

Next, there were two smiling sassy Oxfam girls in neat black T-shirts. One said "How you doin' sir?" and wanted my opinion on "What is the biggest killer of children in the world?" "Malaria," I guessed. "No, it's diarrhoea," she answered and went on, with blithe determination, to explain how a monthly payment would make all the difference. I said she must get a lot of refusals and she said "Yeah. We get all the excuses – 'I'm in a hurry', 'My pay day's tomorrow', 'I have to ask my wife.'" What was important was to be likeable. "People decide in three seconds whether they like you. They give you their credit-card details in the street, so they have to like you." I told her I was already signed up, we high-fived, and I moved on.

Then I found an untidy row of protesters slumped in the shade of a casuarina tree next to a tragically scrawled sign in felt-tip pen that said "Welcome to Occupy Melbourne". A good-natured young woman pushed a petition into my hand. While I filled it in, she explained that the police had come along that morning and arrested their table. They'd already posted the video on Facebook. It was hilarious, she said. I said I'd check it out.

A few metres away, I noticed that nine slender ghost gum trees outside the Westin hotel had been cloaked in long, fabulously colourful knitted socks, in a dazzling variety of patterns, by the Yarn Corner Group. At 6 metres per tree, that was over 50 metres of creatively knitted hosiery, a most impressive effort.

In Federation Square I was drawn to a surreal contraption made of hundreds of lengths of PVC tube that walked along on a dozen or so articulated legs. It was an artificial life form by Dutch artist Theo Jansen. Two university students had been employed for a month to invite passers-by to push this artwork around as part of Federation Square's Creative Programme. When I got there, a delighted group of young adults with Down's Syndrome were taking turns to push it around. I had a go too. Considering how big it was, it was remarkably mobile. Leonardo da Vinci would have loved it.

All these small public efforts had something in common. Each one, requiring persistence and resilience in various degrees, was being done by a group of people. Not by an individual.

Pick up any newspaper any day and read behind the stories. It's almost always groups that are the active players – corporations, political parties, business associations, unions, action groups, sports teams, criminal gangs. Where individuals are the subject, there's usually been some ghastly accident or tragedy.

Our environment is not just physical, it's social. It's populated by groups of people. We are a social species; yet, for some reason, we persist in imagining that history is made by individuals. Not so. Groups are the operative units in our society.

Lone humans tend not to achieve much when it comes to social change. Isolation is disempowering and depressing. When lone individuals do achieve great things, they are often driven insane by loneliness and fear, like so many famous celebrities, artists and inventors.

The message is: if you want to empower people, start a group.

Malnutrition is a keystone problem for those mired in poverty in a country like Bangladesh. Malnourishment during the first three years of a child's life tends to cause stunted growth, poor brain development and low immunity. Often it's an inter-generational problem: malnourished mothers giving birth to malnourished children.

Development experts have long recognised that women's empowerment transforms outcomes for their families. The trick is how to do it on a large scale. In 2005, the development agency CARE rose to the challenge and built women's empowerment into the heart of a major development programme.

The result was SHOUHARDO, a $US126-million, four-year effort in 2,400 Bangladeshi villages and slums, in partnership with the Bangladesh government and numerous local non-government organisations.

When the results of this programme became available in 2009 aid experts were stunned. In less than four years the stunting rate among babies in participating communities had fallen from 56.1 per cent to 40.4 per cent, a 15.7 per cent drop. This figure dwarfed the 0.1 per cent decline in Bangladesh as a whole and easily beat the 2.4 per cent annual decline seen in the average USAID food security programme.[14]

The result was even more dramatic considering that global food prices had risen dramatically in those years, and Cyclone Sidr had ruined much of the Bangladesh rice crop in 2007. Yet, as the price of rice and cooking oil doubled, the proportion of SHOUHARDO households with three square meals a day increased from 32 per cent to 74 per cent.

SHOUHARDO's innovation was to mix a range of traditional development interventions – sanitation, increased food production, food rations, village savings groups, and community-based development committees – with women's empowerment groups, called EKATA groups.

EKATA groups of 20 women and 10 teenage girls would meet regularly, discuss their circumstances and propose solutions to their problems. Girls would learn from the women's life experiences and the women would commit to protecting the girls from violence and abuse. The EKATA slogan was "I am not alone. Together we can achieve something. Together we can change our lives."

The groups drew graphs and maps to understand power relations in their families and villages. They talked about barriers holding them back, like lack of decision-making power, violence, early marriage and lack of education. And they got training in reading and maths and learned the basics of Bangladeshi law – many were surprised to learn it was illegal for girls to marry before 18.[15]

One of the biggest barriers to women's participation in Bangladeshi society is public harassment by groups of young men that prevents women from walking freely to markets and actively participating in community life. "In some villages EKATA members formed support networks to confront young men who sexually harassed women and girls in the streets. The result: the catcalling stopped. And teenage girls began walking freely. The women's groups also sought legal action when men beat their wives, sending a strong signal in the community that the violence had to stop."[16]

As women's voices increased in household and village decision-making so the nourishment of their children improved. One of the evaluators concluded, "What we saw was a clear pattern. Women who participated in the empowerment interventions were getting better antenatal care, eating more nutritious food and getting more rest during pregnancy. They and their children also had better diets in terms of the variety of foods."[17]

Because only 408 of the 2,342 participating villages and slums had EKATA groups, it was possible to draw a comparison between the impact of EKATA groups and the more traditional development approaches. It was startlingly apparent that no single intervention reduced stunting as much as the groups of women and girls getting together and talking about solutions to their problems.

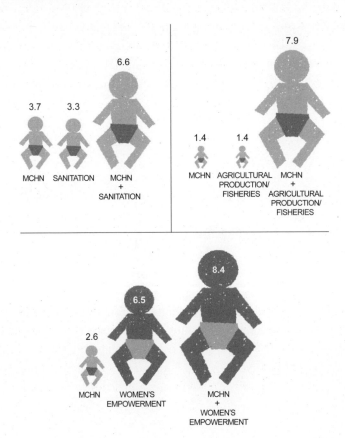

No single intervention reduced stunting as much as women's empowerment groups. (MCHN – maternal and child health and nutrition).[18] Reproduced with permission from CARE International.

Purposeful social interaction does many things. It creates joy. And confidence. And commitment. And accountability. And optimism. But where groups make a real difference to social change projects is in increasing people's resilience – their ability to endure and persevere in the face of the challenges and setbacks that inevitably litter the path to a better future.

Business researchers Chip Heath and Forest Jourden investigated this effect and found that being a member of a group has a remarkable effect on people's perceptions of success and failure. In a series of experiments they asked lone individuals and groups to solve puzzles. They found that, on average, most of the individuals (64 per cent) thought that they performed *below* the median. But most members of groups (59 per cent) thought their group performed *above* the median. The results were especially skewed at the low end: 30 per cent of individuals ranked themselves in the bottom 10 per cent of performance. Heath and Jourden speculated that group membership might cause people to hold more positive illusions about their performance.[19] And the reason they do so, I suspect, is because people like being part of a supportive group, and a dash of denial in the face of setbacks helps a group stick together.

The tendency of groups to find the silver lining in even the most abject of failures has been called 'The Buffering Effect of Groups'. It's especially important in change projects because making social change almost always takes longer than anyone thinks. And there are inevitably numerous setbacks and defeats along the way. How we interpret those setbacks determines whether we are disheartened or invigorated. The saving grace of a group is that it buffers people against those setbacks by changing the way their members interpret them.

If we want to change the world, then it will almost certainly be through the actions of a group or groups rather than through the lone actions of dispersed individuals who don't meet each other. The creation of small communities or teams is behind many successful change efforts. WeightWatchers works, not just because people count calories, but because they become members of purposeful groups. The same applies to Alcoholics Anonymous.

Purpose-built teams are everywhere. They include action groups, health support groups, Green Teams, discussion groups, exercise groups, buddies, study circles, social clubs, communities of practice, leadership programmes, and online networks.

Interestingly, one of the most underrated groups is the team of two. I recently finished a project where I was in a team of two with an energetic bicycling advocate. The teamwork was enjoyable and effortless. We found the complexities of working with a large team vanished – every phone call, for example, was a team meeting. I can't imagine it being that way with a larger team.*

Groups, of course, bring their own challenges. Not all groups are happy. We all know of dysfunctional groups where bad leadership, bullying or failure to delegate wears down the members to the point where the group disintegrates or splits in a mass of anger and blame.

A group can bring perseverance, optimism, accountability and joy, or it can do the opposite. The proviso is to *make sure there's halfway decent leadership or facilitation*. Properly functioning groups are those that pay attention to the human needs of their members. They get on with the job while also making their members feel respected, safe and cared for. The trick is to make sure you have leaders or facilitators who understand that – or who've at least had some training in facilitation – and there's a good chance your group will be successful.

Can online communities work as well? There's currently a huge interest in crowd-sourcing and online communities. Web platforms like Facebook, Joulebug, Quirky, FundBreak, Kickstarter and OpenIDEO enable large numbers of strangers to interact and collaborate on positive efforts. They significantly increase the reach of change projects, but can they be as effective as face-to-face groups in creating persistence and resilience? Is it even possible for members of a purely online community to respect and care for each other as individuals? So far, I doubt it. If, however, an online community could create a genuinely personal sense of social support, then, yes, it might be as empowering as a face-to-face community. In the meantime, the most effective groups are likely to be those whose members can share a couch, pour each other a drink and pass the corn chips.

---

* There's an insightful article on the power of buddy teams at: http://www.jpb.com/report103/archive_20100818.php.

2. Create ease

Schools in remote Aboriginal communities in Australia's north often have a terrible truancy rate. In 2010 one school hit a low of 37 per cent and more than 60 schools fell below 80 per cent. Some 2,000 children were not even enrolled.[20]

Truancy is a significant social problem because kids who don't attend school miss out on basic skills like English and Maths that let them function in the modern world. They tend to get stuck in their communities, passively reliant on welfare, and often sink into a miasma of alcohol, drugs and violence.

A bright spark in the administration (an economist, I suspect) decided that the answer was to threaten parents who didn't shape up, dress their kids, feed them and deliver them to the school gate. The result was 'Improving School Enrolment and Attendance through Welfare Reform Measure', a Federal Government programme mandated in 12 communities in the Northern Territory and Queensland in 2009.

The way it works is that parents whose children miss ten or more days of school a term without a good excuse have their welfare payments suspended. They are supposed to attend a conference with school staff and Centrelink officers and agree on a plan to change their behaviour. Then, if they fail to carry out their plan, they get their payments suspended again. By 2011 there had been 380 suspensions of payments for an average of 21 days.[21]

A long-serving public servant described this as "the last straw in Aboriginal affairs policy. I am absolutely opposed to it. This is bad public policy, it is morally objectionable, and it will not work."[22]

According to the 2010 evaluation report, the threat-based programme did seem to cause an improvement in attendance rates. It found a 5 per cent increase in attendance by targeted children in the Northern Territory and 4 per cent in Queensland. But on closer inspection, the improvement was short-lived. Truancy dropped during the compliance period but just 2 months later kids were just as truant as ever. Interestingly, the rate for the worst six kids was a textbook example of resistance, showing immediate compliance but much worse behaviour over time.

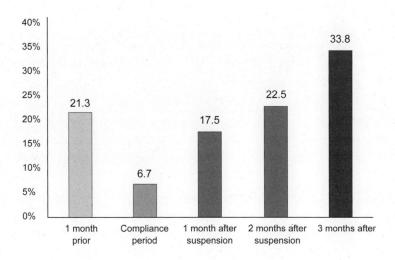

The signature of resistance: immediate compliance followed by more extreme levels of truancy. Source: Department of Education, Employment and Workplace Relations (2012). [23]

The government evaluators concluded: "It appears that many families faced complex and significant barriers which thwarted their attempts to make sure their child attended school. Results show one quarter of all notified parents took reasonable steps to improve their child's school attendance although this was not always reflected in an actual improvement in attendance."[24]

Following this evaluation, the Federal Government expanded the programme to a further 16 communities in 2011 in the face of widespread condemnation – surely a tour de force of bureaucratic obstinacy.

Meanwhile, the remote community of Gunbalanya, nestled in the foothills of the Arnhem Land escarpment 300 kilometres east of Darwin, was taking a different approach. The principal of Gunbalanya School, Esther Djayhgurrnga, and her deputy, Sue Trimble, knew they had a truancy problem but noticed that it was worse during the dry season from June to September.

Sue described their solution:

We could see that in the early part of the year most kids were at school . . . and the second part of the year most kids were out of the community. So we took this to the school council and . . . said 'we should have the school operating when most of the children are in school which is the first half of the year'. We took the indigenous calendar and broke it up into segments and asked the school council to map what was happening at this time in their lives. Were they out hunting? What seasonal factors were happening? And underneath that we listed how many children were at school . . . so the picture was drawn that the school should be open early in the year.[25]

Their modification was deceptively simple: start the year three weeks earlier and have an extended eight-week holiday in June-July-August when families leave town for outstations, hunting, visiting and ceremonies. It made sense because the community is cut off for months during the wet season and the kids hang around with nothing to do. The Northern Territory Education Department supports this experiment but it must have been challenging to overturn the time-honoured customs of the white teachers' year. Recalling white teachers early from their Christmas holidays into the soaking humidity of the wet season can't have been easy.

Instead of forcing kids to fit the school, Esther and Sue made the school fit the kids by matching the school year with the community's climate-driven rhythms. There's no official evaluation available yet but (as of 2012) there's robust praise for this experiment, including from the kids.

At its core, Esther and Sue's idea was simple. They made going to school easier for those kids.

Ease means reducing the mental and physical effort of an action as close to zero as possible. In practice, ease often includes reducing the number of steps or decisions and making each remaining step or decision as mentally unchallenging as possible.

But ease is more than simplicity. This story demonstrates that it's about *fit*: carefully matching the action with the realities and rhythms of people's lives and, if necessary, redesigning the action and its context to improve the fit. Creating ease therefore starts with learning about people's lives.

Designing for ease is what the best professional designers have learnt to do very well. They spend time with users, observe how they do things, see where they fail, and devise ways to smooth the path to action. Their system of practice, called 'design thinking', is well suited to ironing out the kinks and irritating complexities that make products hard to use.

Creating ease requires us to think like designers, observe how people struggle with their current environment, and experiment with tweaks that create a new path of least resistance.

3. Lowering the price of desired behaviours

Nic Frances is an ex-priest who resigned as CEO of the Brotherhood of St Laurence in 2003 and decided to do something about climate change. With a friend, Chris Tierney, he set up a company called Easy Being Green to help people retrofit their homes to make them more sustainable. They bought a few pallets of compact fluorescent lamps (CFLs) and, with a team of youthful assistants, began selling them at a discount price at open-air markets around Sydney. People seemed interested but sales were poor. Nic and Chris were charging A$10 for a pack of six CFLs which was good value compared with, typically, $20 to $40 (£13 to £25) at the supermarket. But the most they ever sold in one day was 91 packs. In desperation, they lowered the price to $5 (£3) but sales didn't improve.

Then, while talking to a Greenpeace campaigner, Nic had an 'ah-ha moment'. New South Wales (NSW) had introduced a carbon-trading scheme in 2003 (it was one of the first states in the world to do so). Doing the sums, Nic figured out that the dollar value of carbon abatement from a single CFL was greater than its purchase price. In other words, by funding the purchase of CFLs through an emissions trading scheme he could give away the CFLs for free. In fact, he could cover the programme management, distribution and advertising costs and still come out ahead.

Ambitiously, Nic tied up a deal with NSW's biggest daily newspaper, *The Daily Telegraph*, for a CFL giveaway campaign that would become one of the largest carbon trading-projects ever undertaken in NSW.

Easy Being Green gave away three million CFLs (in packs of six plus a water-saving showerhead) to about 500,000 households, aggregated the carbon savings, converted them into carbon credits, and sold the credits to pay for the whole project.[26]

After that massive effort, Nic decided the Sydney CFL market was saturated. Which was true enough: by late 2006 Easy Being Green and other players had distributed free CFLs to about 70 per cent of NSW households.[27] So Nic decided to export the model overseas. He started another company, CoolNRG, and repeated the exercise in the UK, this time distributing 4.5 million CFLs in a single day ('The Great British Light Switch').

Next, he set his sights even higher, organising the largest single light bulb distribution in history for a scheme in Mexico to be funded through the Kyoto Protocol's Clean Development Mechanism. Nic points out that, by saving a million poor Mexican families the equivalent of two weeks wages a year in energy costs, it could also be one of the largest poverty-reduction projects in Mexican history.[28]

Nic is a born-again market evangelist. He might not love capitalism but he believes it's the most powerful mechanism for driving human behaviour. In his view, we can use markets to reward people for doing good just as easily as we can reward them for doing evil. It only takes a little imagination and, of course, governments that have created carbon-emissions trading schemes.

I met Nic at a conference and asked him, "Installing a CFL is just about the easiest thing we can ask someone to do, but what about the hard stuff: leaving cars at home, retrofitting homes, becoming active citizens. How can the market help there?" Quick as a flash, he replied "Any human activity that reduces carbon, and can be measured, can be turned into cash. We could literally hand someone a cheque for leaving their car at home two days a week."

He has a point and he's busy proving it. There's a stack of lessons in Nic's story, told simply and inspiringly in his book *The End of Charity: Time for Social Enterprise*, but the one I want to draw out is about the role of price in a social-change project.

There's a time in the evolution of products and behaviours that price matters but it's not at the beginning. Price matters little to early adopters. For them, it's all about the dream. Costs aren't costs, they're investments. But as we ramp up our efforts to go beyond early adopters into majority audiences (that is, when we exceed about 20 per cent take-up in a given population) the rules change.

What stymied Nic's early attempts to sell CFLs was that around 30 per cent of NSW households already had them. The enthusiastic early adopters were already on board. That left Nic with a tough audience: the pragmatic majority.

Interestingly, once they had Nic's free CFLs in their hands, four out of five installed them within 12 months[29] which shows that the majority did actually appreciate the CFLs and understood the benefits. They apparently wanted them but just not enough to fork out $5 for a pack of six.

The 60 per cent or so of people in the 'majority' are tough customers. They care about the environment and the future of the world (so the research says) but their passion is lukewarm. They almost certainly do have passions in their lives, it's just that they don't interact with this particular project. They might be passionate about coaching their daughter's soccer team or becoming the world's No.1 Wikipedia editor. But when it comes to helping to save the environment (and saving money) by installing a CFL bulb, their motivations are cool.

In other words, when you are working with majorities, that is, once you pass about 20 per cent take-up of a new behaviour or product, cost and convenience really do matter, and the further you move into majority markets they matter more. By the time you move into the late majority, that is, past 50 per cent take-up, you really need to have pared the cost down to a bare minimum and ramped up the ease and simplicity to a maximum.

Nic Frances and his team found it very hard to sell CFLs in a market where CFL take-up was already around 30 per cent. The early adopters already had their CFLs. Nic had to leap across the chasm into the majority market, and since installing a CFL was already as simple as it could be, price was the key. By giving away CFLs for free, he found the way to leap the chasm.

This story demonstrates how, even in situations where saving money is not people's main motivation for acting, price might still need to be lowered before people feel able to act – something that's very likely to be the case when adoption of a behaviour exceeds 20 per cent in a given population.

4. Raising the price of undesired behaviours

'Price elasticity of demand' is a fundamental concept in classical economics. It also seems to exist. It's the effect on demand caused by changes in price.

An area where the price elasticity has been studied comprehensively is tobacco sales. In 1999, World Bank consultants reviewed past studies and concluded that, all else being equal, a price rise of 10 per cent was likely to produce a reduction of tobacco consumption of about 4 per cent in developed countries and 8 per cent in developing countries.[30] Later on, economists Craig Gallet and John List analysed 86 studies and found a mean price elasticity of -0.48, meaning that, on average a 10 per cent increase in price is likely to be followed by a decrease in consumption of 4.8 per cent.[31]

Interestingly, because young people have less cash and are less likely to be addicted, their tobacco price elasticity is relatively huge. Gallet and List found an average price elasticity of -1.43 for teenagers and -0.76 for young adults. That means that a 10 per cent increase in tobacco price is likely to cause a 14.3 per cent reduction of use by teenagers.

Wikipedia lists a number of price elasticities. The figures below show the reduction in demand likely to be caused by a 10 per cent increase in price:

Beer -3% to -9%
Wine -10%
Spirits -15%
Coca-Cola -38%
Mountain Dew -44%
Bus travel -2%
Car fuel -0.9% (short run); -3.1% (long run)
Paediatric visits -0.3% to -0.6%
Live performing arts -4% to -9%

These elasticities suggest an interesting proposition, that price elasticity is inversely proportional to people's deep desires. People don't care much about fizzy drinks but they do care passionately about their children's health.

In all likelihood, there's a price elasticity for every human behaviour – although, since the price might be time or humiliation, it might be beyond the bounds of economics to measure it.

Nevertheless, if a behaviour has a dollar or pound cost and you can raise it you're probably going to see less of the behaviour.

But beware of resistance. People work hard to maintain their liberties. As an indication, there's evidence that the effect of tobacco tax hikes is largely limited to preventing new smokers starting. Existing smokers, it seems, prefer to pay the higher cost.[32]

And people are inventive in their resistance. For instance, it's well established that tobacco tax hikes cause a rise in the use of roll-your-own tobacco, which is much more toxic than the packaged variety. And Gallet and List noted that, when smuggling was taken into account, the tobacco price elasticity for adults was lower (-0.36).

A perfect illustration of the resilience of resistors comes from a study by economists Jerome Adda and Francesca Cornaglia. They chose an innovative way to measure the effect of tobacco price rises on smoking behaviour. Rather than counting the number of cigarettes sold, they measured changing concentrations of cotinine, a breakdown product of nicotine, in people's saliva, drawn from a huge medical database covering some 20,000 individuals.[33]

They found that, although increases in tobacco taxes during the 1990s did cut the number of cigarettes being sold, the amount of cotinine found in smokers' saliva stayed remarkably constant. They thought the reason might be that, although smokers were smoking fewer cigarettes, they were inhaling each cigarette more deeply! That's resistance.

5. Thwarting

Thwarting means making a behaviour hard to do. Daniela Santucci and Margaux Park, resource recovery officers at Bankstown City Council in south-west Sydney, decided to stop despairing about the high number of plastic bags contaminating recycling bins in apartment blocks – a small issue for you and me but a chronic problem for the waste industry. Instead, they decided to carry out an experiment. Inspired by Goldstein, Martin and Cialdini's *Yes!: 50 Scientifically Proven Ways to Be Persuasive*,[34] they decided to test some social persuasion techniques.

The basic technique they tested was the 'smiley face emoticon' feedback technique pioneered by Robert Cialdini. The idea is to use a little icon of a smiley face to send a subliminal message of social approval, hopefully making people feel better about doing the right thing. This method has been making an impact in the US power industry through the work of Opower where Cialdini is a consultant. The use of smiley face emoticons, combined with data showing how the recipient's power use compares with their community-at-large, has been shown to reduce power use in US cities by 2 to 3 per cent – a respectable amount from the point of view of an energy utility.[35]

In addition to the social persuasion methods, Daniela and Margaux added a couple of environmental tweaks: handing out kitchen tubs and giving people recycling bins with holes in the lids. The tubs were a way to transport recycling from kitchen to bin without needing to use a plastic bag. And the holes in the bin lids were too small for people to push a full plastic bag into the bin. Daniela said she got the idea from seeing the rubbish bins in public places and had been thinking about it for years.

Here are the results of the 14-week trial:

Smiley face cards alone = 0–6 per cent reduction in contamination
Smiley face cards + recycling tubs = 16 per cent
Smiley face cards + holes in recycling bin lids = 25 per cent
Smiley face cards + face-to-face pledges to council staff = 25 per cent
Smiley face cards + door knocking by council staff = 30 per cent

Which one is the winner? The bin lids with the holes was clearly superior. It not only reduced contamination from 30 per cent to 5 per cent but was a method that could be sustained at no ongoing cost to the council. It was powerful because it was a permanent change to the infrastructure people used. Even though the kitchen recycling tubs achieved only a 16 per cent reduction, they deserved to be continued too, for the same reason.

Why did the holey bin work so well? It might be because bins are perceived to be dirty and people prefer not to touch them if they can avoid it. The hole gives people a way to insert their recyclables without touching the bin but thwarts anyone trying to push in a full bag. Thwarted by a combination of the hole and their own disgust, residents were forced to remove their bottles from the plastic bags they used to transport them from kitchen to bin area. Hey presto, fewer plastic bags in the recycling![36]

A great many behaviour change efforts are based on thwarting, for example:

- Machine guards and safety screens in factories, one of the great behaviour-change interventions in history.
- Safety-by-design: urban design principles that aim to thwart criminal acts in public by ensuring observation at a distance and by removing the shady, concealed spaces criminals depend on for their nefarious acts.
- Reducing the number of parking spaces, a method businesses and councils use to reduce car use.
- And, as an extreme case, gastric banding surgery for the morbidly obese that simply makes it impossible to eat more.

However, keep in mind that, although thwarting is a widely used behaviour-change technique, it's also an attack on people's customary liberties, so there will be resistance.

One of the most controversial social interventions in Australia in recent years has been the BasicsCard. BasicsCard is part of the Northern Territory Intervention, a vast expert-led service-delivery programme that is supposed to improve social order and child safety in Aboriginal communities. BasicsCard is a password-protected debit card that restricts 50 per cent of an individual's welfare income to rent, utilities, fruit and vegetables, healthy food and clothing from approved stores. Spending on cigarettes, alcohol, gambling and pornography is banned. In 2008, BasicsCard became compulsory for every welfare recipient in the 73 communities covered by the Intervention.

Putting aside the Kafkaesque perversity of trying to force people to take responsibility for their finances by depriving them of responsibility for their finances, has it worked? The most positive evaluation reported 50 per cent of recipients claiming they were eating more fruit and vegetables, 61 per cent claiming there was less alcohol abuse, 63 per cent claiming there was less gambling, and 66 per cent claiming an improvement in children's welfare.[37]

Other reports contradicted these results; for example, a 'Whole of Government Monitoring Report' in 2009 found substance abuse up 77 per cent and domestic violence up 61 per cent.[38]

Whatever the benefits, people's own words reveal the galling humiliation of losing control over their spending:

"I just didn't have the energy to fight them. I went into shock. It made me feel like a piece of shit."

"When it was pushed on me, I was really angry because they didn't look at the big picture. They didn't look at who I am. It doesn't look at why people are spending money the way they do. You can't force people to spend money only in major stores."

"BasicsCard no good. Hard to remember PIN. Don't understand how it works. Hard to understand how much money. People in shops are not nice, no good, if not enough money to pay for food. Where the money goes, I don't know." [39]

And that humiliation was driving resistance, hints of which appear in government reports which revealed that spending on tobacco, and fruit and vegetables might not have changed[40] and that the currency of gambling was changing from cash to food, clothing, and even the BasicsCard itself.[41]

BasicsCard warns us that thwarting is an attack on people's liberties and hence their dignity. And, as a result, they'll be motivated to circumvent it whenever they can, using all the creativity humans are endowed with.

6. Regulation

Regulation means declaring a behaviour to be a criminal act, punishable by law, in the hope that the threat will prevent the behaviour.

Seatbelt laws are a celebrated and oft-quoted social change success story based primarily on regulation. They produced a revolution in community behaviour in a remarkably short period of time and made us all a lot safer. Or did they?

Australian states were the first to introduce mandatory seatbelt laws in 1970-71. The effect was dramatic. Rates of seatbelt use shot from 20 to 25 per cent in 1970, to 75 per cent in 1971, reaching 85 to 90 per cent by the late 1970s, all with surprisingly little objection from drivers. Meanwhile, traffic fatalities began a long steady period of decline.[42]

Propelled by the success of the Australian experiment, legislatures around the world followed suit: New Zealand in 1972, France in 1973, Spain and Sweden in 1975, and Germany in 1976. The UK resisted until 1983. Finally, the US states began to fall in line. New York passed its law in 1984 and New Jersey in 1985. At first, the laws covered only front-seat occupants, but during the 1990s the laws were expanded to include all occupants. By 1996, every US state except New Hampshire, which still resists, true to its motto 'Live free or die', had mandated seatbelt use.

Even in the USA, a nation notorious for its aversion to state intervention, the effects on behaviour have been striking. The number of buckled-up Americans has grown steadily every year, reaching 81 per cent in 2006. Eleven states now exceed 90 per cent compliance.[43]

Brilliant! What a success! That was until John Adams, Professor of Geography at University College London, rained on everyone's parade. In 1981 Adams published a paper comparing death and injury rates in states with and without seatbelt laws. The paper revealed something odd, as you can see in the figure below.

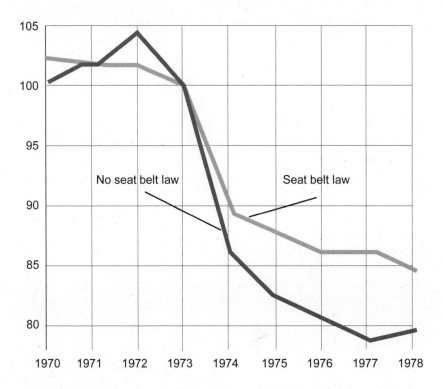

It wasn't supposed to be like this. Death rate indices in 13 seatbelt law countries, compared to four non-law countries. Source: Adams, J. (1986)[44]

In the 18 countries he surveyed, accounting for about 80 per cent of the world's motoring, those with seatbelt laws were no safer and in some cases (Sweden, Ireland and New Zealand) less safe than those without laws. Adams's data suggested that seatbelt laws might be counter-productive, increasing fatalities rather than reducing them.

Adams' paper appeared at a precarious moment for the UK's seatbelt advocates. Parliament was about to debate a mandatory seatbelt bill. No doubt in a prickly mood, Britain's Department of Transport quickly commissioned an internal critique of Adams's work. To their horror, the critique agreed with Adams. It concluded: "Available data for eight western European countries which introduced a seatbelt law between 1973 and 1976 suggests that it has not led to a detectable change in road deaths . . ."[45] Significantly, the internal paper also noted that pedestrian deaths had *increased* slightly in the eight countries since their seatbelt laws were passed. The Department suppressed the critique until Parliament passed the law. Adams's research was denounced by a succession of MPs as 'spurious', 'eccentric', 'preposterous' and 'bogus'.

Adams's observation has remained a thorn in the side of seatbelt advocates to this day. As a result, proving or disproving the benefits of seatbelt laws has become something of a minor industry for statisticians.

A 2000 study for the Automobile Insurers Bureau of Massachusetts analysed 15 years of state-by-state data and concluded that the effect of seatbelt laws "was low, at most, each increase of 1 per cent in the occupant safety belt use in a given state is associated with 1.15 fewer deaths." [46]

Harvard economists Alma Cohen and Liran Einav crunched the data again in 2001 and found that early studies had overestimated the death and injury reductions from seatbelt laws by a factor of two.[47]

In 2002 Brendan Maguire and colleagues at Western Illinois University re-crunched the data and concluded that "For several years traffic fatality rates have been declining in roughly equal proportions in both law states and non-law states . . . while seat-belt legislation is positively associated with increased safety belt use, neither seat-belt laws nor seat-belt use rates are associated in any substantial way with traffic death rates."[48]

There are also a number of research studies to the contrary, so, in fact (and amazingly) the jury is still out on whether seatbelt laws have saved lives. Perhaps a conservative position is that mandatory seatbelts might have saved lives but at nothing like the levels claimed by their advocates.

So what's the explanation? It seems that two psychological effects may be at work: risk compensation and resistance.

Adams proposed risk compensation as the cause of the apparent ineffectiveness of seatbelt laws. The idea is that people get used to, enjoy and need a certain degree of risk in their lives. If that level is reduced, they compensate by increasing their risks in other ways. That makes it a form of resistance.

So, buckled-up drivers feel safer and, to compensate for that reduced risk, they tend to drive a little more dangerously, causing more frequent and more violent accidents that increase the risk to other drivers, bicyclists, pedestrians and their own unbuckled passengers.

That claim set off a new cycle of research among statisticians and psychologists, some of which supported the existence of a risk-compensation effect[49,50] and some of which didn't.[51,52]

The second explanation involves resistance by habitually dangerous drivers. A 1990 study in North Carolina where seatbelt use was then 80 per cent found the remaining 20 per cent tended to be male, under-35-year-olds, driving older vehicles, preferring pickups, having poor driving records, being less likely to have health-care cover, more likely to have consumed large amounts of alcohol in the past year, and more likely to have an arrest record.[53] Another study found non-users in North Carolina had 35 per cent more accidents and 69 per cent more violations than users.[54]

Other researchers agree: "we believe that recent increases in safety belt usage may not be primarily responsible for the observed decrease in road fatalities. The population safety belt usage increase may be due to risk-averse 'good' drivers and their children occupants increasing their usage rate while risky 'bad' drivers and their children occupants maintain their current behaviour."[55]

In the Australian state of Victoria, for instance, only 3 per cent of drivers don't regularly wear seatbelts, but they're involved in 33 per cent of fatal crashes and 58 per cent were drunk at the time![56]

So, although most people buckle up, a small minority of unbuckled drivers may be causing a wildly disproportionate amount of damage.

As a possible example for this effect, when the Western Australian Premier recently increased the first offence for driving without a seatbelt from

A\$150 (£95) to A\$500 (£320), the number of unrestrained deaths increased from 41 (28 per cent of all vehicle occupant fatalities) to 63 (36 per cent of all vehicle occupant fatalities).[57] This would be perfectly consistent with a resistance effect.

The case of seatbelt laws demonstrates that even when laws have overwhelming public support and are backed by continuous education and aggressive enforcement, there are aspects of human nature that can negate many of their hoped-for benefits.

Nevertheless, regulation is widely used to control behaviour. Successful examples include industrial safety, food standards, disease control, building codes, sanitation and protection of the water supply. In these fields rigorous systems of monitoring and enforcement, and engineering, have proven more successful at controlling behaviour than appeals to voluntary change.

But regulation also has a dark side, which is well illustrated by the story of seatbelt laws. The history of alcohol and drug prohibition and many other attempts to use criminal law to regulate behaviour demonstrate similar pitfalls. Despite this, legislatures remain ever ready to criminalise behaviours they deem to be harmful. Recent notable examples include banning Islamic headgear in France, criminalising overseas surrogacy in some Australian states, and the use of anti-social behaviour orders in the UK.

The history of seatbelt laws provides important lessons for would-be regulators.

- If you can avoid regulating a behaviour, do so. Resistance and unexpected blow-backs can fundamentally undermine your efforts.
- Don't even think about regulation until you have overwhelming community support and a high degree of voluntary compliance in the target population. In effect, regulation should be considered only when it reinforces existing social norms.
- There will always be a small number of resistors and they are likely to cause a disproportionate amount of harm. Therefore understand that regulation requires a significant, ceaseless investment in monitoring and enforcement. Weakness in this area is likely to fundamentally undermine the impact of legislation.

Conclusion

Because behaviours are enabled or disabled by their environments, modifying the environment almost always matters when we aim to influence behaviour.

A recent US National Research Council report, for example, gave a nice summary of what might be needed to tackle childhood obesity.

- Incentives to lure grocery stores to move into underserved neighbourhoods
- Eliminating outdoor ads for unhealthy foods and drinks near schools
- Requiring calorie and other nutritional information on restaurant menus
- Implementing *Safe Routes to School* programmes
- Regulating minimum play space and time in child-care programmes
- Rerouting buses or developing other transportation strategies that ensure people can get to grocery stores
- Using building codes to ensure facilities have working water fountains.[58]

All these are environmental interventions.

In the case of behaviours like alcohol abuse, overeating and speeding, environmental modifications may be the *only* possible tools, because people may have no inner motivations we can work with.

The third ingredient of change, therefore, is that a change effort should contribute to sustained changes to the environment in which people make their choices.

That means that the entire environment should be open to analysis and, potentially, modification, including infrastructure, services, social organisation, leadership, technology, pricing, regulation, governance – literally anything that could exert a positive or negative pull on a specific behaviour.

That implies that the job of designing a change programme is necessarily a multi-disciplinary activity. Your brains trust should therefore include the diversity of professionals you might need to create a broad range of interventions; for example, economists, facilitators, regulators, engineers and architects.

Of course, environmental changes are harder to achieve than the comparatively pleasant and quick work of designing ad campaigns and phone apps but they have fantastic advantages of efficiency. Once environmental changes are in place, they affect everyone, and their impact continues indefinitely, often with little additional effort.

If the aim is sustained change it makes no sense to rely solely on messages and marketing techniques that can produce only short-term changes in behaviour. Terrible rates of death and injury at work in the early twentieth century were not tamed by persuasion but by a constellation of permanent regulatory, institutional and technological changes. Do the challenges we now face deserve any less?

Method

Making a theory of change

A theory of change is a testable, measurable, cause-and-effect hypothesis about what changes could cause progress towards your desired future.

The aim is to identify a series of concrete initiatives by specific players to drive environmental changes that, in turn, will make your long-term goal possible. Here's an example of a theory of change:

> **IF** council agrees to a corporate plan that requires a park within ten minutes walk of every home;
> **AND IF** council ensures each park is well-maintained, with shade trees, lighting, exercise equipment for different ages (and, ideally, proximity to a coffee shop);
> **AND IF** the state government establishes a park improvement fund;
> **AND IF** residents join Friends Groups that participate in designing park improvements, and can add their own sculptures and play equipment;
> **THEN** there will be a reduction of obesity, crime, heart disease, depression, and a higher sense of belonging and community resilience in these communities.

There are two stages in creating a theory of change. First, brainstorming *any* actions that could make a difference, even unlikely ones. Second, prioritising a limited number of actions to form your theory.

The 'quality controls' that determine the effectiveness of your theory are:

1. the diversity of your brains trust
2. how inspired and well-informed you've made them

3. how open they are to seemingly wacky and left-field ideas.

Remember, your theory doesn't have to be perfect – the aim is to create a well-informed hypothesis. The effort that results will be an experiment that tests that hypothesis.

The method described below is one of many ways to develop a theory of change. I like this one because it's fast to do.

Rapid theory generator

Instructions:

1. Bring together your diverse brains trust.
2. Inform and inspire them with your research results.
3. Brainstorm using these rules:

a) Draw up a sheet of paper or whiteboard like this:

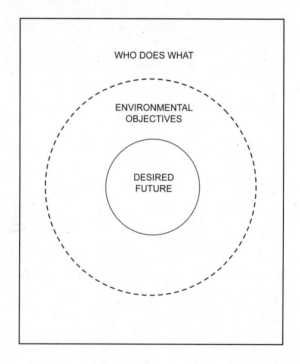

WHO DOES WHAT

ENVIRONMENTAL
OBJECTIVES

DESIRED
FUTURE

b) Brainstorm the question: "For progress towards the desired future, what needs to happen?"

Private writing = 2 minutes
Brainstorming = 15 minutes

c) Keep adding ideas and links until you identify real actions by real people or organisations (as in the diagram below).

d) Record environmental changes in the middle circle of 'environmental objectives'.

e) Don't include activities that are done directly by your project team e.g. "new signage" or "Street Pride campaign". The idea is to identify actions done by others. You can then organise your team to support them.

f) Avoid referring to intangible mental states like 'awareness' or 'attitudes' or vague ideas like 'sustainable', 'accessible' or 'resilient'. Instead, focus on concreté, observable actions by identified people or institutions. Vagueness in describing actors and actions is one of biggest causes of failure in social change efforts (this really can't be overemphasised, and you'll need to be active in enforcing it as the brainstorm proceeds).

g) Be biased towards permanent alterations to the social or physical environment. They're the ones that will result in sustained change.

h) Avoid discussing or judging other team members' contributions. Respect all ideas, however left-field. It's a brainstorm – just get those ideas down!

i) You have permission for wacky ideas. Successful change projects are never boring or predictable. It's the wacky ideas that get people talking and coming along. And remember that every great idea seemed wacky the first time it was proposed!

j) Be positive. Focus on ideas for success, not reasons for failure.

4. Weighting:

In silence, each person distributes 10 dots (as in the example below) between the items they think would have the biggest impact on the desired future (and are realistically achievable). *Weighting time = 5 minutes*

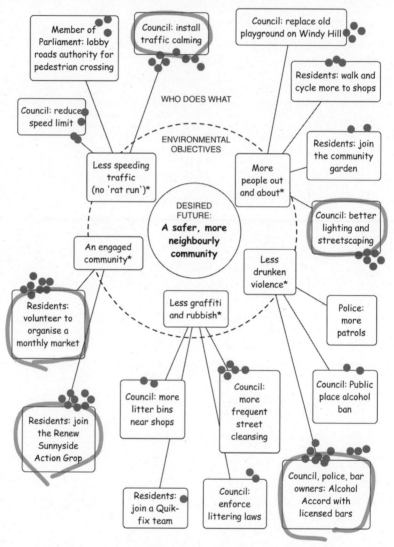

Usually brainstorms start with vague ideas like 'less traffic' or 'fewer drunks'. The trick is to keep going until you get to *concrete actions* by *real people or organisations*.

5. Add up the dots. The 3-6 actions with the most dots become your theory of change (they are the ones circled in the example).

6. Record the details on the table below.

7. Add indicators so your can track the progress of your project.

Note: To track long-term progress like an evaluation professional, you'd also decide on indicators for the environmental objectives (the ones with an asterisk in the diagram) – that will give you a 'trail of logic' and finer-grained measures of progress.

ACTION OBJECTIVES	INDICATOR(S)	DATA SOURCES	TARGET
Residents: join the Renew Sunnyside Action Group	Number of active members	Head count	30
	Number signed up	Member list	500
Residents: organise monthly market	Number of volunteers	Head count	20
	Number of markets held	Number held	12/year
Council: better lighting and streetscaping	Money voted	Council minutes	£100,000 by June 201X
Council: install traffic calming measures	Money voted	Council minutes	£150,000 by Nov 201X
Council, police, bar owners	Signatures on Alcohol Accord		All by June 201X

A table like this helps you monitor and evaluate progress in your efforts.

Now you have a theory of change. In this example, the theory would be:

> **IF** at least 500 residents join the Renew Sunnyside Action Group to lobby council and other agencies;
> **AND IF** at least 20 residents volunteer to organise monthly markets;

AND IF council installs traffic-calming measures PLUS new lighting and streetscaping;

AND IF all parties agree to an Alcohol Accord;

THEN there will be a safer, more neighbourly Sunnyside community.

AND THAT'S OUR THEORY OF CHANGE!

Some good things about this theory are: it's a *pattern* of changes rather than a single all-or-nothing activity; it's about changing the environment rather than changing people's minds; and it was created by a diverse, well-informed and inspired brains trust that probably includes many of the people and organisations who will need to act on it.

Ingredient 4

Design a sticky solution
How reinvention drives change

Noel Kesby is the CEO of the Southern Rivers Catchment Management Authority in New South Wales. His agency's task is to change the behaviours of tens of thousands of farmers over an area the size of Belgium. The official agency-speak for this mission is 'River and Wetland Protection and Restoration'. But if you ask Noel, he pitches it differently: "Our job is to give farmers the edge in their business."

Noel has spent his whole professional life working with landholders and he knows it's farmers who protect the environment, not government. And he knows the bottom line, which is that government programmes must deliver on what matters to farmers, in this case, water and productivity. In the Bega Valley in southern NSW his agency is delivering 'incentive products' to dairy farmers. Each incentive product combines a dollar grant with advice and technology for environmental practices like fencing streams, providing off-stream watering points for cows, planting tree belts, and so on. Each of these practices provides a mix of environmental *and business* benefits, which explains why around 90 per cent of Bega Valley farmers have signed up for them. As proof of their commitment, each farmer has more than matched the government funds with their own hard-earned cash.

Noel got the framing right.

Framing hit the headlines a few years ago when George Lakoff, a linguist at the University of California, Berkeley, wrote a book called *Don't Think of an Elephant: Know Your Values and Frame the Debate*. He wanted to educate Democrats about how Republicans had cleverly framed their language around people's hopes, fears and prejudices: 'War on Terror', 'tax relief', 'free market', 'pro-life', 'Patriot Act', 'Operation Enduring Freedom', and so on.

Framing, of course, is often a lie. Clever framing can work, at least temporarily, in politics, because voters are often too busy and distracted with their own lives to add things up. But in their private lives, farms and businesses people are much better at doing the sums.

Noel Kesby understood this. He went much further than just framing his messages in the language farmers liked to hear. His teams constructed products that genuinely solved farmers' problems. Because farmers got real-life benefits they valued, those new farming practices were more likely to stick.

Borrowing a term from Malcolm Gladwell's *The Tipping Point*, let's call this the *stickiness factor*.*

Stickiness is the make-or-break factor in a change project. Getting the stickiness right means genuinely being at the service of people, recognising their frustrations and intentionally constructing solutions that solve their problems. More than any other factor it determines whether people will be genuinely motivated to adopt a new behaviour or product and continue its use long into the future.

This chapter is about how to get the stickiness right.

Three über-wants

Stickiness is about constructing solutions to people's problems. The better the solution, the more likely it is to stick.

The 'solution' is the behaviour or product you want people to adopt; for example, 'install a thermostat', 'fence your creek', 'use a nicotine patch' or even just 'come to the meeting'.

Keep in mind that solutions are never as simple as they sound. The solution 'leave your car at home', for instance, is really a direction to use different modes of transport, so the design of those modes of transport is inevitably

---

* Gladwell used 'stickiness factor' to mean the content of a message that made it memorable. But, as we'll see, there is a lot more to stickiness than the wording of the message.

part of the solution, right down to their comfort and safety, fares, timetables and frequencies, ticketing systems, the location of bus stops, the quality of bus shelters, the amount of traffic congestion along bus routes, as well as intangibles like commonly held beliefs about the safety of the bus system. In this sense, behaviours and products are almost always complex packages with lots of variables that can be manipulated to increase their adoptability. Changing these variables is what it means to 'design' a solution.

Could there be any general rules for designing the kinds of solution that people will *want* to adopt?

I think so, but before I get to the rules, I want to squash one common assumption about what makes people *want* things. I'm willing to bet that, if you ask almost any group of people about their hot hopes, saving money, if it appears at all, will be low on their list of priorities.

It's true that cheapness sells groceries. All other things being equal, people will choose the cheaper of two different brands of cheese. But behaviour change is not a marginally different kind of cheese. It's a new and often quite scary departure for the self. For most people, saving money alone is a weak justification for the risk and effort involved in personal change. That doesn't mean that economic factors don't affect behaviour. The threat of losing money,[1] in particular, can certainly be a strong motivator. And price, as we noted in Ingredient 3, can be an obstacle for majorities. Nevertheless, when the financial motives of real groups of people have been compared with their non-financial motives, saving money and even being given money tend to pale in significance compared with other motivations.

It's been shown, for instance, that:

- Voting in Congressional elections is more influenced by party loyalty, perceived risks to the environment and health, and altruism ('doing the right thing'), than by economic self-interest.[2]
- Farmers' decisions to adopt conservation practices are more influenced by attachment to the land, wanting to make their farms appear well managed, and aesthetic appreciation than by financial incentives.[3]
- Patronage of public transport is influenced more by frequency and convenience than by the price of fares.[4]
- Recycling is influenced more by consumer knowledge and environmental commitment than by financial incentives.[5]

The common assumption that 'saving you money' is a strong motivator for new behaviours turns out to be an instance of Man is Bad Bias. As we noted earlier on in the book, that bias tends to blind us to the richness of motives that really drive human behaviour.

There are, however, three über-wants that practically everyone is motivated by: wants they can never get enough of; wants they will gladly shell out hard cash for; wants that, if your change effort delivers on even one of them, will give you people's allegiance and affection, plus a devastating advantage over your competition. The power of these wants is so fundamental that, should your project threaten even one of them, you could easily end up with a passionate resistance movement on your hands.

Those three über-wants are: control, time and self-esteem.

Control

I used to be a mediocre gardener. My gardens were patches of dry dirt with stunted vegetables poking up through a scatter of weeds. The chasm between the garden of my dreams and the garden of my reality had made me frustrated for years.

Then I discovered mulch. To be more accurate, I was asked to write a brochure advocating the 'Marvel of Mulch' to my fellow citizens. The discrepancy between my brochure and my garden finally overwhelmed me, and so I decided to get some mulch. I figured I could keep weeds down and have a neat, trendy-looking garden at the same time. So I ordered a load of mulched tree bits and spread it out. Nice. Neat. Fashionable. It was months before I discovered what the marvel of mulch really was. In the middle of a drought, when I hadn't watered the garden for weeks, the soil beneath my layer of mulch was moist, warm, black and full of worms and bugs. Mulch had given me more control over my garden than I had imagined possible. I can plant what I want, where I want, and get beautiful results with a high degree of certainty.

Mulch is supposed to be good for the environment but, frankly, that's just a collateral benefit. I keep using it because it gives me control over my garden.

I like to maximise my freedom of action and minimise uncertainty. I'm a bit of a control freak, but aren't we all?

The human need to maximise personal control and reduce uncertainty explains the competitive advantage enjoyed by most successful products. It explains why people prefer cars to trains, trains to buses, iPods to Walkmans, mobiles to land lines, drip irrigation to open trenches, owning to renting, detached houses to apartments, driving to walking, democracy to dictatorship.

People have a profound need to feel in control of their lives. It's well established that feeling in control of one's work has a strong effect on the well-being of workers.[6] Lack of control causes stress, burnout and physical illness.[7,8] For example, a well-known study by Michael Marmot and colleagues at University College London found that the incidence of heart disease in workers varied directly according their degree of control over their work. Compared with workers who have the highest degree of control, those with middle control had 20 per cent more heart disease, while those with the lowest control had 50 per cent more.[9]

The drive for control also explains why people like democracy. Nations that protect individual liberties and rights tend to score higher in well-being than those that don't.[10] Swiss economist Bruno Frey compared the happiness of citizens in Swiss cantons which had the *most* frequent citizen-initiated referenda, with the happiness of those in cantons which had the *least* frequent referenda. When all other factors were excluded, the difference in happiness roughly equalled doubling people's income.[11]

The drive for control also explains some regrettable aspects of Western civilisation: SUVs, air-conditioners, firearms, security systems, gated communities, domestic violence, anorexia, Human Resource Management, neo-conservatives.

Control is about how you get results. The more control you have, the more certain you are of getting the results you want with a minimum of disruption, delay, danger, doubt and uncertainty. Put simply, any behaviour, gadget, technique or process that increases people's *certainty* of getting their hopes fulfilled is very likely to spread, and any one that doesn't will almost certainly languish and die.

Time

Time is the ultimate, finite, non-stretchy, non-bendy limit on what we can do with our lives. The average person has 16.5 hours of consciousness to play with each day. Though we may try to borrow more from the Time Bank, by not sleeping, sooner or later we have to pay it back. Because time doesn't stretch, the only way to improve our lives is to adopt behaviours and products that require less of it. That means there's a huge premium on any idea or invention that shortens the time it takes to do something. Saving time is the breakthrough quality that guaranteed the success of some of the major inventions that define the twentieth century, from Rudolf Diesel's internal combustion engine (1897) and Johan Vaaler's paperclip (1899) to the ATM machine (1967).

Diffusion scholar Everett Rogers tells a nice story about the difference a time-saving innovation can make:

> 'Thump-thump-thump' is the usual sound heard in an African village as women pound grains and nuts with heavy wooden pestles. But recently this sound changed to 'chug-chug-chug' in one West African village, Sanankoroni, Mali. A woman brings a sack of peanuts into a small mud-brick shed that houses a diesel engine and a variety of contraptions that it powers. She pours her load into a funnel that leads to a grinder and blender, pays 25 cents, and ten minutes later, scoops thick peanut butter into a dozen jars. The woman says it would previously have taken her all day to pound and grind the sack of peanuts. Now she can sell the jars of butter in the village and then take a nap.
>
> The women of Sanankoroni, who own and operate the durable, uncomplaining machine, refer to it as 'The Daughter-in-law Who Doesn't Speak'. It was invented ten years ago by a UNDP development worker in Mali to ease the domestic labour of women.
>
> A forty-five kilogram sack of corn that required three days pounding is now ground in fifteen minutes. Girls who previously had to stay home to do domestic work can now go to school. Mothers now have free time to enrol in literacy classes or start a small business. The men of Sanankoroni approve of the women's progress. One said, "Our wives aren't so tired anymore. And their hands are smoother. We like that."[12]

Here's a kind of research result you hear a lot these days:

A recent survey conducted by Newspoll shows that overall 48 per cent of mothers with young children claim they have two hours or less a week for themselves, including 20 per cent who say they have no time at all.[13]

I read somewhere that consumers in developed countries are supposed to have less time for leisure, family, friends and community than at any time since the Middle Ages. (And what do we spend that leisure time doing? Watching TV and shopping: two activities guaranteed to increase our dissatisfaction. Great system eh?)

Today, just about everyone is stressed about time. Merciless corporate competition and technological change mean that most of us are now doing jobs that were once done by several people. And, to emphasise the sheer heartless cruelty of it all, there are now so many more thrilling and must-do things to squeeze into our miserable shrunken stubs of leisure time.

Frozen food, microwave ovens, automatic dishwashers, online banking, cheap flights are successful because they replace tedious drudgery with free time. (And, once there's enough bandwidth, online conferencing will be huge for the same reason.)

Unfortunately, most environmental, social and health changes seem to require *more* of people's time. Cycling to work, mulching the garden, volunteering, turning off unused lights, insulating a home, voting and driving under the speed limit all take more time. This limits their stickiness. But there's a solution: although these activities may look like they have fixed speed limits, what really slows them down is often not the activity itself, but the *hassle rate*. Hassles are the annoying disruptions and obstacles that get in the way of actually doing something. Like the number of times your car gets stopped in traffic. Solution: a car-pool express lane!

By making your innovation less fussy you'll increase the likelihood people will do it. People hate being forced to think or plan, so the less of that the better. Simplifying instructions and paperwork are ways to minimise the hassle rate. So is reducing the number of choices people have to make.

Amazon's innovation of one-click buying and Apple's annihilation of the instruction manual are classic examples of hassle elimination:

Cliff Kuang, editor of *Co.Design*, wrote:

All throughout the 1970s to the 1990s, if you ever opened up a new gadget, the first thing you were ever faced with was figuring how the damn thing worked. To solve that, you'd have to wade through piles of instruction manuals written in an engineer's alien English. But a funny thing happened with the iMac: Every year after, Apple's instruction manuals grew thinner and thinner, until finally, today, the instruction manuals have become a scant couple of pages that basically say, 'Welcome'. The assumption is that you'll be able to tear open the box and immediately start playing with your new toy. Just watch a three-year-old playing with an iPad. You're seeing a toddler intuit the workings of one of the most advanced pieces of engineering on the planet. At almost no time in history has that ever been possible. It certainly wasn't when the first home computers were introduced, or the first TV remotes, or the first radios.[14]

Even if we can't *give* people time, we need to take away as little of it as possible. The less time we take, the more people are likely to adopt the solution.

A nice example is the evolution of Weight Watchers.

The Weight Watchers method originally involved counting calories, a laborious, time-consuming task. In 1997, to make it quicker and easier, Weight Watchers introduced a 'Points Value' system so, for example, an apple is one point and a cup of rice is four points. People are given a goal, say 25 points per day. If they stay under it, they are told they will lose weight. The system is flexible because people can add extra points for special treats or outings and average them out.

However, it still takes time and discipline to count points and stick with plans. So, in 2004 Weight Watchers launched an even simpler system: a 'no-count' diet called the Core Plan. On the Core Plan, people don't count points but simply eat a variety of wholesome foods. It was designed for those who don't have time to plan meals or who are too busy to think about points.

Time and control together explain why most people drive cars everywhere, despite the appalling costs and stresses. In a survey of Dutch drivers, for instance, 'rapidity' and 'independence' were rated as their top motivations for choosing cars over public transport. Significantly, that study was in Gouda, a city with excellent and pervasive public transport. Even there, cars had the edge over public transport in the terms that counted.

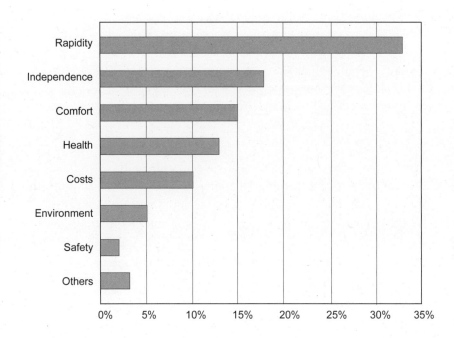

Why people drive. Speed and control trump comfort and health. Source: Tertoolen, G. et al. (1998).[15]

The lesson for public transport authorities is: if you want more people to catch trains, then comfort, health, safety and environment are nice optional extras, but getting people to where they want to go *quickly* is what counts.

Self-esteem

One of my students told me how pleased she was to have recently purchased a house with a chicken shed and a family of chickens. I asked her about the satisfactions of owning chickens. With commendable personal insight and candour, she replied, "They make me interesting".

Is it possible that happiness is social? When happiness researchers Ed Deiner and Martin Seligman examined the characteristics of the happiest individuals, they found without exception that they were highly social, had stronger romantic relationships, were more extroverted, more agreeable and less neurotic, than less happy individuals.[16]

People need relationships. They seem to be essential for self-esteem[17] and are associated with healthy hearts and immune systems.[18] "Although lay people probably understand that close friends and family are correlated with happiness, they may not realise that they are *necessary* for happiness, as well as for health and optimal cognitive functioning," wrote Ed Deiner and another happiness researcher, Shigehiro Oishi.[19]

On the other hand, broken relationships provide some of the greatest anguish in life. This explains why divorce and unemployment have disastrous emotional effects. Studies tracking people's journey in and out of employment show that the emotional impact of financial loss pales in significance compared with the loss to self-esteem and dignity from ceasing to be needed.[20]

Self-esteem, of course, depends to a very large degree on what others think about us. It's no wonder, then, that we are always on the lookout for excuses to engage with others and present our best selves. Products and experiences are essential props in this process. As a result, they have social value quite apart from their practical utility. They help us interact with people, express our dynamic specialness, brag about our successes, and demonstrate our social status.

How we consume the social value of objects and experiences is by buzzing about them with important people in our lives, as my student did with her self-esteem-building chickens. Half the fun of shopping, for instance, is telling our friends about the fantastic bargains we discovered or the delicious luxuries we afforded. A study of 364 Finnish shoppers at a large department store compared three shopping motives: pleasure, utility and social value. The researchers found that utility and social value were about equal influences on the decision to purchase (both slightly ahead of pleasure), except on Saturday, when social value exceeded both utility and pleasure together.[21]

Social value is important, even in seemingly mundane household tasks. A fascinating study of 60 households in Santa Cruz County, California, sought to explain why homeowners spent thousands of dollars on solar water heaters, woodburning stoves, insulation and greenhouses, but ignored caulking and weather-stripping – simple actions that were just as effective at warming homes and lowering heating costs. Even when caulking was offered for free, people were reluctant to take it up.

The reason, the researchers found, was that caulking and weather-stripping were seen as dirty jobs, lacking in glamour, compared with the highly visible and heroic business of house renovation. Americans, they observed, were proud of improvements that added value to their homes. Caulking, by comparison, suggested a leaky or old house. It was something people couldn't talk about it without feeling slightly ashamed. It had no social value. " . . . other energy retrofits are visible to neighbours, serving social ends," they wrote, "the gurgle of water in hot water pipes is seen as rewarding and is pointed out to guests, as is the heat from a woodstove, even when hands are burned and the room smells of smoke. Weatherisation [by comparison] offers little feedback and few opportunities for bragging."[22]

Intriguingly, it appears experiences tend to have greater social value than objects. In a national survey, a cross-section of 1,279 Americans were asked to compare the happiness they obtained from experiences and from products: 57 per cent rated experiences as more happiness-making than products. Just 34 per cent said material objects made them happier.[23] Even accounting for income levels, "not a single segment reported being happier with their material buys." The researchers speculated that the difference may be partly due to the higher social value of experiences: a game is easier to share than a chandelier, and because experiences typically have a beginning, middle and end, they make better stories. The same researchers later observed university students having conversations about their experiences or objects they'd purchased. They found that the students who talked about experiences liked each other more than those who talked about material objects.[24]

Volunteering, sport, political activism and gardening are examples of experiences whose social value generally exceeds their utility value. The same, of course, goes for smoking[25], drinking, drugs, speeding, littering, unsafe sex, tanning and every other kind of risk-taking behaviour.[26]

Objects and experiences also confer social status. In prehistoric times a good hunter might have worn a tiger tooth around his neck as a sign of courage and strength. Now Lexus and ski holidays in Switzerland signify economic prowess. These things are desired because they demonstrate social prestige.[27] No one spends £16.95 on a salmon and pesto focaccia with drizzled balsamic vinaigrette simply because they're hungry.

Remember the deluded self? The self that must, in order to optimistically face each tedious new day of anxieties, trials and humiliations, not to mention the existential terror of death and annihilation, maintain a vainglorious image of its own splendid character and illustrious destiny. Self-deception is so much easier to maintain when others agree with us. That's why it can be desperately important to have the jeans, car, phone, recreational drugs, and solar water heaters that we think others admire and want for themselves.

Most human beings believe that every observable object or behaviour in their lives will be assessed by their peers as a sign of their position in a social pecking order. Those same objects and behaviours therefore have the capacity to threaten or enhance social status and the self-esteem that's attached to it. If Californians believe that owning a Ford Super Duty F450 pickup makes them a better person than owning a Fiat Bambino (and if Europeans believe exactly the opposite) then that's the landscape change makers have to work with. If people believe that a Toyota Prius confers social status, then that subjective belief is just as important as its objective fuel efficiency. In fact, if we want people to reduce their carbon emissions, it may be more important.

If you accept this, you'll agree that the social value of a solution matters a lot. In short, if people think a new behaviour makes them seem cool, it will take off; if they think it makes them uncool, it will crash and burn.

Fortunately, since social value is simply a belief, it's quite malleable. There are lots of ways to raise the perceived social value of an otherwise uncool innovation. Here are three proven techniques that marketers use every day.

Rarity: Objects and experiences that are hard to get or 'hot off the press' have extra status. Owning a rare one suggests that you too are rare and exceptional. Like the must-have Wattson electricity meter, that gives you a real-time display of household energy use. It's sleek, iPod-esque, hip and gorgeous, but what's also great about it is that your friends don't have one.

The impression of rarity is extremely easy to manufacture, for example:

- "Only 12 volunteer positions available."
- "Applications close 17 April."
- "First 20 applicants only."
- "Limited to one per customer."

Expense is a good proxy for rarity, but not the only one; for example, those fabulous charity shop bargains confer just as much self-esteem as more expensive buys.

Association: Think like Nike. If high-status people want it, own it or endorse it, some of their status will rub off. This is the method of choice to promote products that are virtually indistinguishable from their competitors, such as cars, sneakers, beer and politicians.

Story: Some things come with inherently interesting backstories that add to their buzz value. As we noted in an earlier chapter, the stories with surprise+emotion tend to create their own buzz and spread contagiously. Just enter 'Free Hugs' or 'Numa Numa' into YouTube and see what I mean.*

The danger of heroic solutions

Control, time and self-esteem seem like the sure-fire universal qualities of successful solutions. But don't be too sure.

Remember Heroic Agent Bias? It's the belief that we know best. Everett Rogers, one of the founders of diffusion research, called it 'pro-innovation bias'. He issued a stern warning against righteous change makers imposing their half-baked ideas on the world.

Pro-innovation bias, he said, is the assumption that an innovation is good, that it should be spread, that it has no disadvantages, that it should not be reinvented or rejected. Rogers called this a "troublesome and potentially dangerous" intellectual failure that causes change makers to ignore evidence of rejection and overlook possibilities for reinvention.[28]

The fact is, many solutions don't deserve to succeed.

Some are naïve.

The direction to simply 'Quit Smoking' is an example of a naïve solution. It fails to acknowledge the benefits smoking provides, like stress relief, social connection and weight control. And it ignores the challenges and discomforts involved in beating an addiction. It also assumes people live in a bubble, whereas in reality smoking and quitting are socially driven behav-

---

* For a delightful and insightful talk on the intangible value of products, see the TED talk by ad man Rory Sutherland:

http://www.ted.com/talks/lang/eng/rory_sutherland_life_lessons_from_an_ad_man.html

iours. That's why many anti-smoking campaigns now only ask people to consult the pharmacist, call a Quit Line, or use nicotine-replacement patches, instead of simply quitting.

And some innovations are counter-productive. Everett Rogers offered this *mea culpa*:

> In my 1954 Ph.D. dissertation research, I gathered data from 148 farmers in an Iowa farm community about their adoption of such agricultural innovations as 2,4-D weed spray, antibiotic swine feeding supplements, and chemical fertilisers. These chemical innovations were recommended to farmers by agricultural scientists at Iowa State University and the Iowa Agricultural Extension Service. I accepted the recommendations of these agricultural experts as valid. So did most of the Iowa farmers I interviewed. One farmer, however, rejected all of these agricultural chemicals, because, he claimed, they killed the earthworms and songbirds in the fields. At the time, I personally regarded his attitude as irrational. He was classified as a laggard on my innovativeness scale.

By the 1970s, however, the US Environment Protection Agency had banned 2,4-D and antibiotic swine supplements because biomagnification in the food chain made them a threat to human health.

"Today, looking back five decades," wrote Rogers, "the organic farmer I interviewed has had the last laugh over agricultural experts. My 1954 research classified him as a laggard. By present-day standards he was a superinnovator of the then-radical idea of organic farming."[29]

Just because we think a solution is right, just and better, doesn't mean it is. We all have a tendency towards Heroic Agent Bias. There is really only one way to control it. That is to directly involve users in the development and testing of solutions.

How to be sure the solution fits

Once you think you've got a solution to someone's problems, it's time to do some field testing. Testing the workability of your ideas is the basic insurance policy against Heroic Agent Bias.

One way is to watch people trying out your solution.

Surprisingly, some of the most wholehearted advocates of rigorous product testing have been tax authorities. The Australian Tax Office (ATO), for example, constructed a state-of-the-art simulation centre in Brisbane to design new tax forms. It recreated a real office environment with people in one room trying to fill in the forms, while in another room tax staff attempted to decipher and process them. One-way mirrors and cameras allowed designers to observe the bewilderment, dithering and panic that resulted. The ATO claims to have used 30 user clinics, eight creative retreats and 54 observation sessions to create just one suite of tax forms. "Nothing goes out without assurance that users were involved in creation," said one tax officer.

You may not need to go to such lengths to observe users trying your solution. Just watching them at work on the farm, factory floor, pub or health centre might be enough. Or you could talk to users directly. That's what focus groups are for. Talking over your idea with potential users can avoid fundamental design flaws and also give you great ideas for improvement.

Another way is to try it yourself. A road-safety educator told me how she found out what was stopping truck drivers from taking rest breaks. Her method was: she climbed into the passenger seat of a big rig and accompanied a trucker for a thousand or so kilometres across south-east Australia. She discovered that whether truckers took rest breaks had a lot to do with the quality of the rest stops provided by the state road authority. Many of the official rest stops were on sloping ground, or in the baking sun, or lacked water. Suddenly, the issue of rest breaks stopped looking like a behavioural problem and more like an infrastructure problem.

Watching users, talking to users, or doing it yourself are essential insurance policies against the effects of Heroic Agent Bias.

Another reason (as if there needs to be one) why audience research is vital is that there can be huge diversity inside neighbourhoods, socio-economic groups, professions, age groups, cultures and sexes. As an example, studies of Canadian households showed that people from different incomes tend to have different energy-saving preferences. Those on high incomes tended to pay more for energy to maintain their existing high-consumption lifestyles, those on middle incomes tended to choose more efficient products (like home retrofits or more efficient cars), while those on low incomes tended to wear jumpers, enduring hardship as a result.[30]

I've steered away from the effects of individual, sexual and cultural differences in this book because I'm trying to keep a lid on its complexity, but it goes without saying that any change effort must account for these kinds of variable, and user involvement in designing and testing is the best way to do it.

A peek at Diffusion of Innovations

Remember Ryan and Gross, the Iowa University researchers who practically invented Diffusion of Innovations theory back in 1943 when they studied the spread of hybrid corn seed across the American Midwest? It's almost impossible to have a discussion about the spread of new ideas without the concepts that first emerged in their work and were refined by later scholars. So let's briefly look at those ideas. Skip this section if you're already acquainted with diffusion theory.

Diffusion researchers believe that, no matter what the idea, product or behaviour, a population can be broken into five different segments based on their propensity to adopt that particular innovation:

- innovators
- early adopters
- early majorities
- late majorities
- laggards.

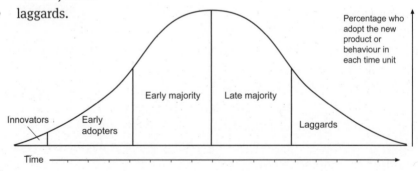

The bell curve. In diffusion theory, products spread not because people change but because the products themselves evolve to better fit the needs of increasingly demanding and risk-sensitive groups. Source: Rogers (2003) p.281.

Each group has its own personality, at least as far as its attitude to a particular innovation goes.

The adoption process begins with a tiny number of visionary, imaginative *innovators*. Tech evangelist Guy Kawasaki calls them 'thunderlizards' (I'm not really sure what he means but it captures their out-there-ness). They are few in number: 1 per cent or less in a given population. They often lavish immense time, energy and creativity on their inventions. And they love talking about them. Right now, they're the ones building stills to convert cooking oil into biodiesel, and making websites to tell the world about it. They have enormous energy and focus, although their one-eyed fixation on the new behaviour or gadget can make them seem dangerously idealistic to the pragmatic majority.

Their evangelical advocacy sets tongues wagging. People watch to see whether they prosper or fail. Meanwhile, the innovators are proving whether the idea works or not.

Once the benefits start to become apparent, *early adopters* leap in. They are typically around 16 to 20 per cent in a given population. They love getting an advantage over their peers and they have time and money to spend. They're often fashion-conscious and love to be seen as leaders: social prestige is one of their biggest drivers. Their natural desire to be trendsetters causes the innovation to take off. What's more, they become the new test bed, reinventing the solution to suit more mainstream needs. They tend to be more economically successful and hence socially respected and well connected. And they like to talk about their successes. So the buzz intensifies. What early adopters say about a solution determines its success. The more they crow and preen, the more likely the new behaviour or product will be seen positively by the majority of a population.

Fortunately for us, early adopters are an easy audience. They don't need much persuading. They are on the lookout for anything that could give them a social or economic edge. When you call a public meeting to discuss energy-saving devices or new farming methods, they're the ones who turn up. They're the first people in your street to install a water tank, mulch their garden, buy laptops for their kids, install solar panels, or buy the next pretentious gizmo.

Some authorities talk about a 'chasm' between visionary early adopters and pragmatic majorities.[31] They think the chasm explains why many products are initially popular with early adopters but fail to reach mass markets. Everett Rogers disagreed with the idea of a chasm.[32] He thought early adopters and majorities form a continuum, although *most* early adopters still have radically different interests and needs from *most* majorities. So even if there's no real chasm, it's a useful mental construct that warns us against the easy assumption that one size fits all.

A lot of new gadgets and lifestyle practices that become popular with early adopters stop at the edge of the chasm and fail to spread further. What makes products or practices bridge the chasm is not persuasion. It's reinvention (which I'm about to describe).

Assuming the solution leaps the chasm, it may spread to the *early majority*: typically around 30 per cent of a population. Early majorities are sympathetic to your idea but, really, they're just too busy getting the kids to football and running their businesses to go out of their way to adopt it. If they do have any spare time, they're not going to spend it fussing around with complicated, expensive, inconvenient products or behaviours: they want to hear (or read) reassuring phrases like 'plug-and-play', 'no sweat' or 'user-friendly'. They're also cost-sensitive, so they want 'value for money'. And they are followers, they want 'industry standard' and 'endorsed by respected people' on the label.

Assuming you meet the early majority's demanding needs for proven performance, low fuss and low cost, you get to the *late majority*. The late majority, again typically around 30 per cent of a given population, are a tough group because they're more than uninterested, they actively dislike your solution. Their stance is one of resistance. To them, the new gizmo or practice is irrelevant and irksome. Yet they have one weakness – they want to fit in. So, when it comes time to market your solution to the late majority, you should emphasise the indispensable normalcy of the solution, for example: "Join the 70% of people who've discovered they can't live without [solution X]." We'll talk more about this method, called 'social proof' in the next chapter.

Meanwhile, *laggards* hold out to the bitter end. They are often around 20 per cent of a population. They are people who see a high risk in adopting a particular practice. Some of them are so worried they stay awake all night, tossing and turning, thinking of arguments against it. And don't forget, there's always the possibility they're right! They may be laggards for very good reasons.

Each of these adopter personalities is very different. So it's vital to know which one you're addressing (and no, you probably can't address them all at once. Why? Because your solution isn't ready for everyone. I'll explain why in a moment). You only need one simple fact – the percentage take-up in that group or population – to tell you which adopter personality you're talking to next. That one fact alone tells you a great deal about how to design your product and how to pitch your invitation. So, for instance, if 20 per cent of a population have already taken up an innovation, it means your early adopters are fully engaged, so your *next* target will be the early majority; and you can guess some useful things about them: they're probably open to your idea in principle, but risk-averse and cost-sensitive, as well as distracted and time-poor. That gives you a lot of clues about how to design and pitch your solution.

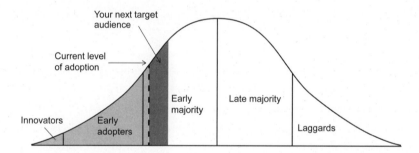

You can't target everyone at the same time. Inevitably, your next target audience is the next slice of your bell curve.

Of course, no one is an innovator or a laggard all the time. It would be too exhausting. In reality, most people are majorities about most things, and only innovators or laggards about certain specific things. We wouldn't say "John is a laggard", we'd say "John is an *iPod* laggard" or "George Bush snr is a *broccoli* laggard".

Why reinvention is more important than persuasion

Even when users participate in design, don't expect your solution to be perfect. Most great ideas start out clunky and only gradually evolve to fit the needs of more and more people. The way solutions evolve or reinvent themselves reveals an important and counter-intuitive fact about social change, which is that the spread of solutions is primarily due to changes in the solutions themselves, not to changes in people's fundamental hopes and desires.

Consider the mobile phone.

In 1983 Motorola introduced the world's first consumer mobile phone, the DynaTac 8000X. It weighed two pounds and cost $US3,995. It had no display, had 35 minutes of talk time and took ten hours to recharge. And there was practically no one to talk to.

In 1995 I bought my first mobile, a Motorola, for $A499 (£240). It was an analog phone with lots of irritating drop-outs, but I could get coverage in any city. The nickel cadmium battery had one-hour talk time and took seven hours to recharge. It was too big to fit comfortably in my pocket so I clipped it to my trouser belt, which was quite a cool thing to do at the time.

When it died, I bought a Nokia: a shimmering blue egg-like object. It fitted into my pocket, which was just as well as it had now become pretentious to hang a phone on your belt. The price was right: it was free, with a two-year contract (which cost about $A200 (£130) a month). It was digital so the reception was better and, best of all, the lithium ion battery took just one hour to charge for 7 hours talk time.

My next phone was a Samsung 330. I bought it in 2006 for $A99 (£42). My call charges were capped at $A49 per month, but if that was too much I could pay-as-I-go. It had a 'fun box', an organiser, a camera, and room for 1,000 phone numbers.

From luggable 'brick' to pocket-sized mini-computer in 13 years. In the same period, the number of users exploded from 30 New York businessmen to over 2 billion souls worldwide.

Then, in January 2007, Steve Jobs, the CEO of Apple Inc., stood up at the Macworld Expo in his blue jeans and tasteless white sneakers and transformed every one of those 2 billion mobile phones into dated technology with his announcement of the iPhone, a hand-held desktop computer the size of an iPod, that also (how handy is this?) makes phone calls.

Now here's a big question. What changed? Did people change or did the mobile phone change? Of course, the answer is that the mobile phone did the lion's share of the changing. It started off as a ponderous block. Then it started evolving. We humans, on the other hand, stayed pretty much the same – busy people, separated from our loved ones, business partners and customers, who just want to talk.

The counter-intuitive point is that most social changes don't involve people changing. Sounds odd, I know, so let me repeat it. *Most social changes don't involve people changing.* People's hopes, wants and motivations stay pretty much the same. Instead, what drives change is the way technologies, systems and practices gradually evolve to become easier, quicker, smaller, hipper, more powerful and more useful.

The evolution of the recycling bin followed a similar arc, from crumply bag, to messy hand-held bin, to big, tidy wheelie bin, and at each stage the participation rate leapt.

And just to rub the point in, here's an interesting fact about the rise of the digital camera. Digital cameras first appeared on the market in 1996 yet sales increased very slowly with no discernible effect on sales of conventional cameras. However, two processes were under way that would eventually destroy the conventional camera market. Firstly, pixel resolution was steadily increasing, and secondly, the price was falling. Finally, in 2002, a two-megapixel camera hit the market for less than US$400 (£255). From that moment on, sales of conventional cameras didn't just decline, they collapsed.[33]

The mobile phone, the recycling bin and the digital camera demonstrate that persuasion is probably the least important driver of change. What really drives change is *reinvention.*

It's therefore a mistake to assume that, just because you have a few per cent of early adopters taking up your solution, you can just keeping rolling it out as if it's perfect for everyone else. It's not.

The solution that appeals to an early adopter almost certainly won't work with an early majority, and the solution that works with an early majority usually won't work for a late majority. That's because early adopters care about your issue and late majorities don't and you can't make them. Instead, your solution has to continually reinvent itself, getting more useful, easier, simpler, quicker and cheaper, to fit more and more demanding, time-poor and reluctant users.

The next time you hear a colleague moaning that people aren't buying into their supposedly desirable product or behaviour, you might ask them: "How could you reinvent that solution to make it a better fit for those people's lives?"

Learning from innovators

An excellent way to evolve a product or behaviour is to watch what innovators are up to, then cherry-pick their ideas.

In the Arabic smoking case study we discussed earlier, notice how the focus groups allowed the project team to hear stories of Arabic women who had already innovated their own solutions to the problem of tobacco use at home. Those stories became the basis of a successful campaign.

A classic story of user reinvention is Skin-So-Soft body lotion. Avon produced Skin-So-Soft to soften skin. But Royal Marine commandos guarding a submarine base in Scotland found it repelled midges. The story spread, but instead of being affronted, Avon rose to the occasion. They mixed in a real insect repellent, citronella, and later added a block-out as well. So you can now buy Skin-So-Soft Bug Guard Plus Insect Repellent Moisturizing Lotion SPF 30.

Some computer games are now built with the intention that they'll be modified by enthusiastic users. Says consumer behaviour expert, Francine Gardin, "They're actually participating in the design of the game. These consumers are really passionate about the game – it's almost like a cult. They have an incredible sense of loyalty and ownership of that brand. Instead of complaining, they fix the product."[34]

Technology evangelist Guy Kawasaki wrote:

> Communities can't just sit around composing love letters to your CEO about how great she is. This means your product has to be 'customisable,' 'extensible,' and 'malleable'. Think about Adobe Photoshop: if it weren't for the company's plug-in architecture, do you think its community would have developed so quickly? However, giving people something to chew on requires killing corporate hubris and admitting that your engineers did not create the perfect product. Nevertheless, the payoff is huge because once you get people chewing on a product, it's hard to wrest it away from them.[35]

It's possible to go one step further and invite the users to help you design the product from the ground up. This approach is popular in overseas aid projects, rural extension work and health policy development where it's variously called 'participative action research', 'participative learning', 'rapid rural appraisal' or similar permutations.[36]

The essence of participative design is simple: make the users partners in devising the solution.

Here's how Professor Steve Sussman at the University of Southern California invited high-school students to help him design what might be the world's most effective teen smoking cessation programme. He first ran a series of focus groups with troubled students in California's Continuation High Schools, asking them what activities they thought would engage other teenagers like themselves. They suggested activities that focused on quitting while young, alternatives to smoking, yoga and seeing ex-smokers as strong people. Steve's team then took these ideas and built them into 26 classroom activities that included games, puzzles, Oprah-like talk shows, and non-intellectual activities like yoga, healthy breathing and anger management. He then invited students in four schools to test the activities and rate the ones they liked most (the top-rating activity was a talk show that emphasised quitting while young). The top 14 activities were then re-tested on yet another group of students to determine their immediate impact. The top eight activities that survived this brutal elimination process were kept in the programme. The eventual programme, called Project EX, was rolled out with 355 smokers in 12 Continuation High Schools. Three months after the programme finished, 17 per cent had quit, compared with only 8 per cent in a control group.[37]

Incidentally, a secret to improving solutions is to be on the lookout for *unexpected* results. They always have useful messages for us.

Let's imagine you're an environmental educator and you decide to hold a 'clean water fair' and invite the local community along. When you do this, you notice that almost no one pays attention to the 3-dimensional pollution diorama and the weed display but that families flock in droves to the hands-on water bug demo and the canoe tour. You didn't expect this and so it's got a message for you. It's telling you to dump the pollution diorama and the weed display, and ramp up the hands-on living exhibits and river adventures. It's also telling you to reframe your fair as a 'river adventure and bug festival'. If you do that, a lot more people will come next year, your fair will prosper, and its educational impact will increase. However, if you ignore the unexpected message, your fair is likely to shrivel and perish.

Critical mass and tipping point

And while I'm at it, this is a good place to mention a popular but useless idea.

A 'critical mass' or 'tipping point' is the beguiling idea that when a certain number of people adopt an innovation, further adoption is self-sustaining and somehow inevitable.

Critical mass is an idea from physics. When critical mass is reached in a sufficiently dense chunk of radioactive uranium, a runaway nuclear reaction happens, and you get a big bang. The shape of the take-off curve for internet use and consumer products certainly resembles the exponential take-off of a nuclear reaction.

One justification for the idea of critical mass is that adoption itself can increase the value of an innovation. Take email: as each new person adopted email, its usefulness increased for those who had not yet adopted it, making it more likely they would.[38] Another argument involves peer pressure, as people begin to fear being left out.

'Critical mass' and 'tipping point' are seductive ideas because they suggest that if we could only reach a certain magic number, we could sit back and watch our solution take off without having to put in much more effort.

Critical mass and tipping point are unhelpful ideas for exactly that reason: they encourage complacency. They miss the most important cause of take-off: reinvention. Take email again. Did you ever try to configure an old-fashioned dial-up modem? If you did, you probably recall hours of crazy-making torment.

Email's seemingly inevitable rise-and-rise was only partly due to a critical mass of users. Its main cause was remorseless and imaginative software innovation and massive infrastructure investment that made it increasingly inexpensive and easy.

What will spread your behaviour or product, therefore, is not a magical number of adopters of Version 1.0, but whether you are observant, imaginative and courageous enough to abandon your apparently successful Version 1.0 and invest in an improved, and apparently risky, Version 2.0. And then an even better Version 3.0, and so on.

The hard news for change makers is that social change doesn't get easier once you pass a tipping point. As our innovations move along the bell curve, we are faced with progressively less interested more distracted people who care less about our cleverness and more about just getting on with their lives. The amount of time, energy, enthusiasm, cash and skills they have to invest gets smaller and smaller as we go. Hence the obligation never leaves us, as change makers, to continually reinvent our solutions to better fit their lives.

Conclusion

There is no universal formula for designing a sticky behaviour or product.

Everybody is different, and we can't possibly know what hot hopes a particular group has until we ask them. That's what focus groups are for. But if, for some reason, you don't want to organise focus groups, then just try chatting to people. When you do, find a way to ask: "What's not working for you?" "What would you like to improve?", "What's your biggest frustration?" These questions can take you to the heart of their hot hopes. Then, and only then, you can start thinking about constructing a solution.

Chances are, your solution will need to pass these tests:

- Will it give people more control over their lives?
- Will it save them time, or at least not take more time?
- Will it give them something to talk about with their peers or raise their social status?
- And for majorities: is it as cheap, easy and simple as it could possibly be?

It turns out that changing the world isn't really about persuasion. Persuasion might get people to try a new idea once, but sustained use depends on our willingness to design and deliver solutions that stick because they make a real difference to people's lives.

Like Noel Kesby, you have to make your goal the equivalent of "giving farmers the edge" and then deliver on it.

Method

Testing for stickiness

Stickiness means that the behaviour (or product) is a good fit for people's wants. In other words, in addition to solving large-scale social or environmental problems, it also answers real frustrations and dissatisfactions of the people we hope will adopt it.

To create sticky behaviours:

- Start by getting to know the frustrations of your intended actors. Talk to them. Find out what's not working in their lives. What frustrations or dissatisfactions could you offer a solution to? A good question to ask is: "Thinking about how you live your life (or run your business, or care for your family, or whatever), what are the things you're unhappy about and would like to change?"
- Observe people trialling the desired behaviour in the field, home and workplace. Spend time trialling it yourself. Are there ways you could make it easier and quicker?
- Look for spontaneous innovators. Someone out there has probably already created a better solution you could build upon.
- Keep in mind the three über-wants: control, time and self-esteem. Find a way to increase people's supply of these and your project will almost certainly prosper.
- Beware Heroic Agent Bias. Test your solution before you launch it. Is it an easy fit for people's lives, or is re-engineering required? Don't be afraid to go back to the drawing-board.
- Expect your innovation to evolve. Watch how people use it. Keep your eyes open for unexpected modifications by users. Look for ways to

make it more useful, easier, quicker, cheaper and more pleasurable. If the behaviour doesn't take, don't blame the users. Instead, invite them to become partners in reinventing a solution that's a better fit for their lives.

The stickiness test

Here is a simple way to check the stickiness of a behaviour. Do it with a focus group and/or your brains trust.

How to use it

Ask a sample of the potential adopters to compare the relative advantages of the new behaviour compared with their current behaviour and to give it a score from +5 to -5. A plus score means the new behaviour is better than the existing behaviour, a minus score means it's worse.

Example:
Parents walk their primary-age children to school.

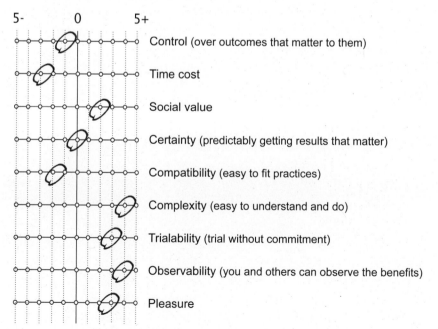

5-	0	5+	
			Control (over outcomes that matter to them)
			Time cost
			Social value
			Certainty (predictably getting results that matter)
			Compatibility (easy to fit practices)
			Complexity (easy to understand and do)
			Trialability (trial without commitment)
			Observability (you and others can observe the benefits)
			Pleasure

What to do with the results

Negative scores point to weaknesses in the design of the solution. They point to where you need to invest effort in improvement. Can you design out the weaknesses or find ways to compensate for them? For example, can you provide incentives, advisory services, free installation, simplified ordering and delivery, discounts, or reduce the number of steps required?

Time will often be a challenge. It reminds us of the eternal importance of simplifying products and processes.

In the example above, the practice of walking kids to school provides some advantages to parents, but also distinct disadvantages, specifically there's a perceived loss of control compared with driving, a significant time cost, and, for that reason, poor compatibility with their daily schedule.

Here's how you could reinvent the desired behaviour to make it a better fit.

Modified behaviour:
Instead of walking their kids to school, parents sign up for a 'walking bus' supervised by a trained volunteer that includes a text message confirming their child's arrival at the school gate.

Of course, that solution might not be perfect either, but now you at least have an idea that's worth field-testing.

Ingredient 5

Expanding the comfort zone
How to help people reduce their fears

Can't do

The South Coast train was packed with exhausted commuters heading home after a long hot day in the big city. I managed to grab one of the seats that slot into the space next to the stairs leading to the upper floor. I was reading, doing my best, like everyone else, to ignore the unpleasant, claustrophobic atmosphere.

But denial wasn't working because sitting on the stairs next to me was a pimply boy, aged around 16, dressed in baggy white polyester 'homey' tracksuit bottoms and a Nike baseball cap. He was moodily flipping back and forth a heavy set of keys, just a few inches from my ear. Krunk-krunk, krunk-krunk. After a while, when it became clear he wasn't going to stop of his own accord, I turned and abruptly asked "Could you stop doing that?" At first he just stared ahead and continued krunk-krunking, as if he hadn't heard me. After a while, he figured out he had to do something, so he turned and glared at me with the kind of vacant-eyed hostility that teenagers do so well. I could tell he wanted to say something but no words came out. Instead, we just stared at each other. After a few seconds he broke eye contact and glared at the back wall of the carriage. All through this stand-off, the krunk-krunking never ceased. I had to endure it for another 20 minutes until he got off the train.

If we had been alone in the carriage I'm sure he would have found an

answer. And if I'd been another hot-headed 17-year-old, it might even have escalated into violence.

The crowded carriage, however, stumped him. He had no idea how to deal with the situation. As he glanced away, I recognised the emotion in his eyes. He had been unexpectedly nudged into his scary zone. He was literally rigid with fear because he had no way to deal with a simple request from a stranger on a crowded train.

A competent adult would have handled this situation differently. They would have backed off, apologised and stopped flipping their damned keys back and forth. A mature adult would have felt the same surge of resistance the teenager felt. No one likes to be told what to do, especially by a stranger. They would have felt the same fight-or-flight emotional arousal, but then their prefrontal cortex would have taken over. It would have judged the situation and responded with a small, painless social concession. It would have done this for two reasons. First, because it was the lesser of two evils – the other being a potentially violent escalation with a complete stranger. And second, because it knew it had the skills to offer that concession easily, without the fear of humiliation or loss.

As I looked at the pimply teenager's frozen gaze, it occurred to me that this is how a lot of violence starts. Not because people want to fight, but because they have no other way to negotiate simple social interactions. Without a set of confident micro-skills to deal with the situation they become helpless to respond any other way.

The psychology of 'can do'

Changing behaviour involves more than creating enabling environments and 'sticky' solutions. Whether people act or not depends on one more factor: their confidence in their own ability to carry off an action with dignity and aplomb.

Unfamiliar actions are scary and people avoid them for good reasons. We all dread humiliation, loss of control and loss of hard-won self-respect. And yet individuals do learn to conquer their fears. They cool off, tell themselves optimistic stories, get new skills, do things in groups. They learn to expand their comfort zones and go ahead and do those risky things like public speaking, bicycle riding or dancing the salsa.

My scared teenager might be a microcosm of the challenge facing change makers in many fields. I suspect that a lot of people find themselves in situations where they *want* to act differently but where wanting is not enough. There's a scary zone to be negotiated – a desolate minefield of vague hazards exaggerated by the delusional perceptions of fragile, emotional selves. Successful change efforts find ways to expand people's comfort zones so those fears are no longer obstacles to action.

Of the many psychologists who've struggled to understand human motivation, one name stands out: Albert Bandura, professor of psychology at Stanford University and one of the great innovators in social psychology.

In the 1970s Bandura and his colleagues were trying to understand the causes of aggression in children. In their famous 'Bobo' experiment they showed that children could learn aggression by watching peers or adults being punished or rewarded for violent behaviour.[1] This led him to explore how humans learn from role models, what he called 'social learning'. He discovered that social learning was more complex than mere imitation: imitation lets people see *how* to do something, but whether they are likely to do it or not depends on whether they see the role model being rewarded or punished for doing it.[2] This eventually led Bandura to make the logical leap to a simple idea that made other psychologists slap their heads, mutter "darn!" and dash back to their drawing-boards. He called it 'self-efficacy'.

The idea of self-efficacy is that, before people can act, they need to have confidence in their own abilities to control the risks and actually bring about the desired results. No matter how great their desire, small gaps in their belief in their own abilities can destroy their self-confidence and create a feeling of helplessness.

Bandura and his colleagues carried out a series of experiments that vividly illustrated the idea.

In one experiment, children were divided into two groups. One group consisted of those who were confident about their mathematical abilities. The other group consisted of those who doubted their mathematical abilities. No matter whether the questions were easy or hard, the children who believed in themselves were quicker to rework the problems they failed and did so more accurately than those of equal ability who were plagued by self-doubt. Positive self-belief turned out to be a better predictor of results than actual mathematical ability.[3]

In another experiment, a group of business managers were led to believe that employee behaviour was hard to change. They rapidly lost faith in their own capabilities, lowered their expectations, and their teams' performances deteriorated, even when the goals were within easy reach. Meanwhile, a second group of managers were led to believe that employee behaviour was easy to change. Their teams showed high degrees of resilience, even in the face of numerous difficulties. They set themselves increasingly challenging goals, used good analytic thinking and worked better as a team.[4]

In another study, Bandura found that teachers' beliefs in their own abilities could either energise or demoralise the social system of a school. He wrote "Schools in which the staff collectively judge themselves as powerless to get students to achieve academic success convey a group sense of academic futility that can pervade the entire life of a school."[5]

Bandura concluded that self-confidence wasn't just about people having skills – it was about their *belief* in their own capacities.[6] "People who believe they can exercise control over events do not conjure up disturbing thought patterns," he wrote. "But those who believe they cannot manage threats experience high anxiety arousal. They dwell on their coping deficiencies. They view many aspects of their environment as fraught with danger. They magnify the severity of possible threats and worry about things that rarely happen." "The stronger the instilled sense of coping self-efficacy," he concluded, "the bolder people are in taking on taxing and threatening activities."[7]

The effect of high self-confidence is to make success seem almost certain, and failure of little concern. Why are attractive women the first to try new fashions? They don't need them. They look good anyway. And that's the reason: they know the risks are low. Even if the outfit looks ridiculous, their self-image won't be shattered. It's the same reason successful corporations are the first to invest in innovative technologies. And why successful farmers are the first to adopt new farm practices. And why small, elite families are the first to adopt family-planning methods in developing countries.[8] Those with the highest confidence tend to act first because they believe they can manage the risks.

How can we instil self-efficacy in people who lack it?

Bandura suggested four techniques:[9]

- Let people experience success – "Successes build a robust belief in one's personal efficacy."
- Let people see others like themselves acting and succeeding – he called this vicarious experience or modelling.
- Have faith in people's capacity to change – he called this verbal persuasion.
- Encourage a positive mood and attitude – he called this positive self-appraisal.*

In a moment, we'll see how these techniques can be built into any change project.

Another insight into 'can do' comes from studies in risk perception.

Paul Slovic is one of a group of risk-perception psychologists who've spent their professional lives trying to understand why people respond in seemingly illogical ways to different hazards. They aimed to explain, for instance, why a parent might happily smoke a cigarette while driving their children over the speed limit (and talking on a mobile phone) to join a protest against the construction of a mobile phone tower near their children's school – a series of logically inconsistent behaviours.

In a tour de force of distillation, Slovic and his colleagues summarised 20 years of research into the perception of risk into just three primary factors. They concluded that people judge risk according to:

- whether they can control their exposure to the hazard
- unfamiliarity – the universal fear of the unknown
- their beliefs [received from the buzz] about the catastrophic potential of the hazard.[10]

These three factors explain the logic behind seemingly irrational judgements of risk: why, for instance, mobile-phone-tower radiation can be per-

---

* Martin Seligman in his book *Learned Optimism* unpacked positive self-appraisal into three dimensions. When faced with difficulties, he concluded, people can define them as temporary or permanent; pervading part of their lives or the whole of their lives; or caused by others or themselves. He showed that people who see difficulties as temporary, non-pervasive and due to external causes tend to recover more quickly and are generally happier.

ceived as more risky than smoking or driving: it's not under the users' control, it's unfamiliar, and people say it causes cancer. Smoking and speeding, on the other hand, seem familiar and under personal control, so they appear much less risky.

Slovic and his colleagues were mainly working for insurance companies and nuclear power utilities so they weren't interested in social risks like humiliation and embarrassment. Still, it's easy to see how similar rules could apply when we ask people to adopt new social and environmental behaviours. If those activities are unfamiliar or if people feel they lack control, chances are the risks will be magnified out of proportion, fear will replace rational judgement, and people will tend to resist the behaviour.

As we're about to see, familiarity and control are two powerful ways to lower the perceived risks of new behaviours.

A third perspective on 'can do' comes from investigations into the 'flow' experience. Way back in 1965, a fresh-faced young psychologist named Mihály Csíkszentmihályi (pronounced shik-sent-me-hi) was studying the experiences of a group of artists. He noticed that they spent hour after hour painting or sculpting with total concentration, absorption and enjoyment, as though it was the most important thing in the world. Yet, paradoxically, when the paint was dry, they abandoned their canvases in a remote corner of the studio and forgot about them. This behaviour made little sense in terms of existing psychological theories that explained motivation in terms of external rewards such as money and recognition. And the object itself – the finished work of art – was clearly not the point either. Something else was going on.

A few years later Csíkszentmihályi came back to the puzzle. With his students, he interviewed more than 200 people who were engaged in strenuous activities that offered little external reward – amateur athletes, chess players, rock climbers, dancers, high school basketball players and composers. But instead of asking about their behaviours and thoughts, Csíkszentmihályi asked them what these activities *felt* like. They described an enjoyable state of deep controlled attention where time disappeared, tasks became effortless and personal concerns melted away. One dancer said "a strong relaxation and calmness came over me. I have no worries of failure. What a powerful and warm feeling it is! I want to expand, to hug the world. I feel enormous power to effect something of grace and beauty". A chess player said "I have a general feeling of well-being, and that I am in complete control of my world."[11]

Csíkszentmihályi called this state 'flow'. He discovered that flow occupies a zone poised between boredom and anxiety, where abilities are exactly matched to the task at hand.* He investigated what conditions caused this state of flow and concluded that flow tended to be produced by:

- a challenging task that matches the actor's skills
- clear and definite goals
- known rules about how the task is to be completed
- clear, frequent feedback so efforts can be monitored and quickly adjusted to maintain the sense of control.

Clear goals, agreed rules, meaningful feedback and skills to match. That's a pretty useful formula for enabling people to act on their motivations.

* * *

Just as an individual can use risk-lowering techniques in daily life, so a change maker can incorporate risk-lowering techniques that expand the comfort zones of participants in a change effort.

The insights of Bandura, Slovic and Csíkszentmihályi into efficacy-building, risk-reduction and flow help explain why these techniques can be so effective.

I'm about to describe nine of these techniques. They're tried and proven comfort-zone-expanding methods that are guaranteed to ease people over the road bumps of their fears. Salesmen, facilitators and organisers use them all the time. They'll make a great difference to your next project.

The techniques are:

- familiarity
- personal control (autonomy)
- discussion with peers

---

* There's an excellent TED video of Csíkszentmihályi describing his research: www.ted.com/talks/lang/eng/mihaly_csikszentmihalyi_on_flow.html

- goals and feedback
- enjoyment
- social proof
- commitment
- labelling
- incentives

I've selected these techniques because there's a lot of evidence about their effectiveness and because they're fairly easy to put into practice. In fact, a huge number of persuasive techniques have been documented. A good summary is *Yes! 50 Scientifically Proven Ways to Be Persuasive* by Noah Goldstein, Steve Martin and Robert Cialdini.

Be aware that it's not a matter of choosing just one technique. Usually you'll be using more than one. In fact, there's no reason why you couldn't use all nine at once! They reinforce each other, so the more you include, the greater your chance of success.

And keep in mind, too, that the best use of these techniques is to stimulate one-off actions. Persuasive techniques don't change people's environments, so by themselves can't be expected to cause long-term changes in behaviour.

Technique 1: Familiarity

If we want people to be less afraid of a novel action, unfamiliarity is probably the number-one obstacle we should tackle. There are three good ways to go about increasing people's familiarity: modelling, touch and feel, and flight simulation.

1. Modelling

Modelling is seeing someone similar perform the exact actions required to achieve a successful outcome and then be rewarded for it.

Albert Bandura thought that modelling might be one of the main ways humans learnt self-efficacy. Any parent, of course, knows modelling is bigger than that – it's THE method par excellence that human beings use to learn everything. One of Bandura's experiments involved a group of four-year-old children who were terrified of dogs. The children were invited to a party where they saw another, similar, four-year-old arrive with a large cocker spaniel. The model child led the dog into a pen on the opposite side of the room, talked to it soothingly and petted it. In following sessions, the children saw the model child climb into the pen, hug the dog and feed it milk from a bottle.

Later the children were left in the room with the dog while the researchers watched. To their amazement they saw the formerly fearful children spontaneously enter the confined pen and play with the dog. Their fears had evaporated. The extraordinary thing is that the change was permanent. When the children were followed up a month later, their confidence was even higher.[12] The same experiment was repeated with children who simply watched a series of films of children becoming progressively more comfortable with a dog. The effect was identical.[13]

The point of this experiment is not just that the children learnt that the dog was safe, but that they learnt *how to play* with the dog enjoyably. They had a chance to observe the specific motions and micro-skills they needed to have the confidence that they knew what to do.

Nothing builds confidence like realising you've just succeeded. Hubert Dixon, from the Centre for Community Change, made the point nicely: "To get over your fear . . . you have to have your first victory . . . you just have to plan it, carry it out and meet your expectations. Then you realise you can do it."[14]

Modelling happens automatically whenever similar people interact, and especially where they form an ongoing group or team.

Modelling easily fits into familiar campaign tactics like 'coffee table' workshops in people's homes, field days on farms, 'tool box' meetings in workplaces and stalls at community fairs. All we have to do is to make sure people see the activity being performed, ideally by someone similar, and then see that their efforts earn them enjoyment, reward or praise.

Here's a nice example from the UK of an anti-obesity programme based on modelling. It aimed to get primary school kids eating more fruit, salads and vegetables. First, plates of fruit and vegetables were put out in lunch rooms. Second, a six-minute *Food Dudes* video was shown at lunch time. The Food Dudes were child cartoon characters who battled against evil Junk Punks who planned to take over the world by depriving children of life-giving fruit and vegetables. The Dudes were often depicted enjoying fruit and vegetables and urging children to keep their Life Force strong by doing the same. And third, children who ate healthy food were given rewards like pens, erasers and rulers.

Over three weeks the children's lunchtime fruit consumption jumped from 21 per cent to 73 per cent, and vegetable consumption from 35 per cent to 68 per cent, with the largest increases among those who ate the least fruit and vegetables at the start.[15] The changes persisted over the next 18 months. Impressed by the results, the Irish government trialled the approach in 150 schools. The results were so striking that the trial was cancelled prematurely and replaced in 2007 by a nationwide roll-out to all children aged 4 to 11.[16] This programme neatly illustrates the essential ingredients of modelling: seeing someone similar successfully carry out a behaviour and then be rewarded for it.[17]

2. Touch and feel

In 1999, Lynette Zelezny, a professor of psychology at California State University, set out to determine what makes the most effective environmental education. In particular, she wanted to know what kinds of educational method had the biggest impact on behaviour. Since most environmental education programmes only measured changes in attitudes (if anything), it was a little difficult to find programmes to evaluate, but eventually she found 18 that measured changes in behaviour as well as attitudes. They included high-school camp workshops, videos, energy use displays and games.

She found, decisively, that the programmes that changed behaviour were those that got people physically involved. Activities like role plays, investigating local issues and workshops had three times the impact on behaviour, compared with those that involved only instruction or information.[18]

Any activity that requires a degree of skill will benefit from touch-and-feel techniques; for example, exercising and cycling, parenting, assertiveness training, sustainable farming, organic gardening, 'no tox' home-cleaning and so on. Part of the trick is to let people experiment with a new behaviour in a safe setting where there are no consequences or judgements for getting it wrong.

Touch and feel can even help to develop intuitive awareness of abstract concepts like biodiversity. Raymond Chipenuik, a professor of environmental studies in Ontario, wondered whether childhood foraging might influence teenagers' knowledge about biodiversity. He gave 106 Ottawa and Niagara teenagers a list of 211 objects – including acorns, violets, crayfish, potato bugs, bullet casings, popsicle sticks and bottle caps – and asked which ones they could remember having collected in their childhoods. Then he gave them a list of different places – like a grain farm, a big stream, a small wood lot, a riverbank with no cottages – and asked them to estimate the local biodiversity.

It turned out that the teenagers who had foraged most when young made the best guesses about how much biodiversity was found at each place. Ironically, the group that did most poorly were those who had studied biodiversity in the classroom.

"It may be that childhood foraging experiences trigger an intuitive sense of biodiversity in much the same way as linguists believe early exposure to speech triggers the development of grammar," he wrote, noting that "virtually all the leading actors in the early American conservation movement were enthusiastic foragers in their youth".[19]

3. Flight simulation stories

A flight simulation is a story that recounts a blow-by-blow description about how similar people achieved the same results. I borrowed this term from Chip and Dan Heath's *Made to Stick*. A good how-to story increases confidence by letting people mentally rehearse the necessary actions in the theatre of their imaginations. Mental rehearsal is a powerful learning tool.[20]

Flight simulation may be behind what is claimed to be one of the most successful large-scale behaviour change programmes in the world, TravelSmart. Invented by Socialdata, a German market research firm, TravelSmart aims to get people using public transport, cycling and walking to work by tackling the micro how-to obstacles that block action.

TravelSmart depends on trained telephone operators who cold-call households in targeted neighbourhoods and ask if they are interested in finding out how to use their cars less. For those who express interest, a conversation follows where the operator attempts to locate people's frustrations with their current travel and then identifies the gaps in knowledge that prevent them trying alternatives to the car. The operator answers the specific doubts they have, sends them information about public transport routes or connects them to bike groups or other services. If they need more help, a consultant visits to discuss the exact routes, times and kinds of support that would help them get out of their cars.

TravelSmart claims to get impressive results: 13 per cent reduction in car trips among 10,000 households in Goteburg, Sweden; 12 per cent reduction among 3,800 households in Viernheim, Germany; and 14 per cent reduction among 15,000 households in south Perth, Australia. Even more impressively, they claim, these results were sustained two to four years after the intervention.[21]

Officially, TravelSmart is supposed to be about information, but I suspect it's really about imagination. The conversations focus people's minds on frustrations they'd been too busy to attend to and then feeds their imagination so they can mentally rehearse the complex task of negotiating an unfamiliar transport system.

Flight simulation can probably even work with print materials like the humble brochure. The trick is to have only one action per brochure and illustrate it with photos or drawings that break the behaviour down into step-by-step micro-actions, so a viewer can easily imagine themselves doing each step. Of course, no print product is ever as persuasive as a human being, but it's a start.

A word of warning. When it comes to familiarising people with new skills, beware of jumping to conclusions about exactly what skills people need.

A European study of sexually active high-school students found that knowing how to use a condom had little effect on the decision to use one. But two factors did have a strong influence: students' perceived ability to control emotional conflicts and their perceived decisiveness and verbal skills in imposing condom use.[22] In other words, if we want to increase the rate of condom use, the skills we need to focus on are assertiveness and emotional intelligence, life skills that have nothing to do with how to use a condom!

And keep in mind that confidence is not simply a collection of skills. Just because we teach a skill doesn't mean we're boosting confidence. It sounds like a subtle distinction, but it can make or break a project. Here's what I mean:

In the late 1990s there was a waste-management crisis as landfill space across Sydney approached exhaustion. The New South Wales Government responded with three years of campaigning to get the public to reduce household waste. One of the most promoted techniques was home composting.

These extensive educational efforts produced a paradoxical result. The more people learnt about home composting, the less they did it. Tracking research in one Sydney region showed that home composting dropped from 53 per cent to 44 per cent of households over the three years. Other Sydney regions produced equally disappointing results, with the overall rate falling from 64 per cent to 58 per cent.[23] What was happening?

The truth about home composting is that it seems easy until someone tries to explain it to you. Then it sounds damnably tricky and complicated. There's so much to think about: temperature, mixtures, moisture levels. Probably not even experienced composters were achieving the level of competence that waste educators were breezily recommending in their beautifully illustrated brochures and displays.

That illustrates the crucial point about self-efficacy. It's not about *being able*. It's about *believing you are able*. Those well-meaning campaigns were increasing people's knowledge about home composting but shattering their confidence to do it.

We've all heard about the 'learning curve' in education. Well, there's an 'efficacy curve' in behaviour change. Too much information can easily damage self-efficacy. We can make things seem too complicated, unwittingly pushing people into their scary zones. It's therefore vital to demonstrate only the first simple steps on the path we hope people will follow. Once they take those first simple steps and get the thrill of success, their confidence will skyrocket, and self-learning will likely propel them the rest of the way.

Technique 2: personal control (autonomy)

Novel actions seem less risky when we can control how and when we do them.

In 2005 celebrity chef Jamie Oliver accepted the seemingly impossible challenge of getting all primary schoolchildren in an entire London borough to eat healthy school lunches. After a heroic struggle, Jamie eventually got most children in one school eating fruit and vegetables at lunchtime.

But there were about a dozen kids who resisted. They stubbornly refused to eat anything except chips, burgers and Turkey Twizzlers (a disgusting fake food made from deep-fried turkey parts). One actually said, "There's no advantage in taking a risk".

So Jamie tried something new. He invited the dozen ultra-laggards to a special cooking class. He asked them to chop and mix ingredients for a salad and make up some marinated chicken drumsticks. The drumsticks were cooked and Jamie plonked them on the table and said, "If you want 'em, you want 'em; if you don't, you don't". Then he turned his back and walked away. And a beautiful thing happened. The most resistant kids in the school start milling around the bowls of food they've just prepared. First gingerly, and then eagerly, they begin to devour the very foods they've been rejecting for months.

I think Jamie was illustrating the effect of personal control. He put the kids in charge of preparing the food and then let them decide whether to eat it. And their fears disappeared.

It got me thinking. In our household we occasionally minded a ten-year-old boy named Toby who was phobic about a lot of foods. He wouldn't eat most fruits and vegetables. In fact, he gave quite rational accounts about how oranges, carrots, lettuce had injured him in the past (like "the orange squished me in the eye" – wow, that must have hurt!).

I thought I'd try Jamie's trick. The next time Toby visited, we asked him to help make dinner. We laid out minced meat, carrots, coriander and garlic, and invited him to grate the carrots and mix the ingredients into meatballs, and then do the cooking. He energetically grated the carrots and squished the meat and he enjoyed the cooking. But, disappointingly, the trick failed because he showed no interest in eating the result. His phobias were intact. "So much for the Jamie trick," I thought.

But the next time he visited, lacking any other way to amuse him, we repeated the method. This time, to our relief, he ate a meatball that he'd mixed with some grated carrot. Triumph!

A couple of weeks later, we repeated the process, and this time he voluntarily consumed three or four meatballs packed with coriander, carrot and garlic. He accidentally put so much garlic in one meatball that it burnt his mouth. We could see his eyes watering, but he was determined to eat what he had created.

So the 'Jamie method' works. It just takes time.

Why should personal control matter so much? Because the fear of losing control, of being at the mercy of another's whims, matters intensely when the stakes seem high. It means that, if we want to reduce someone's fear of an unfamiliar activity, putting them in control of the process can make a difference. Sharing control over decision-making will always be essential in high-stakes situations such as elderly people learning to exercise, parents deciding whether to let their children walk to school, householders deciding whether to accept a hazardous waste plant, or farmers any time. But risk, of course, is in the eye of the beholder, and there's hardly any situation where a degree of shared control will not increase the likelihood of people acting.

Personal control (also known as autonomy) not only lowers the perceived risks of people acting, it's probably a want or motivation in its own right. Try this little experiment. Take a piece of paper and draw on it a day-by-day diagram of your last week (I won't tell you how to do it, I know you'll be good at it) and mark on it the times you felt most highly motivated (that is, the times you least wanted to be doing something else). I guarantee those were also the times you were exercising the most autonomy. Probably you were socialising, playing, exercising or doing a hobby, or getting ready to do those things. Autonomy and high motivation go hand in hand.[24]

Kurt Lewin was one of the first social scientists to focus on the relationship between autonomy and motivation. Comparing the effect of autonomous versus authoritarian teaching styles on young students he wrote: "There have been few experiences for me as impressive as seeing the expression in children's faces change during the first day [in a controlling environment]. The friendly, open, and co-operative group, full of life, became within a short half-hour a rather apathetic looking gathering without initiative . . ."[25]

Authoritarian environments have exactly the same corrosive effect on adult motivation. For example, when workers' control over decision-making is high, they feel and perform better. Autonomy is associated with athletic, academic and job performance, as well as concentration, task persistence, physical and mental health, and longevity.[26]

Autonomy is the idea behind harm-minimisation programmes in drug education, community development programmes like Landcare, and aid schemes like the Grameen Bank's microcredit loans. It's a basic principle in adult education and social organising. Even a command-and-control field like emergency management is slowly recognising the importance of autonomous decision-making in communities subject to flood or fire hazards by establishing autonomous citizen fire-response units like Community Fire Guard in Victoria and Community Fire Units in NSW.[27]

Personal control can even help control one of the most ineradicable forms of bad behaviour – school bullying. Bullying's clandestine nature and complex emotional causes make it one of the most difficult behaviours to prevent. An international comparison of 13 anti-bullying programmes in Europe, Canada, the USA and Australia showed that only one caused a measurable reduction in bullying.[28] That programme, in a suburban Australian high school, encouraged students to start their own anti-bullying committee which autonomously hatched its own initiatives, and included a peer helper group that counselled both the bullies and the bullied, a public speaking group that addressed meetings on anti-bullying, a drama group that created school performances on the issue, and a welcoming team to support new students. This autonomy-based approach resulted in fewer reports of bullying, fewer students being threatened, and more students feeling safe at school.[29]

Some of my students recently gave a perfect example of personal control in practice. A team of council environmental officers were designing a project to stop SUV-drivers driving over sand dunes, an activity that destroys vegetation and bird nesting sites. Their idea was to establish cordoned tracks to the beach and encourage drivers to use them. But instead of just ploughing ahead and establishing the tracks, they decided to invite local beach drivers to a BBQ to help plan the best places to put them. Brilliant! That's putting the principle of personal control into practice.

Technique 3: discussion with peers

Autonomy is more powerful when it's exercised by a group.

During World War Two the United States shipped so much beef, lamb and pork to troops overseas that authorities began to worry about malnourishment at home. They worried so much they set up a Committee on Food Habits under Margaret Mead, the renowned anthropologist, to find out how to overcome housewives' aversion to kidneys, brains and hearts (i.e. offal). The committee employed some of the leading psychologists of the day to grapple with the problem. Notable among these was the pioneering social psychologist Kurt Lewin.[30]

In 1942, while trying to figure out how to educate housewives about the advantages of offal, Lewin performed a seminal social psychology experiment. He selected 85 housewives from Cedar Rapids, Iowa, and divided them into two groups. One group had a 30-minute lecture on the importance of offal meats to the war effort and their nutritive value, plus advice on how to prepare them. The other group were given a short intro on the same matters and then led by a facilitator on a free discussion that first focused on seeing the problem more concretely, then deciding what action they could take about it.

One week after the experiment, 10 per cent of the lecture participants had served offal meats to their families, but an impressive 52 per cent of the 'group decision' participants had served offal.[31]

The only difference between the groups was that the second group had a chance to discuss the issue with their peers. For those women, the fears and risks of serving offal seemed to have declined dramatically.

The outbreak of AIDS in San Francisco in the mid-1980s led to a large-scale intervention based on Lewin's approach. The programme, called STOP AIDS, was organised by gay men. It was based on small group meetings in homes around the Castro Street district and other neighbourhoods where gay men lived. The project trained 7,000 outreach workers, all gay men, often HIV-positive, to run meetings of 10 to 12 people in local homes, where discussions included issues like HIV transmission and safe sex. At the end of each meeting, the participants were asked to raise their hands if they intended to practise safe sex or were willing to organise further small group meetings. The large scale of the project was driven by the idea, drawn from Diffusion of Innovations, that a critical mass was needed for safe-sex practices to be adopted by the majority of a population. About 30,000 men attended these meetings, 21 per cent of the total gay population in San Francisco.

What was the impact? In the two years from 1983 to 1985, the number of new HIV infections in San Francisco dropped from 8,000 to 650 and the rate of unprotected anal intercourse fell from 71 per cent to 27 per cent. The number of AIDS-related deaths dropped from 1,600 per year in the mid-1980s to only 250 in recent years. Of course, all these results can't be attributed to just one programme, but it's likely it made a contribution.[32]

Lewin formulated principles that suffuse the adult education and community organising movements today. There are lots of different statements of these principles, but most go a little like this:

Adults are motivated to learn by what:

- is perceived to be relevant
- builds on their previous experience
- actively involves them and is participatory
- is problem focused
- enables them to take responsibility for their learning
- can be applied in practice immediately
- involves a cycle of action and reflection
- is based on mutual respect and trust. [33]

The key principle is participation. In practice, it means having discussions, brainstorms, debates or deliberations where the aim is for a group of people to speak their minds and make a collective judgement, and where all present have a fair chance to have their say and are listened to. Naturally, these discussions benefit from having agreed ground rules, and someone to act as a facilitator. It helps immeasurably, too, if the tone of the discussion is optimistic and positive.

Kirsty Norris, from Action for Sustainability, UK, shared a story that captures perfectly how autonomy plus group discussion can drive motivation:

> I worked with a business client whose office waste system of choice was replacing individual desk bins with communal recycling and waste stations. They were predicting resistance for this because people would have to walk to the communal stations. We realised that without buy-in there'd be misuse and contamination. We called together reps from various departments along one corridor of the organisation, including the senior management team, HR and IT. We discussed the waste issue with them, what we would like to do (remove desk bins, install communal facilities), *and left them to*

debate it. They decided on a month pilot of their corridor to test out removing desk bins. We reviewed this with them every week. Sorted out the little niggles (communal facilities not quite in right place), shared 'coping stories' with each other (i.e. different ways different people have set up systems to deal with the change). They had the option at the end of the month to have their desk bins back. They were adamant, "no way", and determined to make it work. Plus they were already extending this to their own 'take home' composting in some offices! Communal waste stations are now rolled out across the whole organisation to great success.[34]

Technique 4: goals and feedback

Goals and feedback are essential to feeling you're in control. After all, it's hard to be in control unless you know where you're going and whether you're getting there.

Researchers in Perth, Western Australia, decided to test the effect of goal-setting. They recruited two groups of adults. One group was trained in setting personal goals and attended a series of workshops on sustainable living. The second group just attended the workshops. Both groups had similar significant shifts in knowledge. But only the goal-setters changed their behaviours, cycling to work more often, buying more organic foods, and avoiding toxic products.[35]

It's often asked what kind of goals are best: 'stretch' goals or easy goals? Twenty-five years of research into organisational behaviour makes it clear that challenging, but not overwhelming, goals are the most motivating.[36] Challenging goals tend to cause higher performance than easy goals, 'do your best' goals or no goals at all.[37]

But keep in mind that the mere existence of a goal is not enough: people have to believe the goal is worth striving for. The most motivating goals will therefore be ones people choose for themselves. For example, it's been shown that students who set their own goals achieve more than those who have their goals set by teachers.[38]

In addition, the best goals are specific and measurable: for instance, not merely 'saving energy' but 'achieving 20 per cent energy savings over 3 months'.

Of course, goals work better when there's feedback on progress towards achieving them. But how frequent should that feedback be? Since goals and feedback both enable control, the rule for feedback is that it should be regular enough for people to actively manage their progress towards the goal. So, the closer to real time the better. And remember that the best feedback is warm personal thanks, praise or celebration.

When it comes to reducing energy use, for example, those little graphs on energy bills comparing this quarter's use with the same time last year are interesting and informative, but they arrive a little too late to allow people to actively moderate their demand and, of course, there's no goal to aim for, which is another weakness.

Fortunately, smart meters are coming to the rescue. Smart meters let consumers measure their electricity, gas or water use, in dollars, on a minute-to-minute basis. European and US studies show these devices, combined with tips on energy saving, typically result in 5 to 20 per cent savings in households.[39]

Southern California Edison, for instance, gave 600 consumers an Energy Orb, a softball-sized sphere that, besides having hip decor, glows red during peak energy use when the cost of energy is high, and glows blue during off-peak times. Consumers responded to this simple visual feedback by reducing their peak energy use by 25 per cent.[40] Californian utilities are particularly aggressive in adopting smart meters. San Diego Gas and Energy recently announced the roll-out of 1.4 million smart-meters in a US$572m project.

People love feeling in control of things that matter in their lives. But control doesn't just happen because people are told "OK, you're in charge". That's probably a good way to scare them. Instead, aim to give them the familiarity, skills, goals and feedback that make the exercise of control possible.

Technique 5: enjoyment

Can fun change the world? In 1983 cognitive scientists Eric Johnson and Amos Tversky carried out a seminal experiment which helped answer that question.[41] They divided 557 college students into two groups. One group read newspaper stories about tragic events. The other group read stories about happy events. Afterwards, the students were asked to estimate their own chances of being struck by different kinds of tragedy. The students who read the tragic stories estimated the probability of being a victim of all sorts of tragic events as being higher, despite whether the event was similar or different to the one they read about. So, for instance, reading a story about a fatal stabbing raised their fears of being a victim of violent assault, and also raised their fears of being a victim of an earthquake. Meanwhile, the students who read about happy events became globally less concerned about all sorts of risks.

It seems that happiness, or elation, or just being in a good mood fundamentally alters people's sense of risk. And it simultaneously makes them more persistent at difficult tasks,[42] more creative[43] and more likely to accept requests and invitations.[44]

What's behind this phenomenon? Happiness changes people's mode of thinking. Humans have a number of quite separate systems for making judgements.[45] They either try to logically analyse situations, or they go with gut feelings and intuitions or they use good-enough rules of thumb that allow for quick judgements.[46] When people are depressed or worried they tend to opt for the first. They try to rationally analyse the situation. They mull over the pros and cons. They obsess over the details. They ruminate over the unknowns. That kind of thinking is a sure way to become frozen with indecision. Even when depressed people do succeed in acting, they tend to be more self-critical and set higher, perhaps unattainable, goals for themselves.

Happy people, on the other hand, tend to rely more on emotional factors when making decisions. They are more likely to leap into situations that feel right without calculating the costs.[47] In the words of leading researchers in this field "being in a good mood should facilitate, and being in a bad mood should impair, the impression that attainment of the goal is feasible."[48]

This suggests that enjoyment should not be thought of as an optional extra when you're running a change project. It turns out to be a profoundly important enabler of action. When participants get involved in a process of change, being shifted into a good mood makes them less fearful, more likely to have a go at unfamiliar activities and more creative.

So, yes, fun can change the world.*

---

* Or as my friend Bruce put it "What's fun gets done."

Most activists implicitly understand this. Changing the world may have a deadly serious purpose, but a light touch beats a wrinkled brow any day. Good food, conversation, games, role-plays and humour make all the difference to people's perceived ability to act. A nice example was Danceplant, an event run by a group of youthful green activists. They found a way to combine the two things they loved: dance parties and tree planting. They'd invite their friends to spend a day planting trees on a farm, then at nightfall they'd have a dance party in the bush, grooving to Cuban, reggae or techno music, or jamming on their own instruments. Sometimes they'd show films like *Baraka* or *Blade Runner*. Then they'd camp out, and plant more trees in the morning.[49]

Fun need not be complicated. An example was the 'Hot August Night' extravaganza organised by my friend Geoff Brown.[50] Instead of having a dreary community meeting to launch a new sustainability project in Angelsea, Victoria, he invited the whole community to a party at a local club, with a band and delicious organic food. He spent time facilitating social introductions before kicking off discussions on how to make the town more sustainable.

Technique 6: social proof

Social proof is evidence that plenty of similar people are already doing a particular action.

I used to live in a very laid-back seaside town. It was full of students, artists, retired coalminers and alternative types. It was an easygoing place. If you wanted, you could walk down the main street in your pyjamas and people would hardly notice. I used to enjoy sitting in my favourite café, hair uncombed and wearing a rumpled old shirt. Then we moved to a different town, one that was a bit more middle class and buttoned-up. After we had lived there a few months, I noticed an odd thing happening. Before I went down to the café in the morning, I found myself in the bathroom combing my hair. What's more, I was carefully choosing my best shirt to wear. The thing was, I didn't form a conscious intention to do either of these things: they just happened. That's the awesome power of social norms. They work at a barely conscious level.[51]

Social norms are our rules for what we think is normal or expected in a particular social environment. Usually they are unstated rules. We only sense them by observing the way other people act, dress and talk.

It's easy to see why this social sixth sense is important. We humans depend on each other for survival. Food, shelter, safety, warmth, and comfort depended on maintaining good relationships with the people around us.

As a result, we humans are intensive image managers. We care deeply about the impressions we make on the people around us. Our perceptions about what those other people expect and admire has tremendous power over our personal choices. That's why marketers are always claiming their product is 'fastest-growing' or 'best-selling', trying to create the impression that lots of other people want it. Neuroscientist Read Montague pointed out that humans have "a sort of instinctual response to overvalue something" when we see that others want it.[52]

Social norms change depending on where we are and who we are with. We might wear one set of norms with our children, another with our boss, yet another with our parents, and one at the pub on Friday night, and we'd be in trouble if we mixed them up.

Working out norms is a challenge for human beings because norms can be fuzzy, changeable and hard to define. There's no sign on the edge of my town saying "Only ironed shirts and brushed hair approved in this town".

In fact, norms don't really exist at all except in the minds of observers, which is why social scientists talk about *perceived* social norms. And, being purely mental constructs, people are prone to get them wrong. Famously, high school and university students overestimate the amount of binge drinking by their peers. As a result, something like half the 746 colleges and universities in the US now have programmes that aim to correct mistaken norms about other students' binge-drinking habits.[53]

The subjectivity of social norms makes them highly influenceable, which is good news for change makers.

One way to influence social norms is through social proof – visual evidence that lots of similar people are already doing a particular action. Robert Cialdini and his colleagues demonstrated this in a well-known experiment involving towel reuse in a hotel.

You know those signs in hotel rooms that say "Help save the environment, reuse your towel"? Cialdini wondered whether social proof could get better results. His team randomly allocated two different bathroom signs to

190 rooms in a hotel in the south-west USA.

One sign said "HELP SAVE THE ENVIRONMENT. You can respect nature and help save the environment by reusing towels during your stay." Guests in those rooms reused their towels 35 per cent of the time.

The other sign said "JOIN YOUR FELLOW GUESTS IN HELPING TO SAVE THE ENVIRONMENT. Almost 75% of guests who are asked to participate in our new resource savings programme do help by using their towels more than once. You can join your fellow guests in this programme . . .by reusing your towels during your stay." Guests in those rooms reused their towels 44 per cent of the time.[54] That's a 9 per cent change produced solely by informing people what was normal in that hotel.

Cialdini warns us that we need to be careful when depicting bad behaviour because it's easy to inadvertently promote exactly the wrong result. When we depict people littering, speeding or getting drunk we can easily create the impression that lots of people are doing those things, so they must be normal!

Cialdini demonstrated this negative effect with a field experiment that aimed to reduce the theft of fossils from the Arizona Petrified Forest National Park. Two signs were placed beside trails in the park over different five-week periods.

One sign said "Many past visitors have removed petrified wood from the Park, changing the natural state of the Petrified Forest." The accompanying image showed three visitors taking petrified wood. Over the five weeks, 8 per cent of marked pieces of petrified wood were stolen from that track.

The other sign said "Please don't remove petrified wood from the park, in order to preserve the natural state of the Petrified Forest" and was accompanied by an image of one visitor stealing a piece of wood, with a red circle-and-bar superimposed on his hand. Just 1.7 per cent of marked pieces of wood were stolen from that track.[55]

The effect of the first sign was to make stealing petrified wood seem normal. Messages like "34% of Americans are obese" or "57% of domestic violence victims never seek help" send exactly the wrong message. They make it look like a lot of people are doing the wrong thing. And if a lot of people are doing it, then it must be socially safe! Another of Cialdini's ingenious real-life experiments told Californian householders that they were using *less* energy than their neighbours. Those households then *increased* their energy use to bring it closer to the norm.[56] That's the same effect at work.

Here are a few examples of social proofing in practice:

- a poster that says "I don't smoke, just like 88% of students at this college"
- a sign in a bar that said "Nobody Smokes Here Any More"
- an energy bill that compares your energy use with that of your more efficient neighbours;[57]
- a card on your recycling bin that says "Well Done! This week your household recycled right. 85.7% of households in Bankstown recycled right. Thank you for your efforts."[58]

Technique 7: commitment

When people publicly agree to carry out a small, easy act they are much more likely to accept an invitation to carry out a bigger, more onerous, act later on.

In a former life Karenne Jurd was National Director of The Wilderness Society. Later, she became an environmental manager at Newcastle City Council in New South Wales, but she never lost her flair for interesting approaches to social action. One of her ideas is called 'Gutter Talks'. It's a way to stop people sweeping litter into their street drains and clogging up local streams with plastic bags and bottles.

A Gutter Talk works like this. Imagine you live in a street that's not far from a bushland reserve.

One day you see a poster at your local newsagent that says "A Gutter Talk is coming to a park near you. Have a free cup of tea and swap your old broom for a brand new, premium broom."

Then, one Saturday morning, you see people marching down your street carrying old brooms. You ask what's going on and they say the council is giving away new brooms.

So you grab your ratty old broom and head to the park too. There you see an environmental display, a couple of council officers and a pile of new brooms. You walk up to one of the council officers and ask for your new broom. But before you can take it, there's a conversation. The council officer reminds you that it's important not to sweep plastic, leaves or litter down the street drains and she explains why.

Then she asks you to sign a commitment form. You read the form. There's a list of about 20 environmental actions there. You figure "OK, it won't do any harm" and you sign the commitment form.

And then you swap old broom for new, but before you can walk away, the council officer, in the nicest possible way, invites you to "make the pledge". You can hardly refuse – she's just given you a brand new broom. So you stand with your neighbours, hand on your heart, and repeat the commitments. Just to cap it off, she takes a photo of you all making the pledge and gets you to fill in a photo release form. Lo and behold, a week or so later you see your picture in a newsletter circulated to the neighbourhood, standing with your neighbours, committing yourselves to a different future.

Weeks later, council volunteers go back to the neighbourhoods that have had Gutter Talks and count the litter in nearby streams. They find there's less litter after a Gutter Talk. People seem to have changed their behaviour.

Gutter Talks are an example of the 'foot-in-the-door' technique, beloved of salespeople the world over. The idea is that when a potential customer complies with a small request they are set on a slippery slope. The small, easy request leads to a larger, more difficult request and before you know it you're the proud owner of a $5,000 plasma TV when all you wanted was directions to the post office. In the case of Gutter Talks, the first small request was hard to refuse: swap your crappy old broom for a new premium-made broom. The next, slightly bigger, request was to read and sign a commitment form. After that, most people were hooked whether they liked it or not. Salespeople have always understood that compliance with a small innocuous action inevitably builds commitment towards an eventual sale.

To illustrate the power of this effect, Robert Cialdini explained how door-to-door sales companies managed to overcome the effects of cooling-off laws. The laws allowed customers a few days cooling off after buying an item, during which time they could cancel the sale and receive a full refund. When the laws came into effect door-to-door companies faced an avalanche of cancelled sales. Their response was simple. All they did was ask that the customer, rather than the salesperson, fill out the sales agreement. This innocuous act had the effect of increasing the customers' commitment. As Cialdini noted, people "live up to what they have written down".[59]

The famous experiment that demonstrated the power of the foot-in-the-door technique was carried out by two Stanford University researchers, Jonathan Freedman and Scott Fraser, in 1966.[60] It's already been described in other popular books so I won't repeat it here, but their conclusion was interesting: "Once [the subject] has agreed to a request, his attitude may change. He may become, in his own eyes, the kind of person who does this sort of thing, who agrees to requests made by strangers, who takes action on things he believes in, who cooperates with good causes."[61]

It's as if our words and actions help us to decide who we are.

One of the most impressive field experiments using this technique aimed to reduce the use of natural gas for winter heating by Iowa residents.[62] Two similar groups of households were chosen. For the first group, an interviewer visited each home and offered energy-saving tips with a request to use less gas in future. For the second group, the process was repeated, but with one change: the residents were told that by agreeing to save energy they would have their names appear in a newspaper article as public-spirited, fuel-conserving citizens.

One month later, when the gas meters were checked, the first group used the same amount of gas, but the second group had reduced their gas use by 12.2 per cent.

The researchers then broke their promise. They wrote a letter to the residents explaining that the names would not be published in the local newspaper after all. Did this cause them to return to their wasteful old ways? Not at all. In fact, they saved even more gas during the remaining winter months (15.5 per cent).[63]

The initial savings illustrate the effect of simple public signs of commitment. Believing they'll be seen by their peers to express positive environmental values causes people to act in harmony with those values.

But what caused the savings to *increase further* when they were told their names would not appear? I suspect it's our old friend resistance. Believing their name would appear in a newspaper felt like a kind of pressure and that pressure caused resistance. Remove the pressure and people's strengthened environmental identities had full rein to express themselves.

Don't forget that, to be effective, commitment must be visible to the peers of the person making the commitment. It can include simple methods like asking people to put stickers on their cars, garbage bins, front fences or windows, or have their names appear in a newspaper advert or on an honour roll of supporters or donors displayed in a public place.

One of the simplest forms of commitment is to ask an audience for a simple sign of support by holding their hands up *before* you ask them to do something more committing, like signing a membership form. Their first public display of commitment will motivate them to act consistently afterwards, increasing the number who subsequently sign up (and of course the signing-up should be done in public too).

What about T-shirts? Could just wearing, say, an Amnesty International T-shirt make someone more likely to stand up to racism? It seems the answer is yes. Not only that, but it would also assert an anti-racist social norm. So don't knock the humble T-shirt. It's a powerful weapon in the armoury of social change.

Technique 8: labelling

Labelling means telling people that you believe they're the kind of people who do the right thing.[64]

One of the earliest labelling experiments aimed to reduce littering in a school. Fifth graders were divided into three groups. One group was told they *were* neat and tidy people, while the other group was told they *should be* neat and tidy (the third group was a control). The group who were told they *were* neat and tidy littered considerably less than the others.[65]

Another labelling experiment succeeded in increasing donations to a charity. During a widely publicised local fundraising campaign, a charity worker visited 153 households, asked for donations to The Heart Association. Those who made a donation were told "You are a generous person. I wish more people were as charitable as you". They were left with a card that said "Charitable people give generously to help a good cause and those less fortunate than themselves. Are you one?"

Those who failed to donate were told "Let me give you one of our health leaflets anyway. We've been giving them to everyone, even people like you who are uncharitable and don't normally give to these causes". Attached to the leaflet was a card that said "Uncharitable people give excuses and refuse to help others. Are you one?"

Two weeks later a Multiple Sclerosis volunteer visited the same homes and asked for a donation. Past donors who had been labelled 'charitable' gave an average donation of US$0.70 compared to a control group who gave only $0.40, meanwhile non-donors who had been labelled 'uncharitable' gave an average of $0.23.[66] It seems that, when someone tells us we're good, we like the sound of it and we rise to the occasion!

The easiest way to use labelling is to address a meeting and say something like "You are the leaders in this community. You are the ones others look up to as examples and you're the first to step up and make a difference. That's why you're here." Chances are, they'll rise to that vision.

And don't forget, at the end of a project, tell people they did well because of the kind of people they are . . .they'll be more likely to step up in future.

Limits to commitment and labelling

Commitment and labelling are both identity-based techniques. They manipulate people's sense of who they are. But do these techniques have limits? Can commitment and labelling get people to do anything? The answer seems to be no.

A lot of commitment and labelling experiments have failed. Two professors of marketing, Alice Tybout and Richard Yalch, set out to discover why.[67]

The method was simple: In the lead-up to local elections 162 Chicago voters were interviewed about their interest in politics and elections. Then, irrespective of their answers, half were randomly told "That's interesting, your profile indicates that, relative to others in your community, you are an above-average citizen. Our research shows that you are very likely to vote in elections and participate in political events." The other half were told they were 'average citizens'. They were followed up to see whether they had voted in local elections held one week later.

The technique worked: 86 per cent of the 'above-average citizens' voted in the following elections, compared with 75 per cent of 'average citizens'. However, there was one group that resisted the manipulation: those who defined themselves as non-voters. They seemed not to notice or pay attention to the labelling, because it disagreed with their self-image. What mattered, Tybout and Yalch decided, was whether the behaviour was consistent with someone's self-image: "strategies to influence behaviour, such as labelling, are likely to be particularly effective in situations where individuals have an initial interest in the focal behaviour," they concluded.

So, one limit to commitment and labelling techniques is that you can probably only manipulate people to do things that agree with their existing self-images. The action has to be one that makes them feel they are virtuous in terms of their own values. So in theory it could work for things like giving blood, recycling, voting, saving energy and not littering, but probably not for activities that an audience doesn't identify with, like getting non-cyclists to ride bicycles or teenagers to mow lawns. In effect, commitment and labelling work because they make people bolder in acting on values they already hold.

Another reason commitment and labelling manipulations are liable to fail is if subjects realise they're being manipulated. Pressure causes resistance. So calling a commitment a 'commitment' is a dumb idea. People will immediately figure out they're being manipulated. Such methods work best when they are subtle, under people's radar. People should think the commitment or label is *really* a statement about their beliefs or character.

Nevertheless, self-labelling and labelling are underused behaviour-change techniques. They can be harnessed in very simple ways to increase people's likelihood of acting.

Technique 9: incentives

The techniques we've covered so far are tried and tested and pretty well guaranteed to work in lots of situations. But there's one technique that, despite its popularity, remains controversial: paying people to do the right thing.

New York Mayor Michael R. Bloomberg is an ex-equity trader who understands the motivating power of a cash bonus. He was the force behind a social experiment that paid the poorest kids in New York schools to pass exams. And in a separate programme, the city paid teachers bonuses of around US$3,000 (£1,650) when their schools, as a whole, did well in exams. In all, around 200 New York schools participated in the programmes.[68]

The New York initiatives were based on a similar idea launched in Mexico in 1995. Named Progresa, it was the brainchild of economist Santiago Levy. Instead of the allotments of subsidised tortillas and milk which were the staple of the Mexican welfare system, families received cash payments. Critics predicted that parents would spend the money on tequila. However, most parents seemed to spend the money responsibly, and there's evidence that children aged two to four in the programme weighed more (on average 500g) than those who didn't participate.

New York's experiment was hugely controversial. Some thought it was a monstrous error. "If this programme becomes an expectation on the part of the poor, I think you're going to get a further deterioration of responsible behaviour, not an improvement," argued one critic.[69]

Yet, early feedback was positive. By all accounts, the kids were excited by the cash payments. It's not surprising – some were getting $50 for doing well in a single exam.

So how did it go?

After paying $14 million to 2,400 families, the city quietly abandoned the student and parent incentive scheme in 2010, concluding it didn't work.[70] And the teacher incentive scheme was abandoned in early 2011 following an evaluation by the RAND Corporation.[71] The RAND researchers concluded the programme had produced "no effects on student achievement" and "no effects on teacher behaviours" for $50 million in bonuses.[72] Ouch!

What went wrong? Roland Fryer, the Harvard economist who helped design the programme, wrote that, although students were excited about the incentives, they "had little idea about how to translate their enthusiasm into tangible action steps designed to increase their achievement." He also wondered whether "incentives may need to be coupled with good teachers, an engaging curriculum, effective parents, or other inputs to produce output." He argued that, although paying students for doing well in exams doesn't work, paying them for good behaviours, like attendance, conduct, wearing uniforms and doing homework, can.[73]

Meanwhile the RAND researchers thought teacher bonus schemes may have failed because teachers viewed the payments "as a reward rather than an incentive: It made them feel appreciated for their hard work, but they claimed that they would have undertaken this work with or without the bonus."

There might also, they surmised, be a "flaw in the underlying theory of action for school-based pay-for-performance programmes more generally. As some have argued in the past, motivation alone does not improve schools. Even if the bonus inspired staff to improve practices or work together, it may not have the capacity or resources (e.g. school leadership, social capital, expertise, instructional materials, time) to bring about improvement."

Welcome to the complicated and vexed world of incentives.

One thing's for certain, governments love them. They come in many different forms: emissions trading schemes, tax credits, low-interest loans, cash-back schemes, or subsidies. Often it's just a straightforward cash payment. A consortium including the World Bank paid 15- to 30-year-olds in Tanzania almost $50 a year to stay HIV-negative. The Australian Government is paying parents $5,000 to have a baby. The State of Florida paid up to $100,000 to businesses to install solar cells. The State of Texas paid 75 per cent of the costs for landowners to protect endangered species.

And there's certainly evidence that incentives can encourage action.

Evaluations of health incentive programmes, for instance, show small but generally positive results. Incentives to encourage patients to comply with doctors' directions had an observable, if small, effect;[74] incentives to give up smoking had a measurable effect though probably only for smokers who were already motivated to quit;[75] incentives to improve hospital care had an observable effect but could also cause unexpected negatives like reduced care for the very sick;[76] incentives increased the number of mothers attending a postnatal clinic;[77] and incentives to wear seat belts had observable effects, although mainly in the short term.[78]

Despite this, there's been a long and fierce debate between economists and psychologists about whether incentives make sense.

Economists love the idea of incentives. It fits perfectly with classical economic theory's vision of humans as rational utility-maximising individuals. "People will generally do what is in their own interest particularly their short-term interest," wrote economics professor Paul Ferraro. "If they can receive more benefits from clearing an area of habitat than they could from protecting it, they will clear it."[79]

This idea is so powerful that incentives have spread virus-like into domains once governed by very different value systems. Welfare payments, for instance, were once regarded as social rights but are increasingly seen as rewards for performance.

Psychologists, however, point to the 'hidden costs of rewards'. Essentially, they question whether short-term incentives can ever buy sustained changes in behaviour. They claim that, although an incentive will usually increase people's motivation while it is being offered, once it is withdrawn their motivation may be lower than it was before.

The effect was first pointed out in 1970 when the British social policy expert Richard Titmuss claimed in his book *The Gift Relationship* that paying blood donors would reduce their willingness to donate blood, an effect which actually seems to exist.[80]

In a classic psychological experiment, college students were either paid or not paid to work on an interesting puzzle.[81] When the experiment was over, the students were left in the same room and observed: those who had not been paid played with the puzzle much more than the paid subjects, and reported greater interest in doing so.

Real-world experiments have corroborated this effect. For example, incentives reduced the motivation of elderly people in a nursing home. In return for doing domestic tasks, like making their beds, they were given vouchers. After some time it was found that they were unwilling to do anything at all without getting vouchers. Their internal motivation had declined.[82]

In 1992 a Dutch researcher, Uco Wiersma, carried out a meta-analysis of 20 previous experiments by different researchers. He was forced to agree that external incentives do increase motivation, but only while the incentives last. When the incentives were removed, the motivation to act was less than it was before the incentives were given.[83]

A decade later, three psychologists at the University of Alberta had another look at the research.[84] Their formulation shows how subtle the relationship between rewards and motivation can be. They concluded that rewards can increase motivation when the task is boring. But when the task is interesting, rewards can reduce motivation – but only if the rewards are expected and not tied to performance. When tied to levels of performance, rewards can increase motivation or at least not diminish it. An exception is praise, which reliably increases motivation for all kinds of tasks.

Why should incentives damage motivation? At least part of the explanation is our old friend resistance. Obviously, incentives are used by authorities to manipulate individual choices. If people realise this, they'll be motivated to assert their freedom by rejecting the new behaviour. Here's an illustration:

In 1993 the Swiss government chose two adjacent communities to be potential sites for a repository for mid- to low-level nuclear wastes. A sample of 305 residents was surveyed to determine attitudes to the repository. Half the residents (50.8 per cent) supported the plant even though it was viewed as a heavy burden on their community (thus reminding us of the exceptional civic virtue of the Swiss), even though nearly 40 per cent thought the risk of serious accidents and groundwater contamination was considerable. In fact, 34 per cent thought that some local residents would die as a result of any contamination!

The residents were then told that the Swiss parliament had decided to compensate the host community with amounts ranging from £1,300 to £4,000 per household. In response to this information, the level of acceptance dropped by half, to 24.6 per cent.[85] Similar results were found when tax rebates were offered to neighbours of proposed nuclear repositories in Nevada, Washington State and Wisconsin.

That's the danger with incentives. They can easily say to people, "We don't trust you to do the right thing, we assume you have no inner motivation to act responsibly, so we'll buy your compliance." To maintain their self-respect and assert their autonomy, people are liable to respond by either doing more of the wrong thing or taking the money but thinking worse about the behaviour so that when the incentive stops they are less likely to do it than before the incentive was offered.

How can we avoid being seen as controlling? The trick is to ensure that receiving the incentive doesn't crowd out people's inner motivations.

Firstly, we can make the incentive small or tokenistic, so it's not really an incentive at all, but rather a form of praise that recognises inner motivation.

Secondly, we can require the recipient to provide matching funds. This is common in incentives for environmental restoration, for instance, where farmers might be given just 50 per cent of the funds required to, say, restore a stream.

Thirdly, an interesting recent innovation is to put incentive payments out to tender. This requires potential recipients to compete with each other to get them.

Fourthly, the incentive could recognise a high level of performance, rather than mere participation.

In 2003, Danish marketing academic John Thøgersen posed a novel explanation for the paradoxical effects of incentive programmes. Investigating pay-by-weight garbage services in the Netherlands, he was surprised that the financial incentive seemed to increase people's inner motivation to recycle and compost their waste, rather than decrease it. How could this be reconciled with past research? Thøgersen's thinking is interesting. What matters, he concluded, is not the incentive itself, but how it is understood by the people it's targeted at. If it is seen as controlling, it will reduce motivation, but if it is seen as enabling, it's likely to increase motivation.[86]

Thøgersen's idea is that the *story* an incentive tells is more important than the incentive itself. An incentive may say many things. It may say "we don't trust you or respect your motivations". Or it may say "your action is highly valued by society", "we recognise your superlative efforts and skills", or "we believe in your dream" – such stories are liable to bolster, rather than diminish, inner motivation.

The implication is that there's probably no universal rule for deciding whether a particular incentive is a good idea or a bad idea. Instead, we may have to look at how people interpret the incentive in each situation. What do they think it's saying about the agency's attitude to them? Every situation needs to be tested on its merits, and only knowing the effect on real-life recipients (for instance, through interviews or focus groups) could help us decide what is best in each case.

Conclusion

Early in this book we saw the awesome power of the social immune system. People feel safe in their comfort zones, and the harder we try to drag them out, the more determined will be their denial and resistance. A better way to think of a change maker's job, therefore, is as an expander, not an attacker, of comfort zones. We just looked at nine persuasive techniques that can help do that job.

Persuasive techniques are, essentially, psychological tricks or manipulations that make it easier for people to act by lowering the perceived risks of acting.

But beware persuasion's siren song. Persuasion is seductive for change makers because it seems to promise easy wins at low cost. But persuasion alone is unlikely to cause sustained changes in people's behaviour. That depends on other factors we've already discussed, especially the stickiness of the solution and whether the actors' surrounding environment supports the change.

That doesn't mean that persuasion is dispensable. Persuasion is essential for any kind of change effort because human beings still need to be started on the journey of change. Persuasive techniques are perfect for stimulating simple, one-off, low-commitment actions, like coming to a meeting, signing up, donating money, or trying a new behaviour, that start them on that journey.

Making a theory of action

This method is simple. It's a repeat of the Rapid Theory Generator from earlier (p.140), except this time you place in the centre a specific, measurable action from a specific person, group or organisation and ask: "What would it take for these actor(s) to act?" The aim is to identify concrete ways to lower those actors' perceived risks of action.

Rapid theory generator

Instructions:
1. Bring together your diverse brains trust and make sure it includes some of your target actors. For example, if the action is 'shopkeepers reduce litter', then you'll need to add some supportive shopkeepers to your brains trust. This is a time when it's especially useful to have creative outsiders present, so if you haven't already got an artist, a street performer, a musical director or a poet, now is the time to add them.

2. Inform and inspire them with your research results, especially with examples of what has worked in other places. And don't be afraid to add some left-field solutions or tactics (for instance, check out 'The Fun Theory'* or the work of an innovative community artist like Candy Chang†).

3. Start with a specific, measurable action from a specific person, group or organisation and brainstorm the question: "What would it take for these

---

* http://thefuntheory.com † http://candychang.com

actor(s) to act?" Make sure you focus on concrete initiatives and activities, not vague aims like 'better education' or 'changed attitudes'.

4. Weighting:

In silence, each person distributes ten dots (as in the example below) between the items they think would have the biggest influence on those actors acting (and are realistically achievable). *Weighting time = 5 minutes*

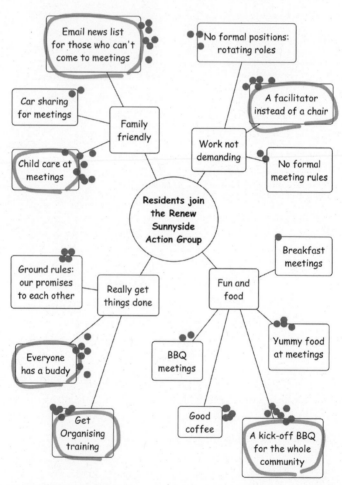

It's OK to start with vague propositions like 'fun and food' or 'really get things done' so long as you keep going until you identify concrete activities you can really imagine occurring.

5. Add up the dots. The 3-6 items with the most dots become your theory of action (those are the ones circled in the example).

6. Record the details on the table below.

ENABLING FACTORS	INDICATOR(S)	DATA SOURCE	TARGET
A kick-off BBQ for the whole community	Number of guests	Head count	200
Child care for meetings	Is the child care adequate?	Feedback from parents	100%
Everyone has a buddy	Happy with the buddy system?	Survey of members	100%
Email news list	Number who participate	Survey of members	40%
A facilitator instead of a chair	How's the facilitator working out?	Survey of members	Great!
Get training in Community Organising	Have we been trained in how to organise?	Yes/No	Yes
	Did it make a difference?	Feedback form	80% benefited

Record the results in a table like this so you can check on progress. Of course, you'll also need a jobs list and a timetable to make sure these things really happen.

Now you have a theory of action

In this example, the theory is:

> **IF** there's a kick-off BBQ for the whole community (with at least 200 guests)
> **AND IF** there's child care at every meeting
> **AND IF** everyone has a buddy
> **AND IF** there's a good email news list
> **AND IF** we have a facilitator instead of a chair

AND IF we get trained in how to organise
THEN there will be at least 30 active members of the Renew Sunnyside
Action Group, and at least 500 signed-up members.
AND THAT'S OUR THEORY OF ACTION!

Some good things about this theory: the potential members created it themselves; it focuses on social pleasures as well as practical action; it learnt
from the mistakes of other groups and abandoned the boring bits that wear
people out.

Ingredient 6

Find the right inviter
Some people we just can't say "no" to

You'll probably hate me for this, but don't buy this book. Instead, go and buy the DVD of *Jamie's School Dinners*. I got mine through Amazon.uk for just £9.97 plus delivery. It's a complete course in being a change maker.

It tells the story of Jamie Oliver's struggle to transform the lunchtime eating habits of 20,000 or so London school kids. I'm not going to tell you the story. Go and watch it yourself. But I do want to celebrate one of the personal qualities he displayed.

The power of passion

As you'll see, Jamie was not objective. He was genuinely affronted at the 'cheap shit' and 'scrotum burgers' that were served as lunchtime meals in English schools. "It's not right," he said. "I wouldn't feed it to my dog." He was so bollocking mad that the DVD comes with a 'swearing deleted soundtrack'. He was practically speechless that primary school kids couldn't name rhubarb, leek or asparagus. "I don't believe it," he said, "I think I'm gonna pass out."

His worst fury was reserved for Turkey Twizzlers, a concoction of turkey parts, fat and salt that was served by a private company contracted to provide the meals in one of Britain's poorest counties. "Fucking Turkey Twizzlers. I tell you what, I'm gonna fuckin' send a bomb around to their factory and shove it right up the arse of their MD. And if you're watching Mr Turkey Twizzlers can you just do me a favour and just . . . phew!"

Jamie's anger gave him the gift of perseverance. He collided painfully with one obstacle after another, but never gave in. Instead, he dusted himself off and tried another angle. When the kids hated his food, he left the school kitchen and entered the classroom. When that didn't work, he went into family homes and worked with parents. When his cooking lessons didn't change kids' attitudes, he tried bargaining: "Throw your packed lunch in the bin if you want to stay in my class." When he noticed the kids who left his class resented being left out, he used the fear of exclusion to get them involved. He manoeuvred his way into this horrendously complex social problem by trying hunches and observing the results. Like a scientist, he proceeded by hypothesis and experiment.

Jamie's case illustrates how passion is often associated with that other quality so often found in successful change makers – naivety. Jamie didn't know he was supposed to fail. He didn't know that one person was not supposed to change the eating habits of a school, let alone a whole borough with 20,000 kids. Thousands of intelligent adults were sitting back helplessly watching a public health catastrophe play out. Why? Because they had the curse of knowledge. But Jamie knew nothing about the school system or the vast weight of institutional habit that contrived to maintain the problem. His ignorance blessed him with optimism.

Passion like this isn't associated with good looks, education, IQ or family money. Anyone can have it. And in case you're thinking Jamie did well because he's a celebrity, let me tell you I've seen plenty of successful change makers who were not famous or fabulously gifted. But they were passionate. They had a dream, lived it in their lives and didn't give up.

Despite innumerable setbacks, Jamie eventually achieved success beyond his wildest dreams. His TV show made unhealthy school lunches an issue in the 2005 UK general election. The government of Tony Blair was shamed into spending millions to raise food standards, including extra funds to renovate school kitchens and retrain school cooks. School inspectors were directed to add the quality of school lunches to their inspections, and a School Food Trust was established to lift nutritional standards.[1]

You'll recall in our earlier discussion about 'buzz' how change so often travels along social networks on a wave of conversation. It travels from believers who are living the dream to those who have not yet, for whatever reason, adopted a change in their lives. Let's call the first group 'inviters' to recognise their role as catalysts who invite change in others. And let's call the others 'actors' to recognise the fact that, provided all the pieces come together, they are the ones who will act in future.

What does it take to be an influential inviter? Can anyone be an inviter? Can the government be an inviter? Could you be an inviter?

Inevitably, good inviters are passionate believers who are living a change in their own lives. Their passion gives them the optimism and perseverance to continue talking about change in a cynical, resistant world. And their contagious optimism helps others believe in their own ability to change. They walk the talk and talk the walk. When Gandhi famously said, "Be the change you wish to see in the world", he was describing the perfect change maker.

But passion alone is not enough to qualify someone to invite change in others. The best inviters embody certain other qualities too: respect, connection, similarity, powerlessness, and belief in people.

Be respected

In February 2007 British billionaire Sir Richard Branson, the ubiquitous head of Virgin Everything, and Al Gore, formerly the next president of the United States, got together to launch Branson's US$25 million (£12.5 million) Virgin Earth Challenge, a prize for designing a commercially viable method to remove greenhouse gases from the atmosphere. That $25 million was just a down payment on the roughly US$3 billion (£1.5 billion) that Branson has pledged to spend on reversing global warming.

What led Branson to make these extraordinary pledges? According to the American Broadcasting Corporation news story:

> Former Vice-President Al Gore convinced him over breakfast one morning.
>
> Branson, in fact, admits to being skeptical about global warming in the past. "I was skeptical, but I've met a lot of scientists. I've read a lot of books. I've had Al Gore spend two hours at my home giving me his personal time to convince me, and sadly, I'm now convinced that the world has a serious problem," Branson said today on *Good Morning America*.

Gore, who appeared on the show with Branson, said he didn't have to strong-arm or lay a guilt trip on the transportation and music mogul.

"We just talked about the facts of the situation," Gore said. "You know, all of us have problems absorbing the reality of what we're facing with this. It's really a planetary emergency."[2]

Facts did not convince Richard Branson. Scientists did not convince Richard Branson. What convinced Richard Branson was two hours with Al Gore, perhaps one of the few people on the planet he was helplessly impelled to respect. What's more, if the article is true, Al Gore didn't even have to ask.

I like to think that everyone has someone they can't say "no" to on a given question. One of the qualities of these people is that we respect them, and one of the unconscious rules of thumb we use to decide whether we respect them is whether that person has social status in our eyes. "Those who have high status, competence and [social] power" make the most influential role models, wrote social psychologist Albert Bandura.[3]

His early experiments showed that children were more likely to imitate a model whose behaviour they saw being rewarded,[4] who was the same age or slightly older[5] or whom they liked or admired.

A classic experiment on respect involved pedestrians obeying or disobeying automatic lights at a pedestrian crossing.[6] The experimenters used a 31-year-old male model who was alternately dressed in high-status clothes (freshly pressed suit, polished shoes, white shirt, tie and straw hat) and low-status clothes (soiled patched trousers and an unironed denim shirt).

When the low-status model crossed against the 'wait' light only 4 per cent of other pedestrians followed him. But when the high-status model violated the signal, the number of followers leapt to 14 per cent.

It seems we look to higher-status peers to help us decide how to act and think. The more prestige or respect they seem to have, the more we instinctively follow their lead. The question for change makers is, obviously, how do you get status? The quickest, easiest way is as a gift. You can be granted status by prestigious local backers or 'gatekeepers'.

Find the gatekeeper

One of the first things I learnt as a facilitator was the importance of being granted status by someone in the group who already has it. So, when I meet a new group, I first ask to be introduced by the most respected person or authority figure in the room. Such an introduction gives me a foot in the door I can build my authority on.

Paul Castelloe and Thomas Watson from the Center for Participatory Change in North Carolina wrote a wonderful article called 'How to enter a community as an organiser'[7] where they explained the importance of gate-keepers:

> Gatekeepers are folks who are well connected in the community, who understand your work, and who are willing to support and sanction it. Such people understand the needs and opportunities of the community, and they are trusted and respected by both grass-roots leaders and formal decision-makers. It gives us so much cred-ibility when I say, 'Yeah, we're new to working in this county, but we've been working for a while with Robin Mauney over at REACH, and she's on our board and she's been helping us. And Lisa Twiggs over at the Family Resource Center, she helped us put this thing together too.' That just gives people an automatic sense of ease, because Robin and Lisa have lots of connections and are trusted in the community.

The power of respect suggests an interesting strategy for social change. It's a little bit like the 'Six Degrees of Kevin Bacon' game. Say you wanted to change the mind of the President, Governor or Prime Minister. You wouldn't lobby them directly. Instead, you'd locate someone they respected. Then you'd do some more research and find out who that person respected. And so on, until, finally, you worked your way down to someone who respected you. Then you'd ask *that* person to lobby their friend to lobby their friend, and so on, all the way up to the President/CEO or whoever. I suspect this is how the political influence game really works. Everyone has someone they just can't say "no" to. The art of influence is to figure out who those respected people are and work with them.

And if you think it's a little cheap to use the same methods as Tupperware, I ask you to consider the awesome power of the Tupperware Party model. The hostess is always someone you know and respect. So, despite your better judgement, you can't say "no" to their invitation, and you go along to the party. You know you can buy exactly the same plastic containers for half the price in the supermarket, but you also know that, despite your better judgement, you'll need to buy at least one item to avoid offending the hostess. You arrive, the hostess introduces the Tupperware demonstrator who then inherits her social status, becoming someone else you also can't say "no" to. The hostess makes the first purchase, setting the social norm for the evening. Basking in the reflected status of the hostess, the demonstrator invites you to buy a completely useless party dip ensemble. You summon up the will to say "no" but instantly feel so bad that you say "yes" to the next offer. The psychology behind this model is potent, and respect is the key element.

Everyone has someone they can't say "no" to. It explains a lot about how changes travel through society. It also explains terrorist recruitment. What could cause well-educated, apparently hopeful young architects, doctors, engineers and family men to become suicide bombers? The answer might be horrifyingly simple: someone they respected asked them.

Be connected

Todd, a 53-year-old man, was sitting quietly playing a poker machine in his local bar on a Saturday night when a drunken 27-year-old Aboriginal man named Peter walked up to him and said "Buy me a beer or I'll punch you in the face." Todd told the stranger to leave him alone and the young man punched him in the face. Bar staff quickly came to Todd's rescue. Peter was later arrested and charged with assault and malicious damage.

Peter had 58 previous convictions, 32 for violence, 27 of which involved prison sentences. At the time of the assault, he was on periodic detention for assault, malicious damage and breach of bail.

If the law was supposed to change Peter's behaviour, then there was a problem with its theory of change. A different approach was required. His case became the first test of 'circle sentencing' in New South Wales.

Circle sentencing originated in Canada in 1992 for the sentencing of indigenous law-breakers and later spread to the United States and Australia. The model is a novel departure from conventional criminal proceedings. Instead of sitting in remote majesty at the head of a court, the magistrate is simply the facilitator of a discussion circle that includes respected community elders, social workers, the prosecutor, the victim, the offender's supporters and the offender. All have the right to be heard and speak their minds. The sentence is agreed through open discussion, and (provided it fits the state's sentencing guidelines) the magistrate confirms it.

In Peter's case the transcript began with the prosecutor asking him why he committed the crime. "I don't know" was his reply. Discussion moved on to the effect alcohol had on Peter. He admitted he had a drinking problem, "I need help, I blame myself," he said. "I'm doing weekends but that still gives me five days to get on the grog. I need to get off the grog."

The elders had known this man all his life so they also knew about his hopes and fears. One said "Do you want the little fellows coming to the jail to visit you, is that what you want, you want them to follow in your footsteps?" Said another "You should be looking after your Nan [grandmother]. What if she dies while you're in jail? You should be alongside her, she needs you now."

One of the qualities of a circle court is that it empowers elders to act like elders. They often make spontaneous offers of support, employment and supervision beyond their formal role in the court. "I'll help you but you'll have to spend time with me," said one in this case.

Together, the circle agreed on three months home detention and nine months good behaviour bond under the supervision of an elder. Before they parted, Peter apologised to the victim.

Six months later the magistrate received a report on Peter's progress. He had started a three-day-a-week job. He had been surprisingly successful at making and selling artwork and had spent the profits to pay off much of his fines and buy furniture for the home he planned to set up with his de facto wife. He hadn't taken alcohol or drugs since the circle court. He'd provided constant care for his grandmother, given counselling to teenagers, and presented talks at community justice seminars. The report said: "The progress [the offender] has made in the past five months is more than he has in the whole of his life. His confidence has improved . . . His artwork has great potential . . . He maintains that the circle sentencing has helped him get his life into perspective and is looking forward to a life without crime . . ."[8]

Peter's is not the only circle-sentencing success story. The process has a powerful effect on the behaviour of offenders, on recidivism rates, and on the happiness of victims. But why?

One reason seems to be the freedom to speak and the dignity given to all, including the victims, who aren't allowed to speak openly in a conventional court. Combined with a caring and supportive environment, this freedom and equality help transform the event from punishment to healing. It's called 'restorative justice' for that reason.

Another reason is its emotional intensity. Offenders report being unprepared for the cathartic emotions that come when they meet those they harmed in the presence of the important people in their lives.

Criminologist John Braithwaite suggests restorative justice works because it uses shame and guilt to reconnect people with their positive hopes for themselves, as well as rebuilding important social ties.[9]

Others researchers have written "By seeing that they are respected and loved by people whom they in turn respect and love, and who condemn their bad behavior but do not view them as a bad person . . . Both their desire to maintain those links and to maintain a favourable sense of self motivate offenders not to reoffend."[10]

The success of circle sentencing suggests that those who are *connected* to us have the power to influence us in ways that strangers cannot.

If you want to be a successful inviter, it will therefore help immensely if you're part of the same circle as those you intend to invite. If you're not part of the circle, then you should aim to find someone who is.

Of course, we don't usually have a bunch of well-connected elders handy. So the question is: Can we create a sense of connection where none exists now? The key might be to bring into existence an ongoing relationship. For example, Water Efficient Durham employed university students to repeatedly visit the same 300 homes to talk about water-saving techniques.[11] That might do the trick. TravelSmart and its offspring, WaterSmart and LivingSmart[12] seem to achieve this with a kind of case-manager approach, where the same telephone operator stays in contact with each particular household. That way the householders get used to hearing a familiar voice and expect they'll hear it again.

But an even better approach is to create a community. Parents' groups, bush regeneration groups, sustainability action groups, community leadership programmes, and so on, all act like social networks where subtle invitations are continually being issued by those who are living their dreams to those who aren't.

Be similar

We are easily influenced by people who are similar to ourselves.

An early social psychology experiment divided boy scouts into two groups. Both groups were shown the same film of a 12-year-old boy playing a war strategy board game.

One group was told the boy was "a boy scout just like you are. He enjoys camping and hiking. He lives here in Twin Cities and goes to the same kind of school as you." That boy was wearing a boy scout uniform.

The second group was told: "This boy doesn't live in Minnesota. He doesn't go to the same school as you. He doesn't like to do the things you do in boy scouts, like hiking and camping. I guess that's why he never joined boy scouts." That boy was dressed in street clothes.

After watching the film, each child was left alone with the board game. All the boys played the game, but the ones who had been told the boy was a boy scout imitated the model's strategies 40 per cent more accurately.[13]

Another experiment involved primary-school children who were poor at maths. Over two days the children watched four videos showing another child successfully solving maths problems. Some of the videos showed similar students solving the problems and others showed a teacher solving the same problems.

When later tested, the students who observed the teacher got 62 per cent more correct answers than the control group, but those who watched similar students beat the control group by 130 per cent.[14]

The consensus amongst psychologists is that role models are most effective if they are a similar age, gender and background to the people they want to influence.[15] So, for instance, if you want to send an anti-drinking message to young men, male role models will be more effective than female role models.[16] The effect can hold true even if the models are similar-looking paid actors, rather than real members of the peer group.[17]

It doesn't even matter whether the similarities are trivial or irrelevant. One experiment showed that people were more likely to comply with a request even if the only thing they had in common with the inviter was the same name, the same birthday, or similar fingerprints![18]

But if the role model is *dissimilar*, the invitation can boomerang. Another experiment showed that seeing similar people enjoy music made subjects like the music more, but seeing *dissimilar* people enjoy the same music made them dislike it![19]

The choice of role models can therefore make or break a change effort. An example of what can go wrong was a £2.4 million anti-smoking ad campaign depicting hip teenage role models aired on MTV Europe in 2001. The evaluators found that teenage viewers were more, rather than less, interested in smoking after watching the ads. They concluded that the campaign flopped for three reasons. First, teenage viewers thought the message was unrealistic and lacking in credibility. Second, the style and execution jarred with their lifestyles. Third, they strongly disliked the central characters in the ads, seeing them as 'too perfect' and 'snobby'.[20]

Jamie Oliver, despite his passion and perseverance eventually realised he was not the best inviter for the school dinner ladies. His celebrity status got his foot in the door but it didn't bring the grassroots credibility he needed to invite dinner ladies out of their comfort zones. Instead, he faced repeated demoralising setbacks.

So what did he do? Finally, in a climactic moment in the series, he found the right person to do the inviting: Nora, the redoubtable head dinner lady. Her request, which I'll reveal at the end of this chapter, was a masterpiece of persuasive invitation.

Be powerless

We've already talked plenty about the dangers of resistance. Resistance happens whenever people think they're being manipulated or pressured.

Resistance is very likely whenever an inviter is perceived to have power, control or authority over an actor. Even when there is no intention to exercise control, the mere existence of unequal power can cause the perception of pressure. The credibility of messages from state agencies and councils, for example, can be undermined by the unstated threat of criminal sanction.

The best way to avoid resistance is to be a neutral, independent person with no vested interest in the outcome - an ordinary Jane or Jamal. Even then, it's easy to use language which unintentionally creates the impression that you're pressuring people to change.

There are a few ways to avoid pressuring language. One is to simply state neutral facts, like this advert in a Toronto lavatory that aimed to get people washing their hands after using the toilet. All it said was:

"Caution. 92 per cent of guys say they washed. 34 per cent were lying."

A second way is to talk about what you are doing, not what they *should* do. This inspires and challenges people with your own commitment but avoids telling them they are wrong.

"Next Saturday I'll vote Green in the Senate." – Murray Black, The Greens
"I'd rather go naked than wear fur." – Joanna Krupa, PETA

A third way is to argue against your own self-interest. This was neatly demonstrated in an early social psychology experiment where subjects were asked to decide between the credibility of two arguments for courts to have more power to convict criminals. In one case the source was Joe 'The Shoulder' Napolitano "serving the third year of his twenty-one-year sentence for smuggling and peddling dope". The other was G. William Stephens, New York prosecutor.[21] The subjects decided that Joe the Shoulder's argument was more credible because he was arguing against his own interest.

If you can't argue against your own interest then you can at least give reasonable weight to the other point of view. There's good evidence that such two-sided arguments have more credibility than one-sided arguments.[22]

Here's how a two-sided anti-tobacco ad might read:

"I love nicotine. It keeps me alert and in control. But I also hate the way it controls me. Giving up was the hardest thing I ever did. And the best."

Two-sided arguments work for two reasons. They make the speaker seem less biased and so more trustworthy. And they turn off the counter-arguing voice in people's heads. Since the counter-argument is being voiced by someone else, the listener is saved the trouble of voicing it herself, neutralising the negative self-talk that's the mechanism for denial.

To summarise, a good inviter is someone who has no power over the actor and who carefully avoids telling them how to live their lives.

Believe in people

Carl Rogers was one of the first psychotherapists to experimentally investigate the effects of personal counselling. In 1956 he wrote an extraordinary paper in which he proposed that just three factors predicted the success of a counselling relationship.[23]

The first factor was whether the therapist was genuinely *himself*. Whether he or she was comfortable in their own skin, natural and not putting on a contrived performance or façade.

The second factor was whether the therapist had empathy for the patient. That is, whether he or she genuinely understood and sympathised with the patient's feelings. For Rogers, accurate empathy meant skilful reflective listening that clarified a person's own experiences and values, without imposing the counsellor's preconceived views. "It is the client who knows what hurts, what directions to go, what problems are crucial, what experiences have been deeply buried."[24]

Recent studies confirm that empathy is vital for successful counselling. In a University of New Mexico study involving alcoholics, psychologists William Miller and Stephen Rollnick found that two-thirds of the change in drinking behaviour after six months could be predicted from the empathy shown by counsellors during treatment. "Those treated by low empathy counsellors", they wrote, "were less likely to improve than if they had been sent home with a good book."[25]

The third factor was whether the therapist had "unconditional positive regard" for the patient. By this, Rogers meant a warm, uncritical acceptance of every aspect of the patient's personality.

Carl Rogers wrote:

When someone expresses some feeling or attitude, our tendency is, almost immediately, to feel 'That's right'; or 'That's stupid'; 'That's abnormal'; 'That's unreasonable'; 'That's incorrect'; 'That's not nice'. Very rarely do we permit ourselves to understand precisely what the meaning of his statement is to him.[26]

It's fascinating to think that the factors that predict whether a client will recover – being oneself, empathy and positive regard – belong to the counsellor, not the client. "People who believe that they are likely to change do so. People whose counsellors believe they are likely to change do so. People who are told they are not expected to improve do not," wrote Miller and Rollnick.[27]

Paul Castelloe and Thomas Watson from the Center for Participatory Change called for a similar state of mind in community organisers:

> Start with a rock-solid belief in everyday people. Your entrance into a community should be upon a core belief that everyday people can come together to create positive change in their community . . . It's important who makes the change in a community. Is it us, as outsiders, or the people themselves? I believe that it has to be the people. So often people have no one who believes in them. And if I can be that one person to believe in somebody, it will help them believe in themselves. Because if they don't believe in themselves, change will not happen.
>
> Also, I have to believe that change can happen. I have to believe that the people can make change. I have to be real clear, and say, "I believe that your ideas can happen. I believe that we can do it." I try to give examples where other people have created similar change. These conversations are the beginning of the seeds that will grow into future community action.[28]

If we are optimistic and believe in people, those beliefs are likely to be contagious. When teachers believe in students those students believe in themselves and do better. When business leaders believe in their teams they do better. When parents believe in their children they do better.

On the other hand, if we are doubtful, cynical and negative then those beliefs are likely to infect our listeners too.

The art of invitation

Here, then, is the model for good inviters:

- They are passionate believers.
- They are similar, respected and connected.
- They are powerless to enforce their requests.
- They believe in the people they hope to influence.
- And, of course, they are dynamic: they *ask* the actors to take that first decisive step to a better future.

When Jamie Oliver met the managing director of Scholarest, the company that supplied Turkey Twizzlers, he ignored the MD's pathetic excuses. Instead, he established who he was, which was not Jamie the celebrity chef but Jamie the guy who just proved he could get a whole school eating healthy meals, on budget. Then he offered an inspiring vision to the MD: "Be the first and ban these reconstituted products." And he made a simple, unambiguous request: "Will you ban Turkey Twizzlers?"[29]

In PR-speak it's called a 'call to action'. Strangely, it seems to be one of the hardest lessons for change makers to learn. Here's a typical invitation scenario created by my students:

Bob Holland, a seasoned oyster farmer, eloquently recounts the tragic tale of how pollution destroyed his oyster farm on Wallace Lakes, and, with a tear in his eye and a choke of emotion, exhorts the meeting of Clyde River oyster farmers to go for "green certification" and "not let the same thing happen here".

Then the project officer takes to the floor, outlines the benefits of certification, thanks everyone for coming, looks a little confused, and sits down.

I'm sitting at the back of the room, thinking "Come on, come on . . . make the call! Ask for action!"

You've got people's attention. They've been touched by hope. They believe the action is do-able and can make a difference. Now they need to know *precisely* what they have to do to get started. So spell it out big and simple: "Sign the expression of interest form and hand it in before you leave." It's the punchline to your invitation: *the simple, precise, first step on the path to a different future.* Spell it out. Make your request. And sit down.

An inviter needs to be dynamic. Their job is to *invite*. So do it. Then be silent and watch what happens.

The virtual invitation

Intriguingly, not all invitations need be verbal or even involve interaction. There can be silent invitations which take place entirely in the actors' imaginations.

One of my students told me this story: She lived on a large block of land which was heavily infested with weeds. She was a council environmental officer and she knew some of those weeds were classed as noxious which meant she could have fined herself for not eradicating them. She knew she had a problem but denied it until a new neighbour moved in. After a few days she heard on the grapevine that the new neighbour was a farmer. That was all it took. Shame, and her imagination, did the rest. She threw herself into spraying and digging until her block no longer looked like a threat to the farming community. She and her neighbour never spoke a word about those weeds. Her change was triggered by a person-to-person interaction but it was one that occurred entirely in her imagination.

This kind of invitation works through expectation. All it requires is that the actor expects that a conversation is imminent and that it could be the kind of conversation that challenges their virtuous view of themselves.

You could use this trick in lots of situations. For instance, here's a way to get doctors and nurses washing their hands more frequently in hospitals (it's one of the biggest infection-control issues facing the health system). All you'd do is put up signs that inform patients they can expect to see doctors and nurses washing their hands with anti-bacterial fluid before touching them. The doctors and nurses would then expect an imminent, challenging conversation with any patient who didn't observe them washing their hands. Those difficult conversations never need occur. The expectation would be enough.

Can governments and corporations be good inviters?

That's an interesting question, and an important one, because so many change efforts are sponsored by government agencies.

There's been a fair amount of research into what makes a corporation or

CHANGEOLOGY

government agency able to influence public opinion.

The key is credibility.

Research by risk communication guru Vincent Covello concluded that the public judges the credibility of government agencies according to four tests:

- Are they empathic or caring? (50 per cent of the judgement)
- Are they competent? (15-20 per cent of the judgement)
- Are they honest and open? (15-20 per cent of the judgement)
- Are they committed and dedicated? (15-20 per cent of the judgement)[30]

Another study found that credible agencies should exhibit competence and expertise, dynamism, lack of bias, fairness, concern for the community's well-being, honesty and openness, and consistency and predictability.[31]

Does your organisation meet these standards in the eyes of its public? Let's be honest. Probably it doesn't. In an age where the media feed every kind of cynicism about institutions it's unlikely that yours has the credibility to invite people on the seemingly risky journey of change.

That's why, if you're in government, it can be a good idea to run joint programmes with respected grassroots community organisations or to invite independent similar-respected-connected spokespeople to endorse your efforts.

What makes a persuasive invitation?

David Suzuki, the great Canadian environmental advocate, recently came to my town and the council organised a public meeting so we could hear his views.

Suzuki is one of the most charismatic public speakers of our time, yet his message was quite gloomy. He berated politicians for sitting on their hands while the world's ecosystems collapsed. I enjoyed his zestful assault on American and Australian politicians. Yet I walked away feeling hollow and somewhat deflated.

There was only one moment that captured my heart and made me buzz with my friends afterwards. At the start of the evening our crusty old Lord Mayor, a local businessman with no renown as an environmentalist, introduced the speakers. Drought is a big issue in our part of the world and it's certainly been worsened by global warming. Therefore water-saving was a hot topic. In the middle of his short speech, the Lord Mayor said "I've got a bucket in my shower. How many of you have a bucket in your shower?" Then he waited, staring around the room as a scattering of hands rose. Then he invited us all to do more to save water. It was humble, simple, and surprisingly arresting.

What made these few words stand out compared with the brilliant pyrotechnics of one of the world's great orators?

The Lord Mayor's words were a nice example of a persuasive invitation. Let's look at the ingredients.

For a start, he was talking about what I was already talking about with my friends and family: drought and water. He connected to the buzz.

Then he caught us off guard. No one expected our Lord Mayor to be personally committed to saving water. His words were stereotype-busting. And they highlighted my own discrepancy: if he was bending over backwards to save every drop of water, why wasn't I?

Those of you who are very astute will have noticed that the Mayor's invitation was a surprising+emotional story. That's right, a persuasive invitation shares the same contents as a contagious story. That's why it got me talking to my friends afterwards.

Then, he proposed a simple action to address my personal discrepancy: use a bucket to collect shower water. He asked me to act.

He got the formula for a persuasive invitation just right. It's an unexpected, emotionally arousing story that reminds the listener of a frustrating discrepancy, offers a credible solution, and asks for the first step along the path.

Our Lord Mayor also added a brilliant optional extra to his invitation. He asked for a show of hands.

Requesting a physical response is a great way to engage people. It forces them to take a position. What's more, they know they are being seen to do so by their peers. As we saw in the previous chapter, visible demonstrations of commitment can be potent methods of influencing people's behaviour.

But he also made a mistake. He asked "Who uses a bucket in the shower?" – which, unfortunately, is an uncommon practice. Even with a green-minded audience he must have known that only a minority of people would raise their hands. He had evoked the wrong kind of social proof. The trick when requesting a sign is to choose a question that a lot of people will respond "yes" to. It would have been better to say, "How many of you saved water this week?" The resounding show of hands would have primed people nicely for his subsequent request to put a bucket in the shower.

Here's a perfect example of a well-crafted invitation. It's dinner lady Nora's invitation from *Jamie's School Dinners* DVD. Jamie wanted to invite scores of school dinner ladies to a special training weekend, so he asked them to a restaurant and invited Nora to address them. Here's what she said. It's a masterpiece of Persuasive Invitation.

> I'm not going to say nothin'. Just ask me questions . . . How horrible it was? It was terrible (chuckles). Everyone moaning. The staff in the kitchen moaning. Teachers moaning. But when you see them eating it, it's just marvellous. I mean, I'm old. I thought I'd give them burgers and chips until I retire, you know. But it's actually put a spurt back into me.

It's got all the ingredients. Passion and optimism. Counter-argument to undercut the audience's doubts. An emotionally touching story. A reminder of frustrated personal hopes. A solution that answers those frustrations. And it was followed by a simple call to action (sign up for the training) that kick-started the audience on their path to a different future.

And here's what she didn't do. She didn't pressure her audience. She didn't argue with them. She didn't whack them with guilt. She didn't talk about childhood obesity, corporate badness or the ruinous impact of junk food on kids' health. Instead, she inspired them with a hopeful personal vision that every one of them could relate to and then issued a specific call to action.

Can you be an inviter?

No one can be a universal inviter, just like no one can be a universal lover. You can love some of the people some of the time, but not all of the people all of the time. Whether you are a good inviter depends on qualities that are hard to fake. It's about who you are and the nature of your connection with those people.

So could you be an inviter? The answer is: with some people yes; with others no. It's important to be realistic about this. You need to think about who you are to those actors. If they see you as passionate, caring, similar, respected, connected and powerless over them, then the answer is yes. If not, then your best role is not to be an inviter yourself, but to be an introduction agency, bringing the right inviters together with the right actors.

Some colleagues in a government agency recently told me about a meeting they organised to tell dairy farmers about the advantages of protecting native vegetation. Instead of fronting the meeting themselves, they drove a grizzled, red-faced, 60-something dairy farmer up from Victoria. His clothes were rumpled. He had no presentation skills. His speech was halting. Yet he had the rapt attention of the other farmers because they knew who he was and what he had achieved on his land. He was the right inviter.

Method

Creating an invitation

Next time you're inviting someone to act, start by finding the right inviter. Ideally, he or she will be:

- Passionately living the dream
- Similar to the actors
- Respected by the actors
- Connected to the actors
- Powerless to enforce their invitation
- A believer in the actors' ability to make a difference.

Of course, it might be impossible to find someone who exactly meets those requirements, but the closer they are, the more influential will be their invitation.

Ten elements that make a great invitation

Every invitation is different, and it's always dangerous to rely on a formula. Still, it's good to have a starting point, so here's a formula you might find useful!

1. Grab their attention.
Written invitations: break their stereotypes about what to expect.
Face-to-face invitations: use some engaging questions, for example

Who's ever waited 5 minutes to cross Forest Parade?
Who wishes it felt safer to walk our streets at night?
Who wishes there wasn't a riot down at the Broken Arms every second Friday
night?

2. Introduce a credible inviter.

Passionate, similar, connected, respected, powerless, a believer.

I'd like to introduce someone many of you know: Bob Buchhorn, aged 87,
chair of the Sunnyside Creekcare Society.

3. Hook their motivations with a surprising+emotional personal story.

Bob Buchhorn: When I was a kid here I spent most of my time down Sun-
nyside Creek catching tadpoles and building tin canoes. Mum would send
me off on my own to the bread shop with 20 cents and never worried about
me walking home from school. There were plenty of people around in those
days to keep an eye out for each other. I'm proud to have been a member
of a group of volunteers that's made a real difference to our natural envi-
ronment and I believe we do the same thing for our streets as well. So let's
get behind this project and give our kids back a little of the safety and
neighbourliness we once enjoyed.

4. Sketch the problem.

Just a few pungent facts and statistics. Don't elaborate or you'll depress
people.

It's not a pretty story. In the last 12 months there have been 15 muggings in
this community. You can all see the vandalism and graffiti. A recent survey
showed that 87% of us are afraid to go out at night and only 12% of us can
name our neighbours.

5. Sketch your inspiring vision.

Our aim is to get back some of the good things about Sunnyside that
seniors like Bob once enjoyed. Streets that our kids are safe to walk in,

parks we can enjoy and neighbours who keep an eye out for each other. And – have some fun while we're doing it.

6. Briefly explain how your project will work, so they know you're serious. And don't forget to mention the investment you're making.

We're starting a Renew Sunnyside Action Group to work with the council, the police and others to get the traffic controls, lighting, landscaping and other changes we need to make this community safe again.

The group will have a professional facilitator and there's $5,000 seed funding for training and expenses for the first 12 months.

If the group thinks it's a good idea, one of the first projects could be a monthly community market in Sunnyside Park selling fresh food from local growers.

We'll also be carrying out a safety audit, listing black spots, making a community plan and inviting the authorities to work with us.

7. Say how you'll expand their comfort zones (lower their personal fears).
For example, a buddy, expert training, funding, just two hours a month, or friendly folks to work with.

It will be a chance to make a real difference, hang out with some friendly folks, and share some delicious food. To make it easy, there'll be a buddy system to share jobs, free child care, and an email news list for those who can't make it to every meeting.

8. Don't forget some enticing instant gratification extras. For example, freebies, food, fun.

We're kicking off the Renew Sunnyside Action Group with a community BBQ on 22 September. There'll be fantastic gourmet sausages from Sam's Butchery, sensational pies from La Petite Tarte, and awesome kids' games from Sunnyside's own Fun Collective.

9. Request a general sign of approval.

Ask for a show of hands for approval of the project's vision (this helps commit people to what you ask next). Make sure you wait for a response before continuing.

> *Who wants Sunnyside to be a wonderful community again?*

10. Lastly, make your specific call to action.

What, exactly, is the first thing you want them to do?

> *I'm circulating a form. Please put down your name and email address to receive an invitation to the Renew Sunnyside Kick-off Party.*

And then sit down and leave it to them.

Bringing it all together
The uses of theory

At the beginning of this book we heard the story of how Peter Clarke and Susan Evans changed the way America feeds its poor. (What, forgotten it already? I'll give you a few minutes to flip back and reacquaint yourself.)

Peter and Susan's story nicely illustrates each of the ingredients in this book: how change depends on a hopeful vision and positive buzz, how solutions always need reinvention, how enablement – changing the environment and reducing fears – lies at the heart of any change effort, and how change is like a dinner party: however much you want to come along, you still need an invitation.

Their story also illustrates a more subtle point: the proper uses of theory.

As my interview with Peter Clarke came to an end, he slipped me a piece of paper. I didn't pay much attention to it at the time but I now realise how important it was to him and Susan. On it, he had written:

Keys to Transplanting Orphan Innovations:
1. Adoption is local. Recognise individual needs. Go onsite.
2. Enlist all participants who must contribute.
3. Identify at least one champion.
4. Provide continuous technical assistance of proven relevance.
5. Deliver funding to seed a startup.
6. Be patient but monitor progress regularly.
7. Cede credit to others.

Peter had given me his theory of change, one that he and Susan had evolved by colliding painfully with the real world, getting knocked flat, picking themselves up and trying a new approach, again and again, over 16 years, learning and refining all the time.

Theories of change are a popular subject among change professionals nowadays, especially those in the health sector.

Many change efforts start by announcing "this project is based on the Stages of Change Model" or "this project is based on The Theory of Planned Behaviour" or on "Social Learning Theory". Peter and Sue started with a theory too: they assumed that the solution depended on education. Then they slowly learnt by trial and error that their first theory was a hopelessly simplistic "colossal mistake".

Their story demonstrates something vital about the role of theories: that the best theory is not the one we assume but the one we discover. A good way to discover it is to form a hunch and test it in the field, learning from what works and what doesn't; all the time becoming more closely acquainted with the realities of the lives of the people we hope to influence. It will always be better to imaginatively create our own theories from the unique situations we encounter than to slavishly follow one-size-fits-all models that others have followed in the past, often with little success.

Six necessary ingredients for change

Having said that, this book does propose a generic theory of change. It outlines six essential conditions for change based on what psychologists, diffusion scholars and practitioners have been telling us for decades about the design of successful change efforts.

This book suggests that, if we want to change the world, all six ingredients will need to be present. Of course, our own efforts need not be entirely responsible for all six, the efforts of other change makers may contribute as well. And some of those ingredients may already be present in a given situation so that no one has to invest time and energy in creating them. Nevertheless, one way or another, all six look like essential conditions for sustained change in a particular group or population.

Start a buzz: Change depends on conversation, or at least interaction, between people in their own social networks. That buzz often begins negatively, as bitching and blaming others for the failures people observe around them. Then, as they feel more able to manage their risks, the buzz becomes positive and focused on the self, and change follows soon after. Surprise+emotion is the key to stimulating buzz.

Offer hope: We humans are motivated to live closer to our dreams and hopes. Unfortunately, life sucks and the painful gap between our hoped-for selves and real life feeds our frustrations, guilts and dissatisfactions. Such is the human condition!

Yet those frustrations are the powerhouses of human motivation and change. When our deep hopes – for self-respect, autonomy, competence and good relationships – are frustrated, we are primed to make changes in our lives.

The proper role for a change maker is not to try to change people's hopes but rather to design change efforts which help people realise the positive, healthy hopes they already have. Therefore, if we want people to be motivated to change, "the proper question is not, 'Why isn't this person motivated?' but rather, 'For what is this person motivated?'"[1] A change effort needs to be framed around outcomes that matter deeply to the people we hope will act.

Create an enabling environment: Every behaviour is enabled or disabled by the day-to-day environments in which people make their choices. If the aim is sustained change, then elements of the actors' environments will almost certainly need to be modified. That might mean changing services, social organisation, leadership, infrastructure, technology, pricing, regulation, governance – anything that could exert a positive or negative pull on people's choices. The most powerful changes are likely to be those that build communities and create ease.

Design a sticky solution: Fortunately, it's not hard to invent solutions to people's frustrations. With a little creativity, most change makers can find ways to deliver on people's universal desires for time, control and self-esteem, while at the same time achieving larger social or environmental gains. However, to do so means thinking like a designer, spending time with people and becoming intimately acquainted with their lives, struggles and frustrations rather than jumping to easy conclusions about what solutions might be right for them.

And remember, too, that reinvention is what drives solutions across social systems. That requires us to have the courage to discard our seemingly successful version 1.0 for the seemingly risky version 2.0, and so on, with a relentless attention to improving easiness, effectiveness, simplicity, pleasure and speed.

Expand people's comfort zones: Change is scary – it's easy, for example, for bicycle riders to forget the terror that can beset those who have never ridden a bicycle before.

Every change effort should therefore expand people's comfort zones so they can act on their motivations without fear, especially without the fear of humiliation. Fortunately, there are plenty of techniques that enable people to manage their fears, like familiarity, autonomy, talking with peers, enjoyment and social proof.

Find the right inviter: Who invites an action can be more important than the character of the action itself. The best inviters are passionate, similar, respected, connected, powerless and believe in the actors' ability to successfully implement a change in their lives.

Each of these six ingredients is a vital link in the chain of what it takes for groups or populations to do things they have never done before. Neglect any one link and a change would be much less likely to be adopted and sustained.

In shorthand, this theory could be written as:

IF there's positive buzz
AND we offer hope
AND an enabling environment
AND a sticky solution
AND expanded comfort zones
AND the right inviter
THEN people will do things they have never done before and sustain those changes.

A good enough theory

There's just one problem of course: "All theories are wrong, but some are useful." Although it's an attractive theory and represents a large body of research and field experience, it's just a theory. The real world is far too complex for any one theory of change to be applied to everyone, everywhere, all the time. In fact, it's deluded and ridiculous to assume that one theory could encompass every human situation. Therefore it's best to think of this theory as 'good enough'. It's a tool to pick up when it's useful and put down when it's not. It's an approximation to human reality, not human reality itself. Its best use is simply to help us think a little more clearly about the business of change.

Peter and Susan's final (maybe) theory for spreading their orphan innovation is a case in point. It doesn't sound like my theory at all. It has special flavours and nuances that are quite different. It might be possible to shoehorn Peter and Susan's principles into a supposedly universal theory. But what would be the point? It would be an awkward fit. Peter and Susan's theory is perfect for their needs. It stands on its own as a hard-won insight into what enabled change in their unique situation.

The best approach is always to make our own customised theory for every situation – perhaps using a process like the one described in the Making a Theory of Change Method – and to regard that theory as a hypothesis waiting to be tested. Your change effort then becomes an experiment that tests your hypothesis. And what you learn helps you develop a better theory.

At the end of this book, therefore, please keep in mind that the proper use of the ideas we've uncovered is simply to help us see better into the situations we encounter. They prepare us, as individuals, for the thinking we need to do to enable change in others. They're not descriptions of the world, they're simply checklists of things to think about.

Final thoughts

Now that we're at the end of this very logical book, I hope I've earned the right to become a little fuzzy and philosophical.

While researching and writing and practising in my day job as a change consultant, I've done a lot of learning, thinking and reflecting over the past four years. Here are some big ideas I'd like to share:

People aren't changed, they change themselves.

I realise now that no one can make other people change their lives. People change themselves. Sustained change always involves people acting on their own inner dreams and hopes. They might comply with incentives or threats in the short term but that compliance is always skin deep. When the incentive ends or the threat fades they'll revert to their old habits. A successful change effort therefore involves increasing people's ability to act on what matters to them.

Love people and put them first.

Ask: will our efforts make people healthier, stronger, closer, freer and more able to live with dignity? And will it do those things on their terms? We may be trying to save the environment or stop disease but unless we are genuinely at the service of people's hopes we have no right to expect their commitment and energy. It's always best, therefore, to treat our target audiences with kindness and respect as if they are intelligent people trying to better their lives in a maddeningly complicated world – people just like ourselves. Therefore never expect perfection, be satisfied with small steps, and don't blame them if nothing happens.

Who we are matters greatly.

As change makers, our stories, our inspirations and how we live our lives or run our businesses are part of the change equation. If we believe a particular change works, others will find it easier to believe in it too. And if we believe in their ability to make change they'll find it easier to believe in themselves. We (and our credible inviters) are the working proofs that change is beneficial and possible.

Face-to-face time matters.

Change is about relationships. Change tends to travel along social networks of people who already know each other. People are courageous when they work in groups. They make sense of their world through their conversations and they learn best by learning from each other. So act like a dating agency and we can't go far wrong.

Be a reinventor.
It's good to think and act like a designer. Failure is never a reflection on our audience but it is a reflection on our ideas. If people seem to reject our solutions then it's time to start wondering how we could reinvent them to better fit their lives and aspirations.

Don't make people wrong.
Don't try to persuade or argue with people. When people think we're making them wrong, denial and resistance are their natural responses.

Inspiration beats information.
Change is, above all else, an act of imagination. People need to see themselves in a better future, and they need to imagine themselves confidently vanquishing every one of the fearful obstacles that litter their path to that future. That's why, at the heart of so many successful change efforts are inspiring, life-affirming, true stories of people who have conquered their own fears, blazed the trail and are proudly sharing their successes.

Process matters.
Successful change efforts happen when engineers, planners, designers, politicians, regulators, facilitators and marketers step out of their professional comfort zones, mix with each other, let their assumptions be challenged, are prepared to defend those assumptions with evidence, and invite the public to genuinely share in the learning and decision-making. Process, therefore, matters greatly.

In terms of process:

Start with a diverse brains trust. Bypass silos, work in multi-disciplinary teams, and invite the users to share the big decisions. Gather all those people who can make a difference around the table before the planning starts. Let them share the inspiration, the thinking, the planning and the credit.

Get inspired by what works elsewhere. Don't start till you've got lost in Google and Google Scholar a few times and been genuinely excited by the methods others have used no matter how wacky and unfamiliar they may seem.

Listen to users and non-users. Go out into the field, watch people, talk to them, listen and don't stop till you've been surprised or confronted by what you hear.

Think in terms of systems. Map the environments that surround people and don't limit your palette of interventions. Act to modify the social, technological and physical contexts in which people make their decisions, and then use communications to draw people's attention to those changes and model appropriate behaviours.

Be ready to abandon your own assumptions. Even the ones you don't know you have. Instead, innovate like crazy, treat each solution like a prototype and every tactic like an experiment.

And then, just maybe, you might succeed in changing the world beyond your wildest dreams.

Further reading

Where to next? Here is a handful of texts I've found both inspiring and informative.

Published resources

Cialdini, R. (1984) *Influence: The psychology of persuasion*. New York: Quill Press. The classic popular text on the psychology of marketing. An enjoyable and insightful read that demonstrates Cialdini's six 'weapons of influence'. It's also an excellent introduction to social psychology.

Virtually alone amongst the crowded field of behavioural psychology books, Chip and Dan Heath focus on making a change project happen in the field:

Heath, C. and Heath, D. (2007) *Made to Stick: Why some ideas survive and others die*. New York: Random House. What makes some ideas travel around the world without needing a marketing budget? This might just be the best book on communication ever written.

Heath, C. and Heath, D. (2010) *Switch: How to change things when change is hard*. New York: Random House Business Books. This focuses on the design of change projects, with inspiring stories and plenty of practical insights.

Rogers, E. M. (2003) *The Diffusion of Innovations*. Fifth edition. New York: Free Press. The authoritative book on how products, ideas and practices spread through societies. Its 550 pages are simply written, effortless to read, and packed with ideas and case studies. If you're serious about being a change maker, read this.

Online resources

Australian Public Service Commission (2007) 'Tackling wicked problems: A public policy perspective'. A brief and elegantly written summary of the literature on wicked problems.
www.enablingchange.com.au/wickedproblems.pdf

Dolan, P. et al. (2010) *MINDSPACE: Influencing behaviour through public policy*. UK: the Institute for Government and the Cabinet Office. Written for practitioners, it sets out nine kinds of 'nudges' that can influence people's choices. www.instituteforgovernment.org.uk/publications/mindspace

Two superb resources on the design perspective in change making, both focusing on collaborative methods and packed with case studies:

IDEO (2009) *Human-centred Design Toolkit*. Second edition. IDEO.
www.ideo.com/work/human-centered-design-toolkit

Murray, R., Caulier-Grice, J. and Mulgan, G. (2010) *The Open Book of Social Innovation: Ways to design, develop and grow social innovation*. London: The Young Foundation, NESTA.
www.nesta.org.uk/library/documents/Social_Innovator_020310.pdf

References and Notes*

Introduction

1. Peter Clarke (2007), personal communication. Also, see Evans, S. H. and Clarke, P. (2011) 'Disseminating orphan innovations', *Stanford Social Innovation Review* 9, 42-7. Or just google 'From the Wholesaler to the Hungry'.

Popular folk theories

1. Gazzaniga, M. S. (1969) *The Social Brain*. New York: Basic Books Inc., p.74.

2. Gazzaniga, M. S. (2005) *The Ethical Brain*. New York: Dana Press, pp.145-55.

3. Motivations of litterers: Curnow, R. C., Streker, P. and Williams, E. (1997) 'Understanding littering behaviour in Australia', Beverage Industry Environment Council.

Motivations of surrogates: Aigen, B. P. (undated) 'Motivations of surrogate mothers', www.surrogacy.com/psychres/article/motivat.html

Motivations of law students: Heath, C. (1999) 'On the social psychology of agency relationships: Lay theories of motivation overemphasise extrinsic incentives', *Organisational Behaviour and Human Decision Processes* 78(1), 25-62.

4. Feagin, J. R. (1975) *Subordinating the Poor: Welfare and American beliefs*. Englewood Cliffs, NJ: Prentice-Hall.

5. Furnham, A. (1988) *Lay Theories*. Oxford: Pergamon Press, p.13.

6. "It seems we define the people who can't be trusted with drugs as everyone but ourselves," concluded the researchers. McNair Ingenuity Research, March 2010, reported on the Australian Broadcasting Company TV show *The Hungry Beast*, http://hungrybeast.abc.net.au/stories/drug-survey-results

7. Miller, D. T. and Ratner, R. K. (1998) 'The disparity between the actual and assumed power of self-interest', *Journal of Personality and Social Psychology* 74(1), 55-62.

8. Frank, R. et al. (1996) 'Do economists make bad citizens?', *Journal of Economic Perspectives* 10(1), 187-92.

9. Beinart, P. (2006) 'We broke it', *The New Republic*, 11 December.

10. Toy, M. (2006) 'Green dream vanishes in a puff of reality', *Sydney Morning Herald*, 26 August.

---

* These can also be found online, with clickable links to the web addresses: see www.greenbooks.co.uk/changeology

11. Thompson, K. (2008) 'The Most Accurate Election Forecast? Hardcore Gamblers', *The Huffington Post*, 2 November, www.huffingtonpost.com/keith-thomson/the-most-accurate-electio_b_140181.html

12. Legal scholar Cass Sunstein summarises the many ways deliberating groups go wrong in Sunstein, C. (2006) *Infotopia: How many minds produce knowledge*. Oxford: Oxford University Press, pp.25-92.

13. Ibid. p.45.

14. "We are primarily concerned with a situation in which the balance of unshared information opposes the initially most popular position. In this case, according to the biased sampling model, the unshared information will tend to be omitted from discussion and, therefore, will have little effect on members' preferences during group discussion. Our results confirm this notion. Group decisions and postgroup preferences reflected the initial preferences of group members even when the exchange of unshared information should have resulted in substantial shifts of opinion. Furthermore, discussion did not increase the recall of unshared information. On the contrary, discussion tended to increase the recall of information that supported the initially most popular (and ultimately winning) candidate even though this information was primarily shared before discussion." Stasser, G. and Titus, W. (1985) 'Pooling of unshared information in group decision making: Biased information sampling during discussion', *Journal of Personality and Social Psychology* 48, 1467-78, http://dimitrivasiljevic.wifeo.com/documents/Stasser_Titus_1985.pdf

15. Fredrickson, B. L. (1998) 'What good are positive emotions?', *Review of General Psychology* 2, 300-19.

16. Fredrickson, B. L. (2004) 'The broaden-and-build theory of positive emotions', *Philosophical Transactions of the Royal Society* 359, 1367-77. www.ncbi.nlm.nih.gov/pmc/articles/PMC1693418/pdf/15347528.pdf

17. For an enjoyable and informative read on the creativity-crushing impact of deadlines and KPIs, see Pink, D. (2009) *Drive: The surprising truth about what motivates us*. New York: Riverhead Books, p.85.

The social immune system

1. Lindner, E. (2000) 'The psychology of humiliation: Somalia, Rwanda, Burundi, and Hitler's Germany'. Doctoral dissertation submitted to the University of Oslo, p.29.

2. Eisenberger, N. I. and Lieberman, M. D. (2003) 'Why it hurts to be left out: The neurocognitive overlap between physical and social pain', *Science* 302, 290-2.

3. Baumeister, R. F. et al. (2002) 'Effects of social exclusion on cognitive processes: Anticipated aloneness reduces intelligent thought', *Journal of Personality and Social Psychology* 83(4), 817-27.

4. Twenge, J. M. et al. (2001) 'If you can't join them, beat them: Effects of social exclusion on aggressive behavior', *Journal of Personality and Social Psychology* 81(6), 1058-69.

5. Baumeister, R. F. et al. (2005) 'Social exclusion impairs self-regulation', *Journal of Personality and Social Psychology* 88(4), 589-604.

6. Sources quoted in Hartling, L. M. (2005) 'Humiliation: Real pain, a pathway to violence'. Preliminary draft of a paper prepared for Round Table 2 of the 2005 Workshop on Humiliation and Violent Conflict, Columbia University, New York, 15-16 December, p.4.

7. Quoted in Smith, D. (2004) 'From the outside, looking in', *Sydney Morning Herald*, 20 March.

8. Resnick, M. D. et al. (1997) 'Protecting adolescents from harm: Findings from a national longitudinal study on adolescent health', *Journal of the American Medical Association* 278(10), 823-32.

9. Lindner, op. cit. (see ref. 1) p.422.

10. Falkin, G. P. et al. (2007) 'Smoking cessation and stress among teenagers', *Qualitative Health Research* 17(6), 812-23.

11. The studies are summarised in a wonderful review of failed health warnings, campaigns and messages in Ringold, D. J. (2002) 'Boomerang effects in response to public health interventions: Some unintended consequences in the alcoholic beverage market', *Journal of Consumer Policy* 25, 27-63.

12. Engs, R. C. and Hanson, D. J. (1989) 'Reactance theory: A test with collegiate drinking', *Psychological Reports* 64, 1083-6.

13. Ringold, op. cit.

14. DeWall, C. N. et al. (2011) 'Forbidden fruit: Inattention to attractive alternatives provokes implicit relationship reactance', *Journal of Personality and Social Psychology* 100(4), 621-29.

15. DiCenso, A. et al. (2002) 'Interventions to reduce unintended pregnancies among adolescents: Systematic review of randomised controlled trials', *British Medical Journal* 324, 1426-34.

16. Naidoo, B. et al. (2004) 'Smoking and public health: A review of reviews of interventions to increase smoking cessation, reduce smoking initiation and prevent further uptake of smoking'. London: Health Development Agency (UK).

17. Foxcroft, D. R. et al. (2002) 'Primary prevention for alcohol misuse in young people', *The Cochrane Database of Systematic Reviews* 3, CD003024.

18. Sewel, K. (2002) 'International alcohol policies: A selected literature review'. Edinburgh: Scottish Executive Central Research Unit, p.17.

19. White, D. and Pitts, M. (1998) 'Educating young people about drugs: A systematic review', *Addiction* 93, 1475-87.

20. Underhill, K., Montgomery, P. and Operario, D. (2007) 'Sexual abstinence-only programmes to prevent HIV infection in high-income countries: Systematic review', *British Medical Journal* 335, 248.

21. Mendoza, M. (2007) 'Review finds nutrition education failing', Associated Press, 13 August.

22. Kolbe, J. et al. (1996) 'Assessment of practical knowledge of self-management of acute asthma', *CHEST: The Cardiopulmonary and Critical Care Journal* 109(1), 86-90.

23. Roads and Traffic Authority (2004) 'Speeding-related injury and trauma in Country NSW'. Issues paper, NSW Country Road Safety Summit 2004, Port Macquarie, 27-8 May.

24. Festinger, L. (1957) *A Theory of Cognitive Dissonance*. New York: Row, Peterson & Company, p.3.

25. Aronson, E. (1999) 'Dissonance, hypocrisy and self-concept', in E. Harmon-Jones and J. Mills (eds.), *Cognitive Dissonance: Progress on a pivotal theory in social psychology*. Washington, DC: American Psychological Association, 103-26.

26. Miller, W. R. and Rollnick, S. (2002) *Motivational Interviewing: Preparing people for change*. Second edition. New York: The Guilford Press, p.22.

27. Festinger, L. and Carlsmith, J. M. (1959) 'Cognitive consequences of forced compliance', *Journal of Abnormal and Social Psychology* 58, 203-11.

28. Axelrod, S. and Apsche, J. (1983) *The Effects of Punishment on Human Behaviour*. New York: Academic Press, p.19.

29. Steketee, M. (2002) 'Cruisers cop it in the end', *The Australian*, 23 May.

30. Australian Department of Family and Community Services (FaCS) (1991, 1996, 2000 and 2004) 'Labour market and related payments: A monthly profile', (Australian Bureau of Statistics [ABS] Cat. No. 6105.0, 6204.0), November.

31. Australian Council of Social Service (ACOSS) (2001) 'Doling out punishment: The rise and rise of social security penalties'. Joint research paper by the National Welfare Rights Network (NWRN) and ACOSS, p.6.

32. Australian Department of Family and Community Services (FaCS) (2002) 'Breaching rules change to protect the vulnerable'. Press release, 4 March.

33. Breach statistics 1997-2001: Sydney Welfare Rights Centre and Australian Council of Social Service (ACOSS) figures cited in Schooneveldt, S. (2004) 'Do mutual obligation breach penalties coerce compliance with government expectations?', *Australian Journal of Social Issues* 39(2), 155-68. Breach statistics 2004-6: Centrelink figures obtained from the Centrelink website at: www.workplace.gov.au/workplace/Category/ResearchStats/PublicBreachData.htm [but since deleted]. Breaching figures shown by the dashed line are estimates because the government has never released them, but welfare organisations believe the rate dropped off sharply from the year 2001-2 down to 102,000 by 2004, when official figures were first published.

Long-term unemployed figures: Australian Bureau of Statistics (ABS) (2006) 'Australian labour market statistics' (ABS Cat. No. 6105.0), January.

34. Australian Council of Social Service (ACOSS), op. cit. p.5.

35. Back in 2000 the single adult unemployment benefit was $A163 a week (around £100). It wasn't much to live on when rent for a single room in a shared house in an Australian city was typically A$100 to A$160 a week. The penalties for breaching were therefore severe. A 2002 survey of 56 breached recipients found that 22 per cent said they needed to move into less desirable housing because they couldn't afford to pay their rent after even the first breach. Three said they moved "onto the streets" and one to "a men's homeless shelter". Schooneveldt, S. (2002*)* 'Do Centrelink activity breach penalties coerce outcomes from unemployed welfare recipients in line with Mutual Obligation policy?' Paper presented to the Social Change in the 21st Century Conference, Brisbane, Australia.

36. Source for robbery statistics: Moffatt, S. and Poynton, S. (2006) 'Long-term trends in property and violent crime 1990-2004', *Crime and Justice Bulletin No. 90*, NSW Bureau of Crime Statistics and Research. The data points are slightly out of alignment because the breaching rates are based on financial years and the robbery rates are based on calendar years.

37. Axelrod, op. cit. p.36. Also see Mohr, L. D. (1997) *Coercive Power in Human Exchange.* Cambridge: Cambridge University Press, p.221.

38. "if a person's behavioural freedom is reduced or threatened with reduction, he will become motivationally aroused. This arousal would presumably be directed against any further loss of freedom and it would also be directed towards the re-establishment of whatever freedom had already been lost or threatened." Brehm, J. W. (1966) *A Theory of Psychological Reactance.* New York: Academic Press, p.2.

Brehm's theory also accounts for denial: "when a communicator tells his audience what conclusion they must draw, there is a significant resistance to attitude change and even a tendency for boomerang attitude change." Ibid. p.121.

Interestingly, reactance can explain why scarcity can make products more attractive. One study involved 27 female college students who disliked the food in the college cafeteria. When told that the cafeteria would close for two weeks, their opinions about the food became much more positive. Brehm, S. S. and Brehm, J. W. (1981) *Psychological Reactance: A theory of freedom and control.* New York: Academic Press, p.43.

39. Ringold, op. cit. (see ref. 11) p.27.

40. Hyland, M. and Birrell, J. (1979) 'Government health warnings and the boomerang effect', *Psychological Reports* 44, 643-7.

41. Feingold, P. C. and Knapp, M. L. (1989) 'Anti-drug abuse commercials', *Journal of Communication* 2, 20-28

42. Bushman, B. J. and Stack, A. D. (1996) 'Forbidden fruit versus tainted fruit: Effects of warning labels on attraction to television violence', *Journal of Experimental Psychology: Applied* 2(3), 207-26.

43. Bushman, B. J. (1998) 'Effects of warning and information labels on consumption of full-fat, reduced-fat, and no-fat products', *Journal of Applied Psychology* 83, 97-101.

Ingredient 1: First, start a buzz

1. Hochschild, Adam (2006) *Bury the Chains: Prophets and rebels in the fight to free an empire's slaves.* New York: Mariner Books, p.7.

2. Ibid. p.158.

3. Ibid. p.78.

4. Ibid. p.156.

5. Zeldin, T. (1998) *Conversation.* London: Hiddenspring, p.7.

6. Pfister, N. (2002) 'Community response to flood warnings: The case of an evacuation from Grafton, March 2001', *The Australian Journal of Emergency Management* 17(2), 19-29.

7. Ryan, B. and Gross, N. C. (1943) 'The diffusion of hybrid seed corn in two Iowa communities', *Rural Sociology* 8, 15-24.

8. Ibid. p.17.

9. Ibid. p.21.

10. Rogers, E. M. (2003) *The Diffusion of Innovations.* Fifth edition. New York: Free Press, p.205.

11. Ibid. p.208.

12. Christakis, N. A. and Fowler, J. H. (2007) 'The spread of obesity in a large social network over 32 years', *New England Journal of Medicine* 357(4), pp.370-79.

13. Christakis, N. A. and Fowler, J. H. (2008) 'The dynamic spread of happiness in a large social network', *British Medical Journal* 337:a2338, pp.1-9.

14. Christakis, N. A. and Fowler, J. H. (2008) 'The collective dynamics of smoking in a large social network', *New England Journal of Medicine* 358(21), pp.2249-58.

15. According to Wikipedia.

16. Rogers, op. cit. p.87.

17. Jones, J. (2006) *Blogging the World Cup with Coca-Cola,* www.marketingvoices.com/830/blogging-the-world-cup-with-coca-cola™

18. See Jeff on YouTube: www.youtube.com/watch?v=VkA2Gvi-8tA

19. Soumerai, S. B. et al. (1998) 'Effect of local medical opinion leaders on quality of care for acute myocardial infarction: A randomized controlled trial', *Journal of the American Medical Association* 279, 1358-63.

20. Lomas, J. et al. (1991) 'Opinion leaders vs. audit and feedback to improve practice guidelines', *Journal of the American Medical Association* 205(17), 2202-07.

21. For a good, readable review of peer-leader programmes, see Parkin, S. and McKeganey, N. (2000) 'The rise and rise of peer education approaches', *Drugs: Education, Prevention and Policy* 7(3), 293-310.

22. Devilly, G. J. et al. (2005) 'Prison-based peer-education schemes', *Aggression and Violent Behaviour* 10, 215-40.

23. Birch, L. L. (1980) 'Effects of peer models' food choices and eating behaviors on preschoolers' food preferences', *Child Development* 51, 489-96.

24. Kelly, J. A. et al. (1997) 'Randomised, controlled, community-level HIV-prevention for sexual-risk behaviour among homosexual men in US cities', *The Lancet* 350, 1500-5.

To help ensure the statistical validity of the results, the characteristics of the eight cities were laboriously compared and similar cities formed pairs, with one member of each pair randomly assigned to the control group and one to the intervention group.

25. Hirst, E. (1989) 'Reaching for 100 percent participation in a utility conservation programme, The Hood River project', *Energy Policy* 17(2), 155-64.

26. Rogers op. cit. (see ref. 10) p.322.

27. Cuijpers, P. (2002) 'Peer-led and adult-led school drug prevention: A meta-analytic comparison', *Journal of Drug Education* 32(2), 107-19.

28. Goleman, D. (2006) *Social Intelligence*. London: Hutchinson, p.15.

29. This was especially so in the pioneering era of environmental legislation in the early 1970s, which saw the establishment of the Environmental Protection Agency in 1970, passage of the Clean Air Act in 1970 and the Clean Water Act and Federal Environmental Pesticide Control Act in 1972.

Agnone, J. (2007) 'Amplifying public opinion: The policy impact of the US environmental movement', *Social Forces* 85(4), 1593-1620.

30. Including Paul Slovic, Howard Kunreuther, Gilbert White, Sarah Lichtenstein, Melissa Finucane, Baruch Fischhoff and others.

31. Finucane, M. L. et al. (2000) 'The affect heuristic in judgements of risks and benefits'. In Slovic, P. (ed.) (2000) *The Perception of Risk*. London: Earthscan Publications UK, p.415.

32. Slovic, P., Flynn, J. and Lennon, M. (1991) 'Perceived trust and the politics of nuclear waste'. In Slovic, op. cit. p.281.

33. Kringelbach, M. L. and Rolls, E. T. (2004) 'The functional neuroanatomy of the human orbitofrontal cortex: Evidence from neuroimaging and neuropsychology', *Progress in Neurobiology* 72, 341-72.

34. Goodman, Andy (2002) *Why Bad Ads Happen to Good Causes: And how to ensure they won't happen to yours*. Santa Monica, CA: Cause Communications.

35. This 1996 Cease Fire ad was designed by BBDO New York. The campaign was funded by *Rolling Stone* publisher Jann Wenner with a small staff in Washington, DC.

36. You can see Amnesty International Hungary's Darfur ad on the Osocio website: http://osocio.org/message/stop_the_daily_rapes_in_darfur/

37. Klein, C. T .F. and Helwig-Larsen, M. (2002) 'Perceived control and the optimistic bias: A meta-analytic review', *Psychology and Health* 17(4), 437-46.

38. Wallston, B. S. and Wallston, K. A. (1978) 'Locus of control and health: A review of the literature (1978)' *Health Education & Behavior* 6(1), 107-17.

39. Burger, J. M (1984) 'Desire for control, locus of control, and proneness to depression', *Journal of Personality* 52(1), 71-89.

40. Sandler, I. N. and Laket, B. (1982) 'Locus of control as a stress moderator: The role of control perceptions and social support', *American Journal of Community Psychology* 10(1), 65-80.

41. Anderson, C. R. (1977) 'Locus of control, coping behaviors, and performance in a stress setting: A longitudinal study', *Journal of Applied Psychology* 62(4), 446-51.

42. Crisp, B. R. and Barber, J. G. (1995) 'The effect of locus of control on the association between risk perception and sexual risk-taking', *Personality and Individual Differences* 19(6), 841-5.

43. Koeske, G. F. and Kirk, S. A. (1995) 'Direct and buffering effects of internal local of control among mental health professionals', *Journal of Social Service Research* 20(3/4), 1-28.

44. Harlan, K. et al. (1996) 'Health optimism and control beliefs as predictors for treatment outcome of a multimodal back treatment programme', *Psychology and Health* 12(1), 123-34.

45. Simoni, J. M., Adelman, H. S. and Nelson, P. (1991) 'Perceived control, causality, expectations and help-seeking behavior', *Counselling and Psychology Quarterly* 4(1), 37-44.

46. Seeman, M. and Seeman, T. E. (1983) 'Health behavior and personal autonomy: A longitudinal study of the sense of control in illness', *Journal of Health and Social Behavior* 24(2), 144-60.

47. Seligman, M. (1990) *Learned Optimism*. New York: Vintage Books.

48. Fredrickson, B. L. and Losada, M. F. (2005) 'Positive affect and the complex dynamics of human flourishing', *American Psychologist* 60(7), 678-86.

49. Miller, W. R. and Rollnick, S. (2002) *Motivational Interviewing: Preparing people for change.* Second edition. New York: The Guilford Press, p.21.

50. Zeldin, op. cit. (see ref. 5) p.16.

Ingredient 2: Offer hope

1. The Otpor story is from Collin, M. (2007) *The Time of the Rebels: Youth resistance movements and 21st century revolutions*. London: Serpent's Tail, p.22.

2. Motivation has no agreed meaning in the literature. In this book, motivation is used interchangeably with hope and desire to mean the feeling of wanting something. Motivation involves frustration, the arousing state called dissonance in the psychological literature and discrepancy in the counselling literature. However, motivation is also a positive act of imagination, evoking an image of oneself leading a better life. Motivation, hope and desire probably cover the same territory as 'intention' used in some behavioural models. Having motivation or desire doesn't mean one actually acts but it does mean one is emotionally predisposed or ready to act.

3. Robinson, S. et al. (2005) 'Distinguishing whether dopamine regulates liking, wanting, and/ or learning about rewards', *Behavioural Neuroscience* 119(1), 336-41.

4. For a fascinating article about the current understanding of dopamine's purpose, see Phillips, H. (2003) 'The pleasure seekers', *New Scientist*, 11 October, p.36.

5. Thank you, Jacquie Anderson, for that useful quote.

6. Aronson, E. (1973) 'The rationalising animal', *Psychology Today*, May, 46-51.

7. Abler, B., Walter, H. and Erk, S. (2005) 'Neural correlates of frustration', *Neuroreport* 16(7), 669-72.

8. Social comparison is said to put people on a 'hedonic treadmill where hoped-for pleasures, once obtained, quickly degenerate into ordinariness, requiring even more expensive and elaborate pleasures to reproduce the initial enjoyment. "As I ratchet up my standards, this reduces the enjoyment I get from any standard of living . . . I compare what I have with what other people have . . . If others get better off, I need more in order to feel as good as before," wrote Richard Layard of the London School of Economics in his famous lecture on happiness. Layard, R. (2003) 'Happiness: Has social science a clue?', Lionel Robbins Memorial Lectures 2002/3. London School of Economics, 3-5 March, Lecture 2, p.5.

9. Kendrick, D. T. et al. (1993) 'Effects of physical attractiveness on affect and perceptual judgments: When social comparison overrides social reinforcement', *Personality and Social Psychology Bulletin* 19, 195-9.

10. Kendrick, D. T. et al. (1989) 'Influence of popular erotica on judgments of strangers and mates', *Journal of Experimental Social Psychology* 25, 159-6.

11. Anecdote about East German happiness from Layard op. cit. Lecture 2, p.8.

12. Kennedy, B. P. et al. (1996) 'Income distribution and mortality: Cross-sectional ecological study of the Robin Hood index in the United States', *British Medical Journal* 312, 1004-7.

13. "When discrepancy becomes large enough and change seems important, a search for possible methods for change is initiated. Given sufficient importance, if people find an avenue for change that they believe will work (general efficacy) and that they believe they can do (self-efficacy), they will often pursue it through behaviour change. If a person becomes alarmed by a discrepancy but perceives no way to change, however, then . . .Instead of changing behaviour, people reduce their discomfort by [denial]," Miller, W. R. and Rollnick, S. (2002) *Motivational Interviewing: Preparing people for change*. Second edition. New York: The Guilford Press, p.11.

14. When I analysed 93 of my students' personal change stories I found feelings of frustration, guilt and unhappiness in 86 per cent of cases. My impression was that the changes they later made in their lives would never have occurred without the driving visceral force of that unhappiness. Robinson, L. (2006) 'The voluntary adoption of new practices', www.enablingchange.com.au

15. According to Albert Bandura, "Most theories of motivation and self-regulation are founded on a negative feedback system. In this view, discrepancy between one's perceived performance and an adopted standard motivates action to reduce the disparity. This is the basic motivator in control theory, homeostatic drive theories, and cybernetic models. Reduction of discrepancy between internal schema and perceived events is also the sole motivating mechanism in Piaget's (1960) theory," wrote Albert Bandura in Bandura, A. (1993) 'Perceived self-efficacy in cognitive development and functioning', *Educational Psychologist* 28(2), 117-48.

16. Hage, G. (2001) ''The incredible shrinking society', *Weekend Review: The Australian Financial Review*, 7 September, pp.4-5.

17. Fisher, R. (2006) 'Just can't get enough', *New Scientist*, 23-30 December 2006, p.36.

18. Fine, C. (2006) 'Your brilliant, cheating, beautiful mind', TimesOnline, 7 January.

19. Brissette, I., Carver, C. S. and Scheier, M. F. (2002) 'The role of optimism in social network development, coping, and psychological adjustment during a life transition', *Journal of Personality and Social Psychology* 82(1), 102-11.

20. Segerstrom, S. C. et al. (1998) 'Optimism is associated with mood, coping, and immune change in response to stress', *Journal of Personality and Social Psychology* 74(6), 1646-55.

21. Satterfield, J. M. and Seligman, M. E. P. (1994) 'Military aggression and risk predicted by explanatory style', *Psychological Science* 5, 77-82.

22. Herbst, K. C., Gaertner, L. and Insko, C. A. (2003) 'My head says yes but my heart says no: Cognitive and affective attraction as a function of similarity to the ideal self', *Journal of Personality and Social Psychology* 84(6), 1206-19.

23. Goleman, D. (2006) *Social Intelligence*. London: Hutchinson, p.54.

24. Damasio, A. R., Everitt, B. J. and Bishop, D. (1996) 'The somatic marker hypothesis and the possible functions of the prefrontal cortex [and discussion]', *Philosophical Transactions: Biological Sciences* 351(1346), 1413-20.

Some psychologists argue that the function of emotion is to help us make approach-avoidance decisions, whereas the role of rationality is to make true-false distinctions. Others argue that emotion's central role is to create or inhibit a state of action-readiness. Zajonc, R. (1998) 'Emotions'. In Gilbert, D. et al. (eds.) *The Handbook of Social Psychology Volume 1*. New York: Oxford University Press, p.591. Also see Frijda, N. H., Kuipers, P. and ter Schure, E. (1989) 'Relations among emotion, appraisal and emotional action readiness', *Journal of Personality and Social Psychology* 57, 212-28.

25. 'It's only logical to be a bit emotional', *Sydney Morning Herald*, 28 December 2001.

26. LeDoux, J. (1996) *The Emotional Brain*. New York: Simon and Schuster, p.19.

27. Schartz, N. and Clore, G. L. (1983) 'Mood, misattribution, and judgements of well-being: Informative and directive functions of affective states', *Journal of Personality and Social Psychology* 45, 513-23.

28. Fessler, D. et al. (2005) 'Angry men and disgusted women: An evolutionary approach to the influence of emotions on risk-taking', *Organizational Behaviour and Human Decision Processes* 95(1), 107-23.

29. Lerner, J. S. and Keltner, D. (2000) 'Beyond valence: Towards a model of emotion-specific influences on judgement and choice', *Cognition and Emotion* 14, 473-94.

30. Garg, N., Inman, J. J. and Mittal, V. (2005) 'Incidental and task-related affect: A re-inquiry and extension of the influence of affect on choice', *Journal of Consumer Research* 32(1), 154-9.

31. Wheatley, T. and Haidt, J. (2005) 'Research report hypnotic disgust makes moral judgements more severe', *Psychological Science* 16, 780-4.

32. "Most people who quit smoking or recover from alcohol do so without assistance from health professionals . . . the stages and processes by which people change seem to be the same with or without treatment. In this sense, treatment can be thought of as facilitating what is a natural process of change." Miller and Rollnick, op. cit. (see ref. 13) p.4.

33. Sheldon, K . M. et al. (2001) 'What is satisfying about satisfying events? Testing 10 candidate psychological needs', *Journal of Personality and Social Psychology* 80(2), 325–39.

34. These results accord with the leading theories of motivation, especially the Self-Determination Theory of Edward Deci and Richard Ryan. They also plug very nicely into Bandura's concept of Self-Efficacy and Csíkszentmihályi's Theory of Flow. Which goes to show that some theories can be useful.

Louis Tay and Ed Deiner published a similar study in 2011 which expanded the sample to over 60,000 individuals in 123 countries. The findings were similar, except, interestingly, they investigated which needs were associated with positive and which with negative feelings. Positive feelings were most associated with being respected, having pride in one's work and having supportive relationships, while negative feelings were most associated with lack of food and shelter, lack of respect, and loss of autonomy. Tay, L. and Deiner, E. (2011) 'Needs and subjective well-being around the world', *Journal of Personality and Social Psychology* 101(2), 354–65.

35. Leading proponents of this idea are psychologists Edward Deci and Richard Ryan. For more, google 'Self-Determination Theory'. Among activists, Tom Crompton at WWF UK is a strong advocate of values-based campaigning. See http://assets.wwf.org.uk/downloads/meeting_environmental_challenges___the_role_of_human_identity.pdf

36. For more on Wieden and Kennedy's OFF ON project, see http://solar-aid.org/about/2010/11/solaraid-is-thrilled-to-announ-1.html

37. Kahneman, D. et al. (2004) 'A survey method for characterizing daily life experience: The Day Reconstruction Method', *Science* 306(5702), 1776–80.

38. Clark, A. (2004) 'Want to feel less stress? Become a fighter pilot, not a commuter', *The Guardian*, 4 November.

39. Schaeffer, M. et al. (1988) 'Effects of control on the stress reactions of commuters', *Journal of Applied Social Psychology* 18(11), 944-57.

And also Evans, G. W. and Wener, R. E. (2002) 'The morning rush hour: Predictability and commuter stress', *Environment and Behavior* 34(4), 521-30.

40. Babalik-Sutcliffe, E. (2003) 'Urban rail systems: Analysis of the factors behind success', *Transport Reviews* 22, 415–47.

41. Perusco, A. et al (2010) 'Evaluation of a comprehensive tobacco control project targeting Arabic-speakers residing in south-west Sydney, Australia', *Health Promotion International* 25(2), 153-65.

42. Jane Halton (2004) 'Social marketing: Helping Australians to help themselves'. Fifth National Public Affairs Convention, Canberra, Media, Entertainment and Arts Alliance, 12 August, www.health.gov.au/internet/main/publishing.nsf/Content/health-mediarel-yr2004-dept-deptspo4003.htm

43. If you really want to freak yourself out, there is a far more disturbing anti-land mine ad on the Osocio social marketing site: http://osocio.org/message/still_waiting_for_a_victim/

44. Rosser, B. R. S. (1991) 'The effects of using fear in public AIDS education on the behaviour of homosexually active men', *Journal of Psychology & Human Sexuality* 4(3), 123–34.

45. Morlet, A. et al. (1988) 'The impact of the "Grim Reaper" national AIDS educational campaign on the Albion Street (AIDS) Centre and the AIDS Hotline', *Australian Medical Journal* 148(6), 282-6.

46. Decades later, in the documentary *Rampant: How a City Stopped a Plague*, The Grim Reaper's funders revealed that they weren't actually trying to change sexual behaviour, they were trying to change the behaviour of conservative politicians who were stalling on funding AIDS-prevention programmes. In that respect, the ad was very successful.

47. Cox, L. S. et al. (2003) 'Change in smoking status after spiral chest computed tomography scan viewing', *Cancer* 98(11), 2495-591.

48. Loewenstein, G., Weber, E. U. and Hsee, C. K. (2001) 'Risk as feelings', *Psychological Bulletin* 127, 267-86.

49. Woolley, J. (2001) 'The South Australian Road Safety Media Evaluation Study: A literature review on best practice with mass media', Adelaide, South Australia: University of South Australia.

50. Witte, E. and Allen, M. (2000) 'A meta-analysis of fear appeals: Implications for effective public health campaigns', *Health Education and Behaviour* 27(5), 591-615.

51. "While fear arousal appears important for attracting attention, its contribution to behaviour change appears less critical than other factors, such as perceptions of vulnerability and effective coping strategies. Furthermore, threatening appeals targeting young males (a high-risk group of concern) have traditionally relied on the portrayal of physical harm. However, the available evidence questions the relevance, and hence effectiveness, of strong physical threats with this group." Lewis, I. M. et al. (2007) 'The role of fear appeals in improving driver safety: A review of the effectiveness of fear-arousing (threat) appeals in road safety advertising', *International Journal of Behavioral and Consultation Therapy* 3(2), 203-22.

52. Tay, R. and Watson, B. (2002) 'Changing drivers' intentions and behaviours using fear-based driver fatigue advertisements', *Health Marketing Quarterly* 19(4), 55-68.

53. Elliott, B. (1993) 'Road-safety mass-media campaigns: A meta-analysis', Department of Transport and Communications, Federal Office of Road Safety (FORS), Australia.

Interestingly, the research showed a difference between the first 40 per cent of the population to adopt new road safety behaviour, and those who come later. For the first 40 per cent, emotional appeals and negative appeals worked best. For the rest, rational appeals and positive appeals worked best. (p.72).

54. Hassard, K. (ed.) (2000) 'Australia's National Tobacco Campaign evaluation report volume two'. Canberra: Commonwealth Department of Health and Aged Care, p.3.

55. Kinsman, T. (ed.) (2004) '1997-2003 National Tobacco Campaign evaluation: Response and recall measures among smokers and recent quitters'. Sydney: Australian Government Department of Health and Ageing, p.17.

56. For example, Scollo, M. M. and Winstanley, M. H. (eds.) (2008) *Tobacco in Australia: Facts and issues*. Third edition. Melbourne: Cancer Council Victoria, chapter 14.4.

57. The cutouts were designed by an advertising agency, Everest Y&R, in Mumbai. Source: *Osocio*, 4 February 2007, http://osocio.org/message/tent_card_cutout/

58. Miller and Rollnick, op. cit. (see ref. 13) p.18.

Ingredient 3: Create an enabling environment

1. Homel, R., Tomsen, S. and Thommeny, J. (1992) 'Public drinking and violence: Not just an alcohol problem', *Journal of Drug Issues* 22, 679-97.

2. Barbara, K. (2001) *The Social Psychology of Aggression*. East Sussex: The Psychology Press, p.87.

3. Troped, P. J. et al. (2001) 'Associations between self-reported and objective physical factors and use of a community rail-trail', *Preventive Medicine* 32, 191-200.

4. Reynolds, K. D. et al. (2007) 'Trail characteristics as correlates of urban trail use', *Health Promotion* 21, 335-45.

5. Cohen, D. A. et al. (2007) 'Contribution of public parks to physical activity', *American Journal of Public Health* 97, 509-14.

6. Frequent metabolically arousing rewards hijack the dopamine system potentially addicting susceptible individuals. One day there will probably be laws against intentionally addicting people; however, for the time being, there's a new field of behavioural manipulation that goes by the name 'gamification'.

7. For more on Let's Move, see www.letsmove.gov/ and www.smh.com.au/lifestyle/wellbeing/first-ladys-war-on-obesity-seeks-an-oasis-for-innercity-food-deserts-20110721-1hqty.html

8. Peden, M. et al. (eds.) (2004) 'World report on traffic injury prevention. Geneva: World Health Organisation, p.13, http://whqlibdoc.who.int/publications/2004/9241562609.pdf

9. da Costa e Silva, V. (ed.) (2003) 'Tools for advancing tobacco control in the 21st century: Policy recommendations for smoking cessation and treatment of tobacco dependence'. Geneva: World Health Organisation, p.1, www.who.int/tobacco/publications/smoking_cessation/recommendations/en/index.html

10. Robinson, L. (2011) 'What enables cycling and safe cycling behaviours?', p.13. www.enablingchange.com.au/What_enables_cycling.pdf

11. Thaler, R. H. and Sunstein, C. R. (2008) *Nudge: Improving decisions about health, wealth and happiness*. New Haven and London: Yale University Press.

12. Ibid. p.179.

13. For a useful taxonomy of context modifications, see House of Lords Science and Technology Select Committee (2011) 'Behaviour change' report, p.10.

14. Care (2012) 'Reaching new heights: The case for measuring women's empowerment', p.2.

15. Ibid. p.8.

16. Ibid. p.10.

17. Lisa C. Smith, quoted in ibid. p.4.

18. Ibid. p.16.

19. Heath, C. and Jourden, F. J. (1997) 'The buffering effect of groups', *Organizational Behavior and Human Decision Processes* 69(2), 103-16.

20. Schliebs, M. (2010) 'Remote Northern Territory schools bleed pupils', *The Australian,* 3 November.

21. Horin, A. (2011) 'Welfare stick fails for NT schools', *Sydney Morning Herald,* 22 December.

22. Turner, P. (2011) 'Cutting Centrelink cash won't stop indigenous truancy', *Sydney Morning Herald,* 25 November.

23. These figures refer to children whose parents had been informed they were subjects of the programme. Australian Government, Department of Education, Employment and Workplace Relations (2012) 'Improving School Enrolment and Attendance through Welfare Reform Measure (SEAM)'. Evaluation report for 2010, pp.34-5, www.deewr.gov.au/schooling/programmes/pages/seam.aspx

24. Ibid q.v. Interestingly, they noticed a 'school effect' where some schools were simply better at retaining their students irrespective of the number of compliance notices issued.

25. Sue Trimble interviewed in West Arnhem College, Gunbalanya Flexible School Year Trial 2012, www.youtube.com/watch?v=U-XHftXOxoY

26. Easy Being Green was very successful. Of the three million compact fluorescent lights distributed, 81 per cent were in use 12 months later. See Cool nrg (2007) 'New South Wales case study: Mass-market energy-efficiency campaign, New South Wales (NSW), Australia', p.10.

27. Frances, N. (2008) *The End of Charity: Time for social enterprise.* Sydney: Allen and Unwin, p.139.

28. The programme was funded in 2012 by the Mexican Government with Cool nrg managing distribution and collecting the carbon credits.

29. Cool nrg (2007) 'New South Wales case study: Mass-market energy-efficiency campaign, New South Wales (NSW), Australia', p.10.

30. Jha, P. and Chaloupka, F. J. (1999) 'Curbing the epidemic: Governments and the economics of tobacco control'. Washington, DC: World Bank, p.41.

31. Gallet, C. and List, J. (2003) 'Cigarette demand: A meta-analysis of elasticities', *Health Economics* 12, 821-35.

32. Kidd, M. and Hopkins, S. (2004) 'The hazards of starting and quitting smoking: Some Australian evidence', *The Economic Record* 80(249), 177-92. This study analysed Australian National Health Survey data on the smoking behaviours of 27- to 3-year-olds and found that, although the price of cigarettes appeared to have an effect on their decision to start smoking, there was no detectable effect on rates of quitting.

33. Adda, J. and Cornaglia, F. (2005) 'Taxes, cigarette consumption and smoking intensity', Discussion Paper No. 1849, Forschungsinstitut zur Zukunft der Arbeit (Institute for the Study of Labour), Bonn.

34. Goldstein, N., Martin S. and Cialdini, R. (2008) *Yes!: 50 Scientifically Proven Ways to Be Persuasive* is summarised at: www.moskalyuk.com/blog/yes-50-scientifically-proven-ways-to-be-persuasive/1624

35. For research papers on Cialdini's work with Opower, see: http://opower.com/utilities/results

36. You can download the full study of the Bankstown City Council experiment at:

www.efslearninghub.net.au/Portals/0/Resources/Publications/Files/1253/BCC%20CRC%20 Progress%20Report%20June%202011.pdf

37. Australian Institute of Health and Welfare (AIHW) for the Department of Families, Housing, Community Services and Indigenous Affairs (FaHCSIA) (2009) 'Report on the evaluation of income management in the Northern Territory'. Canberra: AIHW.

38. Department of Families, Housing, Community Services and Indigenous Affairs (FaHCSIA) (2009) 'Closing the Gap in the Northern Territory', Whole of Government Monitoring Report, pp.34-5.

39. Equality Rights Alliance (ERA) (2011) 'Women's experience of income management in the Northern Territory'. Canberra: ERA.

40. Brimblecombe, J. K. et al. (2010) 'Impact of income management on store sales in the Northern Territory', *Medical Journal of Australia* 192(10), 549-54.

41. Department of Families, Housing, Community Services and Indigenous Affairs (FaHCSIA), op. cit. (see ref. 38) p.48; and ORIMA Research (2010) 'Evaluation of the child protection scheme of income management and voluntary income management measures in Western Australia', p.204.

42. Milne, P. W. (1985) 'Fitting and wearing of seat belts in Australia: The history of a successful countermeasure'. Department of Transport, Canberra: Australian Government Publishing Service, p.11.

43. National Highway Traffic Safety Administration (NHTSA) (2007), 'Seat belt use in 2006: Use rates in the States and Territories', Traffic Safety Facts April, www-nrd.nhtsa.dot.gov/ Pubs/810690.pdf

44. Adams, J. (1986) 'Seat belt laws: A clumsy perspective', University College London, first draft of a contribution to *Clumsy Solutions for a Complex World*. www.cycle-helmets.com/ seatbelts_adams.pdf

45. Quoted in Adams, op. cit. p.10.

46. Derrig, R. A., Segui-Gomez, M. D. and Abtahi, A. (2000) 'The effect of seat-belt usage rates on the number of motor-vehicle-related fatalities', Proceedings of the 2000 Risk Theory Society Seminar, 14-16 April, University of Minnesota, Minneapolis, www.aria.org/rts/ proceedings/2000/seatbelts.pdf

47. Cohen, A. and Einav, L. (2001) 'The effects of mandatory seat-belt laws on driving behavior and traffic fatalities'. Discussion Paper No. 321, The John M. Olin Center for Law, Economics, and Business, Harvard University, Cambridge, MA. www.law.harvard.edu/programmes/olin_ center/papers/pdf/341.pdf

48. Maguire, B., Faulkner, W. R. and Mathers, R. A. (2002) 'Seat belt laws and traffic fatalities: A research update', *Social Science Journal* 33(3), 321-33.

49. Evans, W. N. and Graham, J. D. (1991) 'Risk reduction or risk compensation', *Journal of Risk and Uncertainty* 4(1), 61-73.

50. Asch, P. et al. (1991) 'Risk compensation and the effectiveness of safety-belt-use laws: A case study of New Jersey', *Policy Sciences* 24(2), 181-97.

51. Houston, D. J. and Richardson, L. E. (2007) 'Risk compensation or risk reduction? Seatbelts, state laws, and traffic fatalities', *Social Science Quarterly* 88(4), 913-36.

52. Cohen and Einav, op. cit. (see ref. 47).

53. Reinfurt, D. et al. (1990) 'Characteristics of drivers not using seat belts in a high-belt-use state', *Journal of Safety Research* 27(4), 209-15.

54. Hunter, W. W. et al. (2002) 'Characteristics of seat-belt users and non-users in a state with a mandatory belt-use law', *Health Education Research* 5(2), 161-73.

55. Derrig et al., op. cit. (see ref. 46).

56. Transport Accident Commission (TAC) (2008) 'Seatbelt statistics', published on TAC website but since deleted.

57. Western Australia Government informant (2009), personal communication.

58. Parker, L. et al. (eds.) (2009) 'Local government actions to prevent childhood obesity', Committee on Childhood Obesity Prevention Actions for Local Governments. Washington, DC: Institute of Medicine (IOM) and National Research Council.

Ingredient 4: Design a sticky solution

1. Tversky, A. and Kahneman, D. (1991) 'Loss aversion in riskless choice: A reference-dependent model', *The Quarterly Journal of Economics* 106(4), 1039-61.

2. Holmes, T. P. (1990) 'Self-interest, altruism, and health-risk reduction: An economic analysis of voting behavior', *Land Economics* 66(2), 140-49; and Sigelman, L., Sigelman, C. K. and Bullock, D. (1991) 'Reconsidering pocketbook voting: An experimental approach', *Political Behavior* 13(2), 129-49.

3. Ryan, R. L., Erickson, D. L. and De Young, R. (2003) 'Farmers' motivations for adopting conservation practices along riparian zones in a mid-western agricultural watershed', *Journal of Environmental Planning and Management* 46(1), 19-37; and Erickson, D. L., Ryan, R. L. and De Young, R. (2001) 'Woodlots in the rural landscape: Landowner motivations and management attitudes in a Michigan (USA) case study', *Landscape and Urban Planning* 58(4), 101-12.

4. Cervero, R. (1990) 'Transit pricing research: A review and synthesis', *Transportation* 17(2), 117-39.

5. Hornik, J. et al. (1995) 'Determinants of recycling behaviour: A synthesis of research results', *Journal of Socio-Economics* 24(1), 105-27.

6. Grebner, S. et al. (2004) 'Stressful situations at work and in private life among young workers: An event sampling approach, *Social Indicators Research* 67(1-2), 11-49.

7. Wallerstein, N. (1992) 'Powerlessness, empowerment, and health: Implications for health promotion programmes', *American Journal of Health Promotion* 6(3), 197-205.

8. Maslach, C. (2005) 'Understanding job burnout'. In *Stress and Quality of Working Life: Current perspectives in occupational health,* International Stress Management Association (ISMA), p.44.

9. Marmot, M. et al. (1997) 'Contribution of job control and other risk factors to social variations in coronary heart disease incidence', *The Lancet* 350, 235-39.

10. Donovan, N. and Halpern, D. (2003). 'Life satisfaction: The state of knowledge and implications for government'. Paper presented at the Conference on Well-Being and Social Capital, Harvard University, Cambridge, MA.

11. Frey, B. and Stutzer, A. (2002) *Happiness and Economics*. Princeton and Oxford: Princeton University Press.

12. Rogers, E. M. (2003) *The Diffusion of Innovations*. Fifth edition. New York: Free Press, p.247. The Daughter-in-law Who Doesn't Speak story was based on an article by Thurow, R. (2002) 'Could Just 10 Horsepower Be Enough to Free All the Women of Mali?', *The Wall Street Journal*, 26-28 July.

13. *Newspoll News* (2002) 11(1).

14. Cliff Kuang (2011) 'What made Steve Jobs so great?', *Co.Design*, 25 August, www.fastcodesign.com/1664863/what-made-steve-jobs-great?partner=best_of_newsletter

15. Tertoolen, G. et al. (1998) 'Psychological resistance against attempts to reduce private car use', *Transportation Research-A* 32(3), 171-81.

16. Deiner, E. and Seligman, M. E. (2002) 'Very happy people', *Psychological Science* 13(1), 81–4.

17. Ryan, R. M., Stiller, J. D. and Lynch, J. H. (1994) 'Representations of relationships to teachers, parents, and friends as predictors of academic motivation and self-esteem', *The Journal of Early Adolescence* 14(2), 226-49.

18. Uchino, B. N., Cacioppo, J. T. and Kiecolt-Glaser, J. K. (1996) 'The relationship between social support and physiological processes: A review with emphasis on underlying mechanisms and implications for health', *Psychological Bulletin* 119(3), 488-531.

19. Diener, E. and Oishi, S. (2005) 'The nonobvious social psychology of happiness', *Psychological Inquiry* 16(4), 162-7.

20. Winkelman, L. and Winkelman, R. (1998) 'Why are the unemployed so unhappy? Evidence from panel data', *Economica* 65, 1-15.

21. Rintamaki, T. et al. (2006) 'Decomposing the value of department store shopping into utilitarian, hedonic and social dimensions: Evidence from Finland', *International Journal of Retail and Distribution Management* 34(1), 6-25.

22. Wilk, R. R. and Wilhite, H. L. (1985) 'Why don't people weatherize their homes? An ethnographic solution', *Energy* 10(5), 621-9.

23. Gilovich, T. and Van Boven, L. (2003) 'To do or to have? That is the question', *Journal of Personality and Social Psychology* 85(6), 1193-202.

24. Van Boven, L. and Gilovich, T. (2003) *The social costs of materialism: The existence and implications of experiential versus materialistic stereotypes.* Unpublished manuscript, University of Colorado.

25. Ho, R. (1994) 'Cigarette advertising and cigarette health warnings: What role do adolescents' motives for smoking play in their assessment?', *Australian Psychologist* 29(1), 49-56.

26. Leary, M. R., Tchividjian, L. R. and Kraxberger, B. E. (1999) 'Self-presentation can be hazardous to your health: Impression management and health risk', in Baumeister, R.F. (ed.) *The Self in Social Psychology.* Philadelphia, PA: Psychology Press.

27. Hayden, B. (1998) 'Practical and prestige technologies: The evolution of material systems', *Journal of Archaeological Method and Theory* 5(1), 1-55.

28. Rogers, op. cit. (see ref. 12) p.106.

29. Rogers, op. cit. (see ref. 12) p.193.

30. Ritchie, J. R. B. et al. (1981) 'Complexities of household energy consumption and conservation', *Journal of Consumer Research* 8, 233-42.

31. Moore, G. A. (1999) *Crossing the Chasm: Marketing and selling high-tech products to mainstream customers.* Revised edition. New York: HarperCollins.

32. Rogers, op. cit. (see ref. 12) p.282.

33. Mullins, J. (2004) 'The next generation', *New Scientist*, 16 October, p.25.

34. Quoted in Purcell, P. (2004) 'A quick mod takes gamers beyond their doom', *Sydney Morning Herald*, 23 August.

35. Kawasaki, G. (2006) 'The art of creating a community', on his blog 'How to change the world, 14 February.

36. A really useful guide is Booth, E. M. (1996) *Starting with Behavior: A participatory process for selecting target behaviors in environmental programmes*, GreenCOM, the Environmental Education and Communication Project of the US Agency for International Development (USAID). Washington, DC: Academy for Education Development.

37. Steve Sussman, personal communication.

38. Rogers, op. cit. (see ref. 12) p.344.

Ingredient 5: Expanding the comfort zone

1. Bandura, A., Ross, D. and Ross, S. A. (1961) 'Transmission of aggression through imitation of aggressive models', *Journal of Abnormal and Social Psychology* 63, 575-82.

2. Bandura, A. and Walters, R. H. (1963) *Social Learning and Personality Development*. New York: Holt, Reinhart and Winston Inc., p.58.

3. Collins, L. (1982) 'Self-efficacy and ability in achievement behaviour', cited in Bandura (1993) 'Perceived self-efficacy in cognitive development and functioning', *Educational Psychologist* 28(2), 117-48.

4. Bandura, A. and Wood, R. (1989) 'Effect of perceived controllability and performance standards on self-regulation of complex decision-making', *Journal of Personality and Social Psychology* 56, 805-14.

5. Bandura, A. (1993) 'Perceived self-efficacy in cognitive development and functioning', *Educational Psychologist* 28(2), 117-48.

6. "... perceived self-efficacy is concerned not with the number of skills you have, but with what you believe you can do with what you have under a variety of circumstances." Bandura, A. (1997) *Self-Efficacy: The exercise of control*. New York: W.H. Freeman and Company, p.37.

7. Bandura (1993) op. cit. p.132. He also observed that: "Much human depression is cognitively generated by dejecting ruminative thought."

8. Rogers, E. M. (2003) *The Diffusion of Innovations*. Fifth edition. New York: Free Press, p.295.

9. Bandura, A. (1997) *Self-Efficacy: The exercise of control*. New York: W.H. Freeman and Company, p.79.

10. Slovic, P., Fischhoff, B. and Lichtenstein, S. (1980) *Facts and Fears: Understanding perceived risk*. In Slovic, P. (ed.) (2000) *The Perception of Risk*. London: Earthscan, p.137.

11. Csíkszentmihályi, M. (1991) *Flow: The psychology of optimal experience*. New York: Harper Perennial, p.59.

12. Bandura, A., Grusec, J. E. and Menlove, F. I. (1967) 'Vicarious extinction of avoidance behaviour', *Journal of Personality and Social Psychology* 5(1), 16-23.

13. Bandura, A. and Menlove, F. I. (1968) 'Factors determining vicarious extinction of avoidance behaviour through symbolic modeling', *Journal of Personality and Social Psychology* 8(2), 99-108.

14. Hubert Dixon is quoted from an unpublished research report by Christine Laurence for the Winston Churchill Memorial Trust of Australia, 2002, p.18.

15. Lowe, C. F. et al. (2004) 'Effects of a peer modeling and rewards-based intervention to increase fruit and vegetable consumption in children', *European Journal of Clinical Nutrition* 58, 510-22.

16. Coghlan, A. (2007) 'Superheroes battle the forces of junk', *New Scientist*, 21 July.

17. By the way, it may matter whether the role model demonstrates mastery, that is, flawless performance without self-doubt, or whether they demonstrate 'coping behaviour', where they begin by making errors and displaying anxiety and self-doubt but then gradually demonstrate the tricks that allow them to overcome their fears and eventually achieve mastery. The jury is still out on whether mastery or coping behaviour is best, with some results giving coping behaviour the edge. In one pioneering experiment, for example, high-school students who were

struggling with maths were shown films of similar students displaying either mastery or coping behaviour. The children who observed the coping model had the biggest improvements in personal confidence and subsequent exam results. Schunk, D. H., Hanson, A. R. and Cox, P. D. (1987) 'Peer-model attributes and children's achievement in behaviors', *Journal of Educational Psychology* 79(1), 54-61.

18. Zelezny, L. C. (1999) 'Educational interventions that improve environmental behaviors: A meta-analysis', *The Journal of Environmental Education* 31(1), 5-14.

19. Chipenuik, R. (1995) 'Childhood foraging as a means of acquiring competent human cognition about biodiversity', *Environment and Behaviour* 27(4), 490-512.

20. Driskell, J. E. et al. (1994) 'Does mental practice enhance performance?', *Journal of Applied Psychology* 79(4), 481-93.

21. Ker, I. (2004) 'Household-based voluntary travel behaviour change: Aspirations, achievements and assessment'. Melbourne: ARRB Transport Research.

22. Baele, J., Dusseldorp, M. and Maes, S. (2001) 'Condom use self-efficacy: Effect on intended and actual condom use in adolescents', *Journal of Adolescent Health* 28, 421–31.

23. Kent, J., Robinson, L. and White, J. (2002) 'Sustaining change: Towards a sustainable living programme'. Unpublished report for the Department of Environment and Climate Change (formerly Resource NSW).

24. How motivation and autonomy are associated: Gagné, M and Deci, E. L. (2005) 'Self-determination theory and work orientation', *Journal of Organizational Behaviour* 26, 331-62; Grolnick, W. S. and Ryan, R. M. (1989) 'Parent styles associated with children's self-regulation and competence in school', *Journal of Educational Psychology* 81, 143-54; Black, A. E. and Deci, E. L. (2000) 'The effects of instructors' autonomy support and students' autonomous motivation on learning organic chemistry: A self-determination theory', *Science Education* 84, 740-56; Williams, G. C., Deci, E. L. and Ryan, R. M. (1998) 'Building health-care partnerships by supporting autonomy: Promoting maintained behavior change and positive health outcomes'. In Suchman, A. L., Hinton-Walker, P. and Botelho, R. (eds.) *Partnerships in Healthcare: Transforming relational process*. Rochester, NY: University of Rochester Press, pp.67-87; Williams, G. C. et al. (1999) 'Presenting the facts about smoking to adolescents: The effects of an autonomy-supportive style', *Archives of Pediatrics and Adolescent Medicine* 153, 959-64.

25. Lewin, K. (1948) *Resolving Social Conflicts; Selected papers on group dynamics*, Lewin, G. W. (ed.). New York: Harper & Row, p.82.

26. "More autonomous people tend to demonstrate self-actualisation, self-esteem, ego-development, integration in personality, and satisfying interpersonal relationships . . . compared to control-oriented people who tend to demonstrate public self-consciousness, Type A behaviour patterns, defensive functioning, and placing high importance on pay, status and material possessions." Gagné, M and Deci, E. L. (2005) 'Self-determination theory and work orientation', *Journal of Organizational Behaviour* 26, 331-62.

27. "The NSW Fire Brigades had tremendous success in improving fire preparedness with its street-based community fire units, but only where the communities had initiated them – not when the fire authorities tried to impose them." Lewis, D. (2003) 'Australia burning to learn better bushfire science', *Sydney Morning Herald*, 7 October.

28. Rigby, K. (2002) 'A meta-evaluation of methods and approaches to reducing bullying in pre-schools and in early primary school in Australia'. Canberra: Attorney-General's Department.

29. Petersen, L. and Rigby, K. (1999) 'Countering bullying at an Australian secondary school', *Journal of Adolescence* 22(4), 481-92.

30. Wansink, B. (2002) 'Changing habits on the home front: lost lessons from World War II research', *Journal of Marketing and Public Policy* 21(1), 90-99.

31. Lewin, K. (1943) 'Forces behind food habits and methods of change'. In 'The problem of changing food habits: Report of the Committee on food habits, 1941-1943'. Washington, DC: National Research Council, National Academy of Sciences, p.60.

32. Based on the account in Rogers op. cit. (see ref. 8) p.72.

33. Knowles, M. (1990) *The Adult Learner: A neglected species*. Houston: Gulf Publishing.

34. Kirsty Norris shared her story on a 3 Pillars Behaviour Change Network discussion on Linkedin during 2011.

35. Sheehy, L. and Dingle, P. (2003) 'Goal Setting, Education and Sustainability: Living Smart in the City of Fremantle'. Regional Governance for Sustainability (Third Conference of the Regional Government Network for Sustainable Development), Fremantle, Perth, Western Australia, 17-19 September 2003.

36. Locke, E. A. and Latham, G. P. (2006) 'New directions in goal-setting theory', *Current Directions in Psychological Science* 15(5), 265-8.

37. This is illustrated by an experiment where 80 families were asked to choose either a 20 per cent goal or a 2 per cent goal for energy saving during summer. Half of each group was given feedback three times a week and the other half got no feedback. Only the 20-per-cent-plus feedback group achieved significant reductions (13-15 per cent): Becker, L. J. (1978) 'Joint effect of feedback and goal setting on performance: A field study of residential energy conservation', *Journal of Applied Psychology* 63(4), 428-33.

38. Hannafin, M. J. (1981) Effects of teacher and student goal setting and evaluations on mathematics achievements and student attitudes, *Journal of Educational Research* 74(5), 321-6.

39. Challis, C. (2004) *A Literature Review of Secondary and Smart Metering Knowledge in Managed Housing*, Energy Savings Trust, UK.

40. Thompson, C. (2007) 'Clive Thompson thinks: desktop orb could reform energy hogs', *Wired Magazine*, 24 July.

41. Johnson, E. J. and Tversky, A. (1983) 'Affect, generalization, and the perception of risk', *Journal of Personality and Social Psychology* 45(1), 20-31.

42. Kavanagh, D. J. (1987) 'Mood, persistence, and success', *Australian Journal of Psychology* 3(3), 307-18.

43. Isen, A. M., Daubman, K. A and Nowicki, G. P. (1987) 'Positive affect facilitates creative problem solving', *Journal of Personality and Social Psychology* 52(6), 1122-131; Fredrickson, B. L. (2004) 'The broaden-and-build theory of positive emotions', *Philosophical Transactions of the Royal Society* 359, 1367-77.

44. Schwarz, N. and Clore, G. L. (1983) 'Mood, misattribution, and judgements of well-being: Informative and directive functions of affective states', *Journal of Personality and Social Psychology* 45, 513-23.

45. Most psychologists think there are two modes of human decision-making – rational and intuitive – but others think there are four human thought processes that continually interact: conscious goal-directed calculation; rule-of-thumb or heuristic judgements that depend on repeating behaviours that worked in similar situations; Pavlovian instinctual responses driven by immediate autonomic reactions like fear, hunger, etc.; and habitual behaviours that have become inflexible through repetition, like driving or typing. Kate Douglas (2007) 'The other you', *New Scientist*, 1 December.

46. Slovic, P. et al. (2004) 'Risk as analysis and risk as feelings', *Risk Analysis* 24(2), 1-12.

47. Carlson, M., Charlin, V. and Miller, N. (1988) 'Positive mood and helping behaviour: A test of six hypotheses', *Journal of Personality and Social Psychology* 55(2), 211-29,

48. Schwarz, N. and Bohner, G. (1966) 'Feelings and their motivational implications: Moods and

the action sequence. In Gollwitzer, P. M. and Bargh, J. A. (eds.) *The Psychology of Action: Linking cognition and motivation to action.* New York: Guilford Press, p.133.

49. Danceplant was led by Graham Strong, whose family have farmed near Wagga Wagga, New South Wales, for generations.

50. Geoff is an inspiring facilitator. You can check out his blog at www.yesandspace.com.au

51. In *Social Intelligence,* Daniel Goleman describes 'social receptors' in the brain, regions primarily dedicated to sensing and responding to the people around us, their feelings and intentions. So important are social relationships to humans that these brain areas are always 'on'. "Even while the rest of the brain is quiescent," he wrote, "four neural areas remain active, like neural motors, poised for quick response. Tellingly, three of these ready-to-roll areas are involved in making judgements about people." This, Goleman explains, is why we can make judgements about people around a tenth of a second more quickly than we make judgements about objects. Goleman, D. (2006) *Social Intelligence: The new science of social relationships.* New York: Bantam Books, p.67.

52. Read Montague, Baylor College of Medicine, Houston, Texas, quoted in Spinney, L. (2004) 'Why we do what we do', *New Scientist,* 31 July.

53. Although there's not a lot of evidence these programmes as currently designed work very well: Wechsler, H. et al. (2003) 'Perception and reality: A national evaluation of social norms marketing interventions to reduce college students' heavy alcohol use', *Quarterly Journal of Studies on Alcohol* 64, 484-94.

54. Goldstein, N. J., Cialdini, R. B. and Griskevicius, V. (2008) 'A room with a viewpoint: Using social norms to motivate environmental conservation in hotels', *Journal of Consumer Research* 35, 472-82.

55. Cialdini, R. B. (2003) 'Crafting normative messages to protect the environment', *Current Directions in Psychological Science* 12(4), 105-9.

56. Schultz, P. W. et al. (2007) 'The constructive, destructive, and reconstructive power of social norms', *Psychological Science* 18(5), 429-34.

57. For an evaluation of Opower's use of social proof on energy bills, see Allcott, H. (2011) 'Social norms and energy conservation', *Journal of Public Economics,* http://opower.com/uploads/library/file/1/allcott_2011_jpubec_-_social_norms_and_energy_conservation.pdf.

58. For the story behind Bankstown City Council's smiley-face recycling cards: http://enablingchange.posterous.com/holely-lids-can-we-all-be-scientists

59. Cialdini, R. B. (1984) *Influence: The psychology of persuasion.* New York: Quill William Morrow, p.80.

60. Freedman, J. L. and Fraser, S. C. (1966) 'Compliance without pressure: The foot-in-the-door technique', *Journal of Personality and Social Psychology* 4(2), 195-202.

61. Ibid. p.201.

62. Pallack, M. S., Cook, D. A. and Sullivan, J. J. (1980) 'Commitment and energy conservation', *Applied Social Psychology Annual* 1, 235-53.

63. The team repeated the experiment in summer with Iowa residents who cooled the homes by central air conditioning. The same effect occurred, with an initial saving of 27.8 per cent, rising to a whopping 41.6 per cent when they were informed their names would not appear.

64. A good summary of labelling theory and studies is Cornelissen, P., Dewitte, S., Warlop, L. and Yzerbyt, V. (2007) 'Whatever people say I am that's what I am: Social labeling as a social marketing tool', *International Journal of Research in Marketing* 24(4), 278-88.

65. Miller, R. L., Brickman, P. and Bolen, D. (1975) 'Attribution versus persuasion as a means for modifying behavior', *Journal of Personality and Social Psychology* 31(3), 430-41.

66. Kraut, R. G. (1973) 'Effects of social labeling on giving to charity', *Journal of Experimental Social Psychology* 9, 551-62.

67. Tybout, A. M. and Yalch, R. F. (1980) 'The effect of experience: A matter of salience?', *Journal of Consumer Research* 6(4), 406-13.

68. The New York incentives story is sourced from Grimes, C. (2008) 'Do the right thing', *Financial Times*, 24 May; and Medina, J. (2008) 'Next question: Can students be paid to Excel?', *The New York Times*, 5 March.

69. Ibid. (Grimes).

70. Butler, A. G., Kennedy, K. and Kennedy, M. (2010) 'Paying students for grades: Is it sustainable and should it be?', *Academic Leadership* 8(3), 1-7.

71. Marsh, J. A. et al. (2011) 'A big apple for educators: New York City's experiment with schoolwide performance bonuses, Final evaluation report', Santa Monica, CA: RAND Corporation.

72. Professor Fryer wrote that the failure may have been due to the incentives being too small, the scheme being too complex, group-based awards not being effective, or teachers not knowing how to increase student performance. Fryer, R. G. (2011) 'Teacher incentives and student achievement: Evidence from New York City public schools', National Bureau of Economic Research Working Paper No. 16850.

73. Fryer, R. G. (2010) 'Financial incentives and student achievement: Evidence from randomized trials', National Bureau of Economic Research Working Paper No. 15898.

74. Giuffrida, A. and Torgerson, D. J. (1997) 'Should we pay the patient? Review of financial incentives to enhance patient compliance', *British Medical Journal* 315, 703-7.

75. Bains, N., Pickett, W. and Hoey, J. (1998) 'The use and impact of incentives in population-based smoking cessation programmes: A review', *American Journal of Health Promotion* 12(5), 307-20.

76. Petersen, L. A. et al. (2006) 'Does pay-for-performance improve the quality of health care?', *Annals of Internal Medicine* 15 145(4), 265-72.

77. Kavanagh, J. et al. (2006) 'A systematic review of the evidence for incentive schemes to encourage positive health and other social behaviours in young people'. London, EPPI-Centre, Social Science Research Unit, Institute of Education, University of London.

78. Hagenzieker, M. P., Bijleveld, F. D. and Davidse, R. J. (1997) 'Effects of incentive programmes to stimulate safety-belt use: A meta-analysis', *Accident Analysis and Prevention* 29(6), 759-77.

79. Ferraro, P. J. and Kiss, A. (2002) 'Direct payments to conserve biodiversity', *Science* 298, 1718-19.

80. Mellström, C. and Johannesson, M. (2005) 'Crowding out in blood donation: Was Titmuss right?', *Working Papers in Economics* 180, Department of Economics, University of Gothenburg, Sweden.

81. Deci, E. L. (1971) 'Effects of externally mediated rewards on intrinsic motivation', *Journal of Personality and Social Psychology* 18(1), 105-15.

82. Kazdin, A. (1982) 'The token economy: A decade later', *Journal of Applied Behavior Analysis* 15, 431-45.

83. Wiersma, U. J. (1992) 'The effects of extrinsic rewards in intrinsic motivation: A meta-analysis', *Journal of Occupational and Organizational Psychology* 65(2), 101-14.

84. Cameron, J., Banko, K. M. and Pierce, W. D. (2001) 'Pervasive negative effects of rewards on intrinsic motivation: The myth continues', *The Behavior Analyst* 24(1), 1-44.

85. Frey, B. S. and Oberholzer-Gee, F. (1997) 'The cost of price incentives: An empirical analysis for motivation crowding-out', *The American Economic Review* 87(4), 746-55.

86. Thøgersen, J. (1994) 'Monetary incentives and environmental concern: Effects of a differentiated garbage fee', *Journal of Consumer Policy* 17(4), 407-42.

Ingredient 6: Find the right inviter

1. See www.schoolfoodtrust.org.uk

2. ABC News (2006) 'Breakfast with Al Gore persuades Branson to pledge billions to global warming', 22 September.

3. Bandura, A. (1977) *Social Learning Theory*. New Jersey: Prentice-Hall Inc., p.88.

4. Bandura, A., Ross, D. and Ross, S. A. (1963) 'A comparative test of the status envy, social power, and secondary reinforcement theories of identificatory learning', *Journal of Abnormal and Social Psychology* 67(6), 527-34.

5. Brody, G. H. and Stoneman, Z. (1981) 'Selective imitation of same-age, older and younger peer models', *Child Development* 52, 717-20.

6. Lefkowitz, M., Blake, R. R. and Mouton, J. S. (1955) 'Status factors in pedestrian violation of traffic signals', *Journal of Abnormal and Social Psychology* 51, 704-6.

7. Castelloe, P. and Watson, T. (2000) 'How to enter a community as an organizer', Center for Participatory Change (CPC), Asheville, NC.

8. Potas, I. et al. (2001) 'Circle sentencing in New South Wales: A review and evaluation'. Sydney: Judicial Commission of New South Wales.

9. Braithwaite, J. (1989) *Crime, Shame and Reintegration*. Cambridge: Cambridge University Press.

10. Tyler, T. R. et al. (2007) 'Reintegrative shaming, procedural justice, and recidivism: The engagement of offenders' psychological mechanisms in the Canberra RISE drinking-and-driving experiment', *Law & Society Review* 41(3), 553-86.

11. For a summary of the Water Efficient Durham project, see: www.toolsofchange.com/en/case-studies/detail/156

12. See www.dpi.wa.gov.au/livingsmart

13. Rosekrans, M. A. (1967) 'Imitation in children as a function of perceived similarity to a social model and vicarious reinforcement', *Journal of Personality and Social Psychology* (7), 307-15.

14. Schunk, D. H. and Hansen, A. R. (1985) 'Peer models: Influence on children's self-efficacy and achievement', *Journal of Educational Psychology* 77(2), 313-22.

15. Schunk, D. H. (1987) 'Peer models and children's behavioral change', *Review of Educational Research* 57(2), 149-74; Bandura, A. (1997) *Self-efficacy: The exercise of control*. New York: W. H. Freeman and Company, p.87; Brown, I., Jr. and Inouye, D. K. (1978) 'Learned helpless through modeling: The role of perceived similarity in competence', *Journal of Personality and Social Psychology* (36), 900-8; Emswiller, T. et al. (1971) 'Similarity, sex, and requests for small favors', *Journal of Applied Social Psychology* 1(3), 284-91; Goldstein, N. J., Cialdini, R. B. and Griskevicius, V. (2008) 'A room with a viewpoint: Using social norms to motivate environmental conservation in hotels', *Journal of Consumer Research* 35, 472-82.

16. Bochner, S. (1994) 'The effectiveness of same-sex versus opposite-sex role models in advertisements to reduce alcohol consumption in teenagers', *Addictive Behaviors* 19(1), 69-82.

17. Walter, G. A. (1976) 'Changing behaviour in task groups through social learning: Modeling alternatives', *Human Relations* 29(2), 167-78.

18. Burger, J. M. et al. (2004) 'What a Coincidence! The effects of incidental similarity on compliance', *Journal of Personality and Social Psychology* 30(1), 35-43.

19. Hilmert, C. J., Kulik, J. A. and Christenfeld, N. J. S. (2006) 'Positive and negative opinion modeling: The influence of another's similarity and dissimilarity', *Journal of Personality and Social Psychology* 90(3), 440-52.

20. The campaign was funded by British American Tobacco, Philip Morris and Japan Tobacco International. Devlin, E. et al. (2002) 'Evaluation of the industry-funded "Youth Smoking Prevention" (YSP) campaign'. Proceedings of the 3rd European Conference on Tobacco or Health (ECTOH), Warsaw, Poland, 20-22 June.

21. Walster, E. and Aronson, E. (1966) 'On increasing the prestige of a low prestige communicator', *Journal of Experimental Social Psychology* 2, 352-42.

22. Eisend, M. (2006) 'Two-sided advertising: A meta-analysis', *International Journal of Research in Marketing* 23, 187-98.

23. Rogers, C. R. (1992) 'The necessary and sufficient conditions of therapeutic personality change', *Journal of Consulting and Clinical Psychology* 60(6), 827-32.

24. Rogers, C. R. (1961) *On Becoming a Person, A Therapist's View of Psychotherapy*. London: Constable, p.11.

25. Miller, W. R. and Rollnick, S. (2002) *Motivational Interviewing: Preparing people for change*. Second edition. New York: The Guilford Press, pp.7-8.

26. Rogers op. cit. (see ref. 24) p.18.

27. Miller and Rollnick op. cit. p.9.

28. Castelloe and Watson op. cit.

29. In March 2005, Scholarest banned Turkey Twizzlers from its offering.

30. Covello, V. (1992) 'Risk communication, trust, and credibility', *Health and Environment Digest* 6, 1-4.

31. McComas, A. K. and Trumbo, C. W. (2001) 'Source credibility and environmental health risk controversies: Application of Meyer's credibility index', *Risk Analysis* 21(3), 467-80.

Bringing it all together

1. Miller, W. R. and Rollnick, S. (2002) *Motivational Interviewing: Preparing people for change*. Second edition. New York: The Guilford Press, p.18.

Index

We publish a wide range of books on ecological and cultural issues, including gardening, eco-building, economics, politics and green living. For a complete list, please visit our website:

www.greenbooks.co.uk